Yale Publications in American Studies, 18
Published under the direction of the American Studies
Program

BIRTH CONTROL IN AMERICA

THE CAREER OF MARGARET SANGER

David M. Kennedy

New Haven and London, Yale University Press

Library of Congress catalog card number: 79-99827
ISBN: 0-300-01202-0 (cloth), 0-300-01495-3 (paper)

Designed by John O. C. McCrillis,
set in Baskerville type,
and printed in the United States of America by
The Colonial Press Inc., Clinton, Massachusetts.

Published in Great Britain, Europe, and Africa by
Yale University Press, Ltd., London.
Distributed in Canada by McGill-Queen's University
Press, Montreal; in Latin America by Kaiman & Polon,
Inc., New York City; in Australasia and Southeast
Asia by John Wiley & Sons Australasia Pty. Ltd.,
Sydney; in India by UBS Publishers' Distributors Pvt.,
Ltd., Delhi; in Japan by John Weatherhill, Inc., Tokyo.

For
my mother
Millicent Fowler Caufield Kennedy
and
my father
Albert John Kennedy

Preface

When Margaret Sanger died in September 1966, she was eulogized as "one of history's great rebels and a monumental figure of the first half of the twentieth century." From an unexceptional childhood in Corning, New York, she grew to fame and influence as the world's leading propagandist for the artificial control of human reproduction. She began by defying old conventions and ended the lionized champion of new ones. By the time of her death at age 82, said *Time*, "her vision had been realized beyond her dreams." History records few examples of such successful advocacy of important social change.[1]

Much of that change occurred in the last two decades of Mrs. Sanger's life, after she had retired from official leadership in the birth control movement. At the time she "left the front," as she put it, in 1943, the most commonly used contraceptives were still intravaginal devices and chemicals. By the time of her death, millions of women all over the world regularly took oral contraceptives. That development Mrs. Sanger promoted both indirectly and directly. Not only did it reflect her long years of propagandizing for a simple, inexpensive contraceptive; it also owed in large part to the financial and organizational support she made possible in the post-World War II years to research in hormonal anovulants. Thus did Dr. Gregory Pincus, one of the principal developers of the "pill," inscribe a 1959 report on oral contraceptives "to Margaret Sanger with affectionate greetings—this product of her pioneering resoluteness." [2]

So too did the government which had once prosecuted Margaret Sanger move dramatically, in the years after 1945,

1. *New York Times*, September 11, 1966, sec. 4, p. 12; *Time*, September 16, 1966, p. 96.
2. Inscription dated February 14, 1959, on print of "Field Trials with Norethynodrel as an Oral Contraceptive," MSP–SS.

to realize her vision. The United States Government had quietly supported a few family planning programs as early as the 1930s, but it neither publicly acknowledged nor vigorously pursued those activities. When President Dwight D. Eisenhower was asked in 1959 about the federal government's relation to birth control, he replied: "I cannot imagine anything more emphatically a subject that is not a proper political or governmental activity or function or responsibility. . . . That's not our business." [3] Four years later, however, President John F. Kennedy hesitantly voiced his approval in principle of federal support for contraceptive research.[4] By 1965, Eisenhower had reversed his position on public support for family planning, and had become, with former president Harry S. Truman, a co-chairman of Planned Parenthood–World Population.[5] In the same year the then President, Lyndon Baines Johnson, announced in his State of the Union Message that he would "seek new ways to use our knowledge to help deal with the explosion in world population and the growing scarcity of world resources." [6] In 1966, President Johnson repeated that pledge and sent two strong messages to Congress urging support not just for research but also for family planning services in foreign countries and at home. By 1967, the Agency for International Development was spending almost nine million dollars annually on birth control abroad, and the Department of Health, Education and Welfare, with the Office of Economic Opportunity, spent over twenty million dollars for contraceptive programs in this country.[7]

Margaret Sanger could rightly regard those technological and political developments as important victories for her cause. While they were by no means ultimate solutions to the problems of family planning and world population, they were significant steps in that direction. But for all their

3. *New York Times,* December 3, 1959, p. 18.
4. *New York Times,* April 25, 1963, p. 16.
5. *New York Times,* June 23, 1965, p. 23.
6. *New York Times,* January 5, 1965, p. 16.
7. *Congressional Quarterly Almanac, 23* (1967): 454.

value, those accomplishments were simply consolidations of still more important, if less dramatic, victories won before World War II. What follows is the story of those earlier victories.

This book explores the relation between Margaret Sanger's character and the nature of the movement she led in America between 1912 and the Second World War. It is the story of her public career and is thus both less and more than a biography. It does not deal in detail with Mrs. Sanger's personal life from birth to death. It does try to describe the context in which Mrs. Sanger worked, the attitudinal and institutional responses she evoked; for that reason, she herself is sometimes absent from lengthy sections of the pages that follow.

Perhaps the terminal dates for this study need further explanation. Mrs. Sanger's career in behalf of birth control embraced a period in American history during which contraception was first advocated in an organized way, initially rejected, at least officially, and finally accepted both privately and publicly. The congruence of that cycle with Mrs. Sanger's active adult life was no accident; indeed, she did much to shape its development. But this study hopes to call attention to more than Mrs. Sanger's effective agency. There are historical moments perfectly fitted to the temperaments and personalities of certain individuals. The time from 1912 to the Second World War was such a moment for Margaret Sanger. For innovation and rejection she was ideally suited, but acceptance proved, for her, an uncomfortable victory. Hence this study begins with her pioneering work and concludes with the not fortuitously simultaneous events of official governmental acceptance of birth control and Mrs. Sanger's retirement from leadership of the American birth control movement. It hopes to illuminate, through her life, a part of the life of American society in that period. It treats only briefly and speculatively the advocacy and practice of contraception in the nineteenth century, topics that still need investigation. Neither does it examine the years since 1945. Finally, because of limitations of time and space, this study focuses almost exclusively on the United States. It deliberately, perhaps artificially, ignores the history of Malthusian movements in Europe in the nineteenth century and the story of Mrs. Sanger's not inconsiderable influence on the world birth control movement, particularly in Asia, in this century.

This artificiality, I hope excusable, undoubtedly owes in large part to the origins of the book as a doctoral dissertation in American Studies at Yale University. The dissertation grew from conversations about the place of women in American life with Norman Holmes Pearson, to whom I owe my first debt. Arthur Mann, of the University of Chicago, also provided encouragement in the early stages of the work. Edmund S. Morgan, David Hall, and especially R. Hal Williams, all of Yale University, Lawrence Chisolm, of the State University of New York at Buffalo, William L. O'Neill, of the University of Wisconsin, and David M. Potter, of Stanford University, offered helpful criticisms at various stages of the project. Jon Hirschoff saved me from some errors in Chapter 8. Janet Goodhue Smith was my most devoted critic, and gave support in more ways than I can acknowledge.

My largest obligation is to John Morton Blum, who found time amidst the duties of departmental chairmanship to restrain my errancies, sustain my commitment, and tirelessly edit my prose. The example of his own meticulous scholarship and the conscientious care he gave to me in this study are largely responsible, I trust, for whatever merit the book might have. Needless to say, neither he nor anyone save myself is responsible for any errors of fact, interpretation, or omission that may remain.

I wish to express my appreciation also to Grant Sanger, M.D., of New York, who gave me permission to use his mother's papers at the Library of Congress and at Smith College; to the librarians of those two institutions, who furnished both excellent professional services and a pleasant atmosphere in which to work; to Mrs. Dorothy Dickinson Barbour of Cleveland and to Christopher Tietze, M.D., of

New York, for permission to use the Robert Latou Dickinson papers in Dr. Tietze's possession; to Orm Øverland, of Oslo, Norway, for a number of helpful bibliographical suggestions; to the Graduate School of Yale University for awarding me a Sterling Fellowship in 1966–67, allowing me an undistracted year in which to finish the project; to the Institute of American History, Stanford University, for financial aid in the final stages of preparation of the manuscript for publication; to Mary A. Noonan, Fran Knight, Lois Machado, and Sharon Mosler for assisting in various stages of the transition from manuscript to book; and finally, to Ian Ballantine, Mme. Françoise Delisle, Mrs. Max Eastman, and Stuart Mudd, M.D., for permission to quote from various manuscript sources.

D. M. K.

Stanford, California
August 1969

Contents

List of Abbreviations

ABCL	American Birth Control League
AJOG	*American Journal of Obstetrics and Gynecology*
AMA	American Medical Association
CMH	Committee on Maternal Health, New York Obstetrical Society
FERA	Federal Emergency Relief Administration
IWW	Industrial Workers of the World
JAMA	*Journal of the American Medical Association*
MRC	Maternity Research Council
MSP–LC	Margaret Sanger Papers, Library of Congress, Washington, D.C.
MSP–SS	Margaret Sanger Papers, Sophia Smith Collection, Smith College Library, Northampton, Massachusetts
NBCL	National Birth Control League
NCWC	National Catholic Welfare Conference
NYAML	Library of the New York Academy of Medicine, New York
NYBCL	New York Birth Control League
USPHS	United States Public Health Service
VPL	Voluntary Parenthood League

CHAPTER 1

The Woman Rebel

"No Gods, No Masters," proclaimed the little newspaper from the masthead of its first edition. That slogan expressed the guiding principle of the *Woman Rebel*. Its editor, Margaret Sanger, urged women "to look the whole world in the face with a go-to-hell look in the eyes; to have an ideal; to speak and act in defiance of convention." She had launched her publication, Mrs. Sanger explained, "to stimulate working women to think for themselves and to build up a conscious fighting character." Woman was enslaved "by the machine, by wage slavery, by bourgeois morality, by customs, laws and superstitions." Mrs. Sanger announced a singular proposal to break those bonds: "It will also be the aim of the *Woman Rebel* to advocate the prevention of conception and to impart such knowledge in the columns of this paper." [1]

With that manifesto in March 1914, Margaret Sanger began her long career in behalf of the cause which became synonymous with her name: birth control. The now familiar phrase had not yet been coined, and Margaret Sanger was still just another of the restless young who had streamed to New York City in quest of experience and fulfillment.

Margaret Sanger, like so many others, came to New York from what F. Scott Fitzgerald called "that vast obscurity beyond the city." Her familiar Main Street lay along the banks of the Chemung River in Corning, New York, the factory town where she was born in 1883. There she grew up in a family of eleven children, of which she was the

1. *Woman Rebel*, March 1914, copy in MSP–LC.

sixth-born. Her mother, a frail, patient, submissive woman, died of tuberculosis at the age of 48. Her father, Michael Hennesey Higgins, a stonecutter, Irish-born, iconoclastic, in his daughter's words, "a philosopher, a rebel, and an artist," lived until he was 80. Margaret Sanger later noted the disparity in her parents' life-spans with bitterness. Her mother, Mrs. Sanger implied, had died the victim of her father's passion.[2]

Even as a girl, Margaret had borne her father some resentment. To her had fallen the tasks of nursing her mother in the final stages of illness and of managing the household after her mother's death. She disliked that first experience with enforced domesticity. Housework bored her. Her father became, in her eyes, a "tyrant," running her life with iron sway. He especially objected to her seeing young men. One evening, when Margaret returned home after her father's appointed deadline, he threw the door shut in her face. Echoes of the incident sounded throughout Margaret Sanger's life, just as the slam of another door reverberated for Ibsen's Nora Helmer.[3]

Young Margaret Higgins perhaps harbored even deeper hostility toward her father. She later wrote of "the only memory I have of any sex awakening or a consciousness of sex." The event appeared innocent enough. Margaret was sick; her father went to watch over her and, overcome by

2. Margaret Sanger, *My Fight for Birth Control* (New York: Farrar and Rinehart, 1931), pp. 4–6. The discussion of Mrs. Sanger's early life is drawn almost exclusively from *My Fight* and from *Margaret Sanger: An Autobiography* (New York: Norton, 1938). Use of these two works has been guided by Gordon Allport's insight: "As a rule autobiographical writing seems to be preoccupied with *conflict*, with what Kreuger has called the 'personality-making' situations of life. Happy, peaceful periods of time are usually passed over in silence. A few lines may tell of many serene years whereas pages may be devoted to a single humiliating episode or to an experience of suffering. Writers seem driven to elaborate on the conditions that have wrecked their hopes and deprived them of satisfactions." Gordon W. Allport, *The Use of Personal Documents in Psychological Science,* Social Science Research Council, Bulletin 49 (1942), p. 78.

3. *My Fight,* pp. 28–29; *Autobiography,* pp. 42–43.

drowsiness, fell asleep on top of her bed. But she recalled the occasion with a sense of terror: "Then I heard heavy breathing beside me. It was father. I was terrified. I wanted to scream out to Mother to beg her to come and take him away. . . . I lived through agonies of fear . . . I was petrified. . . . I was cold; I began to shiver; blackness and lights flickered in my brain; then I felt I was falling, falling—and knew no more." [4] The incident seemed to reveal something Margaret could never fully articulate: that the paternal domination she resented was associated in her mind with an aggressive, threatening, masculine sexual instinct. In her mature life, that association continued to color her attitudes toward men and sex.

Yet on a conscious level Margaret revered her father for his warmth, his wit, his free spirit, and especially for his iconoclasm, which she later called "the spring from which I drank." Michael Higgins, from Margaret's earliest memory, had no gods and no masters. A Catholic apostate, he chose as his heroes Henry George, Robert Ingersoll, and Father McGlyn. Any number of proposals, radical by contemporary standards, became his personal causes: feminism, socialism, the single tax. He exhorted his children to approach situations and ideas without the encumbrances of habit or doctrine.[5]

Though he himself could often be stubborn and illogical, Higgins taught his daughter that, to be free from the constraints of custom and prejudice, she must subjugate her emotions to her reason. Under his tutelage, she later wrote, "I realized I was made up of two Me's, one the thinking Me, the other, willful and emotional, which sometimes exercised too great a power; there was danger in her leadership and I set myself the task of uniting the two by putting myself through ordeals of various sorts to strengthen the head Me." [6] Michael Higgins encouraged those ordeals, perhaps because he perceived the pitfalls to which young

4. *My Fight*, pp. 11–12.
5. *Autobiography*, p. 38.
6. *Autobiography*, p. 25.

Margaret's deep-seated, almost compulsive romanticism might lead her. But neither Higgins's precepts nor Margaret's attempts at self-discipline succeeded in establishing the ascendancy of her head over her heart. Throughout her life, her "willful and emotional" nature remained troublingly unsubordinated.

Trouble arose, too, from the very iconoclasm Margaret so admired in her father. Higgins once invited Robert Ingersoll, the famed religious free-thinker, to speak at a public meeting in heavily Catholic Corning. The meeting hall belonged to the local Catholic priest, who predictably barred the door to the heretical Ingersoll. Stopped before the locked entrance, Ingersoll, Higgins, and young Margaret found themselves pelted by "hoodlums" with "tomatoes, apples and cabbage stumps." Margaret wrote of the incident later:

> None of us realized how the Ingersoll episode was to affect our well-being. Thereafter we were known as children of the devil. On the way to school names were shouted, tongues stuck out, grimaces made; the juvenile stamp of disapproval had been set upon us. . . . No more marble angels were to be carved for local Catholic cemeteries, and, while father's income was diminishing, the family was increasing.[7]

The pains of childhood ostracism, for Margaret Higgins, had a sharp association with the Catholic church.

She further blamed the church for her family's economic mediocrity, which she resented intensely. The Higgins family stood somewhere in the middle of the economic scale in Corning. At the bottom were the residents of the flatlands, near the river, and on top the factory managers in grand houses on the hills above the city. Margaret later claimed that from an early age she had associated the flatlands' "poverty, toil, unemployment, drunkenness, cruelty, quarreling, fighting, debts, jails with large families." Her memory of that youthful appraisal of social conditions could

7. *Autobiography*, p. 21.

be discounted as retrospective self-legitimization, but her recollection of the good life on the hills vividly evoked the envy she felt as a child. The wealthy, she wrote,

> owned their own homes, had few children, dressed them well, and kept their houses and their yards clean and tidy. Mothers of the hills played croquet and tennis with their husbands in the evening. They walked hand in hand with their children through the streets to shop for suitable clothing. They were young looking mothers, with pretty, clean dresses, and they smelled of perfume. I often watched them at play as I looked through the gates in passing.

The Higgins children, on the other hand, "knew not where we belonged. Everything that we desired most was forbidden. Our childhood was one of longing for things that were always denied. We were made to feel inferior to teachers, to elders, to all." Since her childhood, she had felt like an outsider.[8]

Margaret Sanger could never look back on Corning with joy. She associated it with dim fears of her father, sorrow and drudgery after the death of her mother, bitterness over the ostracism which a Catholic town dealt the village agnostic's daughter, and jealousy toward the gracious ladies who lived on the hilltops. She had been away at boarding school—at the Claverack College and Hudson River Institute, a Methodist school in the Catskills near the city of Hudson—for two years just before her mother's death, and the sojourn convinced her that the boundaries of experience in Corning were too constricted to satisfy her emotional stirrings. After her mother died, she later recalled, "I wanted a world of action. I longed for romance, dancing, wooing, experience." She rejected the usual womanly employment: "The thought of marriage," she wrote later, "was akin to suicide."[9]

Months of nursing her mother awakened an interest in

8. *My Fight*, pp. 5–9.
9. *My Fight*, p. 31.

medicine. Her father had always told her: "Leave the world better because you, my child, have dwelt in it." [10] So Margaret resolved to become a physician. But for Cornell and medical school she also longed in vain. The family could afford only nursing school, not the protracted expense of college and a medical education. Still, a nurse had nearly as many humanitarian opportunities as a doctor, and a career in nursing would serve just as well to get her out of Corning. In the spring of 1899, Margaret Higgins, fifteen years old, left for the White Plains Hospital, in Westchester County near New York City, to begin her nursing education.

Her three years at the hospital, she recalled, "tested character, integrity, nerve, patience and endurance." [11] The strenuous routine also tested her health, never very strong. Within two years she had to undergo an operation for tubercular glands. The tubercular condition persisted for nearly twenty years more. It constantly drained her energy, which fortunately was immense, and at least once endangered her life.

A student nurse's schedule allowed little time for social life, but when Margaret was transferred to the Manhattan Eye and Ear Hospital for a period of final training, she could at last indulge her desire for "romance, dancing, wooing." At a hospital dance a friend introduced her to a young architect and aspiring painter, William Sanger. The next morning at 7:30 he awaited her on the steps as she came out of the hospital, and he continued to meet her there morning after morning. When she returned to White Plains, he kept up his visits. "He was impatient of conventionalities, intense in his new love, his whole mind concentrated on our future life together," Margaret remembered. One afternoon in August 1902, just six months after they had met, while Margaret had a two-hour break from her hospital duties, William Sanger whisked her off to a

10. *Autobiography*, p. 23.
11. *My Fight*, pp. 32–33.

minister and married her. She was back at the hospital with
time to spare. The wedding had to be kept secret at first, so
that Margaret would be allowed to finish nursing school.[12]

Here was romance. Here was wooing. Here, too, it seemed
for a season, was the promise of fulfillment. Nineteen years
old, newly wed to a dashing architect who longed to paint
and spoke enthusiastically of going to Paris to study with
the masters, Margaret Sanger seemed to be living a fantasy
even she had not dared to dream. But within months after
her marriage her tubercular affliction worsened. Her husband installed her in Dr. Edward L. Trudeau's famed sanitarium at Saranac, in the Adirondacks. There she relieved
the boredom of semi-invalidism by reading in preparation
for the delivery of her first child, Stuart, who was born in
1903. After the delivery Mrs. Sanger and the baby returned
to Saranac for another eight months of treatment. But the
confinement, the routine, the despair over her lack of visible progress against the disease drove her to depths of
nihilism and nearly to a renunciation of her will to live.
She at last quit the sanitarium impulsively, returned to
New York, and began looking with her husband for a home-
site in the suburbs.[13]

They found one in Hastings-on-Hudson, a developing
upper-middle-class community near Dobb's Ferry in Westchester County. Using William Sanger's own plans, they
began to build the home of their dreams. Soon there came
Grant, a brother to Stuart, and, not long after, Peggy, the
little girl for whom the young mother had longed. Margaret Sanger immersed herself in the long-envied life of suburban housewifery. She had her own home on the hillside,
wore clean dresses, and smelled of perfume. She had the
opportunity to play croquet and tennis with her husband
in the evening, to attend card parties and women's meetings, and to buy clothes in Manhattan.

But all that was not enough. Suburban life disappointed
her blissful expectations. Her neighbors, she found, were

12. *My Fight*, p. 35; Margaret Sanger to Mary Higgins, n.d., MSP–LC.
13. *Autobiography*, pp. 58–61; *My Fight*, pp. 36–39.

inclined "to sink back into a complacent suburban attitude,
to enjoy petty middle class comforts." [14] The fatuous whirl
could not still her romantic yearnings. It only agitated what
she called her "world-hunger, the pull toward wider horizons." Had she conquered her despair at Saranac to live
only for this? After ten years of married life, Mrs. Sanger
finally decided that "this quiet withdrawal into the tame
domesticity of the pretty riverside settlement seemed to be
bordering on stagnation." [15] William Sanger felt the same
stagnation, in his work and in his marriage. Besides, the
huge house had become a financial burden now that he
gave more of his time to painting and less to architecture.
In early 1912 he took his wife away from Hastings and together they plunged into New York's Bohemia.

The wider horizons toward which Margaret Sanger was
drawn obviously bounded more than the creature comforts
she had possessed in plenty at Hastings-on-Hudson. Though
she never completely abandoned her bourgeois yearnings,
her anxiety was born of factors more profound than aspi-
rations for upward mobility. Her resentment of the well-
to-do, though it did not nullify her envy, certainly outweighed it and was not so easily allayed. That resentment
grew to a bitter alienation from the American social order
and in New York soon led Margaret Sanger to radicalism.
The Sangers took an apartment "way uptown" but spent
most of their time in Greenwich Village. Times were ex-
citing in New York. What Henry May has called The
Rebellion had captivated the imaginations of youthful intellectuals, and they gathered to debate and compare their
heterodoxies in the Village. There, in the Liberal Club's
loft in McDougal Street, and in Polly Halliday's restaurant
downstairs, Margaret Sanger met the intense young radicals
who began to shape her vague dissatisfaction into a commitment to reform, even to revolution. William Sanger already had several acquaintances among the amorphous

14. *My Fight,* p. 40.
15. *Autobiography,* p. 66.

group of New York artists and rebels. Through him Margaret eventually befriended such activists as Eugene Debs, the famed Socialist leader; Theodore Schroeder, an impassioned antireligionist and champion of civil liberties; Alexander Berkman, who still bore the scars of a fourteen-year prison term for shooting and stabbing Henry Clay Frick; John Reed, a fledgling reporter and revolutionary later to be buried in the Kremlin; the redoubtable Emma Goldman, conspirator, agitator, feminist, and, since 1900, an outspoken advocate of "voluntary motherhood"; and Henrietta Rodman, a dedicated feminist "who was especially in touch with the university crowd and the social settlement crowd, and the Socialist crowd." All these crowds found their way to the Sangers' apartment. And the Sangers, with so many others, found their way to Mabel Dodge's salon.[16]

There, amid the splendor of Mabel Dodge's white rooms and the bright talk of the guests, Margaret Sanger encountered ideas wholly new to her. She heard Big Bill Haywood and Frank Strong Hamilton tell of the "Wobblies," the Industrial Workers of the World. She listened to Emma Goldman defending the anarchist tactic of direct action, to Walter Lippmann explaining Freud, to Will Durant, recently separated from a Jesuit seminary, describing the sexual theories of Havelock Ellis and Richard von Krafft-Ebbing, to John Reed telling of the revolution in Mexico. At Mrs. Dodge's, said a New York newspaper, the guests were "politicians, painters, sociologists, sexologists, futurists, dramatists, sculptors, editors, writers, anarchists, socialists, I.W.W.'s and poets." [17] Mrs. Sanger heard them all, but hers was not a systematic mind and she found the welter of

16. *Autobiography,* p. 68; Henry May, *The End of American Innocence* (Chicago: Quadrangle Books, 1964), p. 249; Hutchins Hapgood, *A Victorian in the Modern World* (New York: Harcourt, Brace, 1939), p. 282; Floyd Dell, *Homecoming: An Autobiography* (New York: Farrar and Rinehart, 1933), p. 247.

17. *New York Morning Telegraph,* February 8, 1914, clipping, Mabel Dodge Luhan Papers, Beinecke Library, Yale University, New Haven, Connecticut.

intellectual discussion at the Salon Dodge difficult to as-
similate. She drank in ideas but did not discriminate among
them, weigh them, or select those that best suited her own
temperament and purposes. Her purposes, in fact, were still
undefined—"feeble efforts," she later wrote, "which at that
time were certainly built on dreams and ideals." [18]

Socialism was the first dream to which Margaret Sanger
committed herself. Her husband had long been a party
member, and now she joined Local No. 5 and became a
women's organizer for New York City.[19] She believed Morris Hillquit when he insisted that the time was ripe for
socialism: industrialism had at last created a proletarian
class-consciousness and a visible enemy in the class of pluto-
cratic bosses. She regularly read the *Masses,* a genteel advocate of the politically and artistically avant-garde. There
she found the congenial argument that the church posed
perhaps the largest obstacle to progress and the triumph of
socialism.[20] And in the daily Socialist *Call,* Mrs. Sanger
read the complaints of a maturing radical feminism. Industrialism, argued the *Call,* had forced the woman out of
the family, both by stripping the home of its productive
function and by paying the husband low wages which compelled the wife to work. Capitalists had contrived that
forced draft of woman's industrial labor, in competition
with men, in order to depress all wages. But that thesis, the
Call maintained, carried its own antithesis; for new requirements of industrial self-sufficiency had destroyed woman's
historical serfdom and slavery and had created conditions
in which "woman had to for the first time resort to her
power of reasoning and concentration, a power that lay
dormant for centuries." [21] All those ideas fired Mrs. Sanger's

18. Margaret Sanger to Mabel Dodge Luhan, March 13, 1937, Mabel
Dodge Luhan Papers.

19. Sanger, *Autobiography,* p. 75; Margaret Sanger to Paul Douglas,
June 12, 1935, MSP–LC.

20. See especially the December 1913 issue of *Masses.*

21. *New York Call,* January 23, 1912, p. 6 and January 30, 1912, p. 6;
see also John Spargo, *Socialism and Motherhood* (New York: B. W.
Huebsch, 1914).

mind and were to influence much of her later birth control activity. But in the prewar years, as she increasingly turned her own reasoning and concentration to the world about her, she began to move away from the relatively conventional program of the Socialists and toward a more revolutionary position. She eschewed the Socialists' political approach and embraced the anarchist tactic of direct action.

In Margaret Sanger's conversion to direct action Emma Goldman was perhaps her chief but not her only mentor. Mrs. Sanger long admired Big Bill Haywood, whose Industrial Workers of the World rejected political activity and directly assaulted the problems of industrial organization, working conditions, wages, and hours. When the IWW struck the Lawrence, Massachusetts, textile mills in 1912, Margaret Sanger helped to evacuate the children of the strikers. In an article for the *Call*, she reported that at Lawrence "capitalism shows its fangs of despotism and murder." She described the young soldiers who guarded the struck mills: "The time has come to educate these boys, to remind them to what class they belong, and when they realize this they will refuse to murder their own working brothers, to serve as hirelings to prop up the profit system, which bases its existence upon the blood of the famished workers." [22] Later, when the Wobblies walked out of the mills at Paterson, New Jersey, Mrs. Sanger dutifully marched on the strike lines and listened to Haywood and John Reed and the radical feminist Elizabeth Gurley Flynn harangue the workers.

The Sangers were also associated with the Ferrer School, a liberal educational experiment begun in 1910 by Emma Goldman, Alexander Berkman, Bayard Boyesen, son of the leading American devotee of Henrik Ibsen, and the educational reformer and civil libertarian Leonard D. Abbott. The school, where Stuart Sanger was enrolled, gained notoriety as a focal point for the activities of "anarchists." When Frank Tannenbaum led a "raid" of the unemployed on New York's churches in 1914, the *New York Times* laid the

22. *New York Call*, February 15, 1912, p. 6.

plot to the group associated with the Ferrer School, whom it branded as the most serious threat to society since the Haymarket conspirators in 1886. The Ferrer School, said the *Times*, "is turning out, and is intended to turn out, graduates filled with a settled discontent with the present social system and a determination to end it." Though the *Times* exaggerated its danger, the Ferrer School had a definitely radical character. Will Durant taught there, as did, occasionally, Lincoln Steffens, Clarence Darrow, and the artist George Bellows. They and other unorthodox social critics such as Emma Goldman and Alexander Berkman also conducted evening classes for adults at the school.[23]

In those classes Margaret Sanger absorbed several varieties of philosophical anarchism. Despite their differences, all the anarchists shared a social outlook that Hutchins Hapgood, a minor writer and chronicler of prewar Bohemia, described as "deeply sympathetic with the philosophy of the underdog." [24] They agreed with Kropotkin's definition of progress as increasing freedom for the individual and they believed in the growth of voluntarism as the basis of social relationships. They damned both church and state as oppressive institutions that checked the development of the natural personality.

The radical IWWs, Emma Goldman, the anarchists connected with the Ferrer School, and many cognoscenti of the Salon Dodge were not satisfied with the Liberal Club's bland resolutions endorsing free speech, nor with the Socialists' time-worn proposals for economic restructuring through political reform. Rather, they harbored a vision steeped in the traditions of romanticism, saturated with intoxicating notions of the dignity of the human personality and the related need for unfettered self-expression. Their message deeply moved Margaret Sanger. Like them, she soon demanded not only political but also aesthetic and especially psychological revolution. And the cutting edge of the new

23. Sanger, *Autobiography*, p. 75; *New York Times*, March 29, 1914, sec. 6, p. 2.

24. Hapgood, *A Victorian in the Modern World*, p. 277.

psychological theories the anarchists constantly invoked aimed at one central fact of life: sex.

When Freud came to Clark University in Worcester, Massachusetts, to lecture in 1909, his was only the most dramatic in a long series of importations of radically new sexual ideas from England and Europe. The United States had known Havelock Ellis's researches in sexual psychology for a decade. Margaret Sanger had certainly read them.[25] She had also read Edward Carpenter, whose *Love's Coming-of-Age* had a wide circulation in America after 1911. Carpenter was perhaps the most bold of the English Edwardian authors who wrote about sex, as Carpenter put it, "with a sense almost of religious consecration." [26] They couched their discussion of sex in a romantic rhetoric which appealed strongly to the American anarchists, and especially to Mrs. Sanger's emotional nature.

The anarchists also found familiar logic in the writings of the Swedish feminist, Ellen Key. From Miss Key, Margaret Sanger took her most enduring ideas of the nature of womanhood and marriage. Echoing Nietzsche's attack on Western ethics, Ellen Key in her books *The Century of the Child* (1909) and *The Woman Movement* (1912) advocated a system of subjective morality. Only sexual love, not law or tradition, Miss Key argued, could make marriage holy and durable. Marriages that denied sexual satisfaction to women violated a higher imperative than mere legality and should be dissolved. The most sacred thing, she said, was individual desire. The inner self, therefore, should be allowed full freedom of expression and development.

Freud added to such notions the suggestion that sexuality was the most important determinant of the self. And Mrs. Sanger, like so many others, frequently exhibited her misunderstanding of Freud when she invoked his authority for the claim that the removal of sexual restraints would

25. *Autobiography*, p. 94.
26. Edward Carpenter, *Love's Coming-of-Age* (New York: Mitchell Kennerly, 1911), p. 26.

automatically liberate the inner being and produce happiness.

The ideas of Havelock Ellis, the Edwardian novelists, Ellen Key, and Sigmund Freud were standard conversational fare with the radicals of the Ferrer School and the habitués of the Salon Dodge. In countless gatherings, Mrs. Sanger heard the rebels and intellectuals try to fit the new sexual theories to their programs for social reform. She came away from those discussions with a sense of the centrality of sex in social reconstruction. For Margaret Sanger, that conviction grew less from her understanding of psychology than from her appraisal of the mystical power of sex and emotion.

"I love being swayed by emotions by romances," she wrote in her journal in 1914, "just like a tree is rocked to and fro by various breezes—but stands firmly by its roots." With so many of her contemporaries, Margaret Sanger admired Nietzsche for his attack on the desiccated rationalism of Western morality, a morality which was the handmaiden of the repressive institutions of church and state. She repudiated "the Christian, democratic, ascetic ideal" in favor of a new ethics which emphasized "life in its fullness and all that is high, beautiful, and daring." Emotion would be the cornerstone of the new morality Mrs. Sanger advocated, and that code would sanction, in terms Ellen Key and the vulgar Freudians would understand, "real" desires. "Those who restrain desire," Mrs. Sanger wrote, "do so because the desire is weak enough to be restrained. Reason usurps its place and governs the weak and unwilling and being restrained, it by degrees becomes passive till it is only the shadow of desire." Reason, the excrescence of past acts and consequences, imposed an external order on man. "Emotion however is that which urges from within, without consciousness of fear or consequences." Emotion, in other words, sustained what Nietzsche described as the will to power.[27]

27. Margaret Sanger, "Journal," entry for November 3–4, 1914, MSP-SS.

Michael Higgins had sensed his daughter's receptivity to such ideas. Now, as a mature woman, Margaret Sanger joined fully in a general movement to apotheosize the irrational. Her commitment to that movement helped to explain both her greatest strengths and her greatest weaknesses.

During her education in the Village, Mrs. Sanger had not neglected her nursing. As a visiting nurse, she usually took obstetrical cases since she could then make arrangements in advance for the care of her own family. Increasingly those assignments took her to the Lower East Side. There, "below Fourteenth Street," she said later, "I seemed to be breathing a different air, to be in another world and country." It was in fact several other countries: "New Israel" in the tenth ward; the "Bloody Sixth" ward or "Little Italy"; Hell's Kitchen, further to the west in the sixteenth and twentieth wards, teeming with poor Irish. And well might there have been "a different air" in those tenement districts: in 1916 over 508,000 people lived below Fourteenth Street and east of Broadway. In the tenth ward alone, 76,000 people were packed into 1,179 tenements.[28]

Although Mrs. Sanger made her own personal discovery of them in 1912, those wretched conditions had been on the conscience of the Progressive generation for years. Concern for sanitation and public health had inspired some of the first slum reforms in the late nineteenth century. Sanitation reformers, prompted both by solicitude for the welfare of the poor and by the desire to insulate the general community from alien contamination, directed their attention especially to the cure and prevention of tuberculosis and venereal disease. That duality of motive was to find its analogue among birth control reformers.

On the Lower East Side, Mrs. Sanger was struck first of all by the incredible ignorance of immigrant women about

28. Sanger, *Autobiography*, p. 88; Roy Lubove, *The Progressives and the Slums: Tenement House Reform in New York City, 1890–1917* (Pittsburgh: University of Pittsburgh Press, 1962), pp. 261–65.

their own bodies and by the resultant high incidence of social diseases. In a series of articles for the *Call*, entitled "What Every Girl Should Know," she dealt frankly with venereal disease and various aspects of feminine hygiene. Her candor offended the Post Office Department, which banned the *Call* from the mails in late 1912. The editors then stopped the series, but retaliated by printing the headline "What Every Girl Should Know" and under it the words: "NOTHING! By order of the Post Office Department." [29] The ignorance such prudish actions helped perpetuate often had tragic consequences. The fecund daughters of Italy and of the ghettos of Eastern Europe found children far more a liability than an asset in crowded New York slums. Without knowledge of an effective contraceptive, they resorted to abortion, which frequently resulted in permanent injury or even death.

Margaret Sanger, as a nurse, undoubtedly saw many women die. But the death from an attempted abortion of one unfortunate slum-dweller named Sadie Sachs, Mrs. Sanger claimed, changed the course of her life. Mrs. Sachs's doctor had warned her that another pregnancy might endanger her life; but the only contraceptive advice he offered was the suggestion that Mr. Sachs sleep on the roof. Sadie Sachs died in the fall of 1912 while trying to terminate prematurely another unwanted pregnancy. Mrs. Sanger, the attendant nurse, overcome by the tragedy, left the death-room, and as she described it later,

> walked and walked and walked through the hushed streets. When I finally arrived home and let myself quietly in, all the household was sleeping. I looked out my window and down upon the dimly lighted city. Its pains and griefs crowded in upon me, a moving picture rolled before my eyes with photographic clearness; women writhing in travail to bring forth little babies; the babies themselves naked and hungry, wrapped in newspapers to keep them from the cold; six-year-old

29. *Autobiography*, p. 77.

children with pinched, pale, wrinkled faces, old in concentrated wretchedness, pushed into gray and fetid cellars, crouching on stone floors, their small scrawny hands scuttling through rags, making lamp shades, artificial flowers; white coffins, black coffins, coffins, coffins interminably passing in never-ending succession. The scenes piled one upon another. I could bear it no longer.

As I stood there the darkness faded. The sun came up and threw its reflection over the house tops. It was the dawn of a new day in my life also. . . .

I was resolved to seek out the root of the evil, to do something to change the destiny of mothers whose miseries were as vast as the sky.[30]

By Mrs. Sanger's own account, Sadie Sachs's death and the "vision" that followed it impelled her to strip off her nurse's uniform, swear never to indulge in mere "palliatives" like healing again, and commence a career dedicated to the emancipation of women. Nowhere, however, did she explain why that one particular death affected her so much more profoundly than the others she certainly witnessed.

Margaret Sanger's reliance on the Sadie Sachs episode to account for the beginnings of her career resembled a common autobiographical ploy of reformers. No doubt the suffering on the Lower East Side moved her as it would have moved anyone with a heart and a conscience. Perhaps, even, she was more moved than most. But the real significance of her description of Mrs. Sachs's death and the "vision" that followed lay in Mrs. Sanger's later relation to the birth control movement.

In some degree, any reformer must embody in himself the force of the moral rectitude he calls upon to sanction his reform. He must communicate to followers, opponents, and the apathetic not only the reasonableness of his proposals, but a sense also of the emotional force of his own

30. *Autobiography*, p. 92; a nearly identical account is in Sanger, *My Fight*, pp. 51–57.

belief. Only thus can he tap the spiritual resources responsive to emotional appeal but so often impervious to logical demonstration.

Yet Mrs. Sanger exaggerated the emotional. She was from childhood a passionate romantic. In New York her "Great Awakening," as she called it, had been essentially an emotional awakening, nurtured by the romanticism of Emma Goldman's anarchism and Bill Haywood's IWW, channeled, even in its ideological aspect, along those lines of the new psychology that emphasized the dignity and desirability of emotional experience. Naturally, then, Margaret Sanger found a sanction for her life's work in a traumatic reaction to a pathetic death.

But there were other, perhaps more compelling reasons for Mrs. Sanger's reliance on that episode. As Mrs. Sanger grew older, the birth control movement became a broadly based, organized social movement, one which elevated many people, including Margaret Sanger, to international prominence. She gave that movement nearly all her productive years. To it she would sacrifice her marriage and, she may have felt, the life of one of her children.[31] But others emerged to challenge her primacy in the movement. She therefore needed not only to symbolize a moral ideal but also to establish, to herself and to others, the historical necessity of her own person, a proof of the uniqueness of her moral insight. What better claim to uniqueness than to base her actions on that most subjective of motives, the command of an emotional impulse? That would enhance her symbolic role, justify the hardships she had suffered in her private life, and legitimize her claim to sole leadership in the birth control movement.

For similar reasons she occasionally perpetuated some transparent myths. After Sadie Sachs's death, Mrs. Sanger claimed, she spent "almost a year" trying to learn about contraception at various libraries, including the Boston public library, the Library of Congress, and the Library of the New York Academy of Medicine. There, she said, "I

31. See Chapter 3, p. 77.

found no information more reliable than that exchanged
by any back-fence gossips in any small town." [32]

She could not have looked very carefully. The *Index
Catalogue of the Library of the Surgeon-General's Office,*
in 1898, at least fourteen years before Margaret Sanger
concerned herself with the subject, listed nearly two full
pages of books and articles on "prevention of conception."
Those works discussed such methods as the condom, vaginal
douching, suppositories, tampons, and the "womb veil" or
cervical pessary.[33] Here was more than back-fence gossip.
No real improvement was made on those basic techniques
until the advent of the anovulant pill in the 1950s.

Yet Mrs. Sanger insisted that she had to travel to France
in 1913 to find reliable contraceptive information. Again,
that account served to establish her historical uniqueness
and to dramatize the dedication she brought to her work.
By making birth control seem an innovation she personally
had imported from France, she conveniently suppressed
some historical facts: that contraception was widely practiced among certain social groups in the United States as
early as the nineteenth century; [34] that the medical profession did have some, admittedly undiffused, contraceptive
knowledge available; and that Emma Goldman had been
advocating contraception for more than ten years. Mrs.
Sanger usually used the myth of the year's fruitless search to
advance her position in relation to the medical profession,
which balked at her nonmedical leadership in a medical
area. Claiming that before her researches in France doctors
knew little or nothing about contraception was one way to

32. *Autobiography,* pp. 93–95.

33. *Index Catalogue of the Library of the Surgeon-General's Office,
United States Army* 2d ser., 3 (Washington, D.C.: Government Printing
Office, 1898): 800–02. An interesting example of the medical literature
on contraception current in the 1890s is William Pawson Chunn, "The
Prevention of Conception, Its Practicability and Justifiability," *Mary-
land Medical Journal* 32 (1894–95): 340–43. The standard general work
on the subject is Norman E. Himes, *Medical History of Contraception*
(Baltimore: Williams and Wilkins, 1936); see especially pp. 286–303.

34. See Chapter 2, p. 44.

establish her legitimacy with regard to organized medicine.[35]

Mrs. Sanger decided to go to France, she wrote in her *Autobiography*, at the suggestion of Big Bill Haywood, who had himself been there in 1908 and was acquainted with the French syndicalists, including Victor Dave, a venerable survivor of the Paris Commune. Mrs. Sanger neglected to mention that Dave had introduced Emma Goldman to contraceptive ideas in 1900, when he took her to the secret meeting of the Neo-Malthusian Congress in Paris.[36] Presumably Dave had discussed such ideas with Haywood as well, and now Haywood, Mrs. Sanger claimed, urged her to go to France and learn for herself about contraception.[37]

Most probably, however, Mrs. Sanger made the trip at the insistence of her husband, who had long promised her a stay in Paris. During an idyllic Cape Cod summer in the company of Hutchins Hapgood, Mary Heaton Vorse, and the Provincetown Players, Mrs. Sanger chafed increasingly at the mediocrity of her marriage, while her "world-hunger" went unsatisfied. William Sanger probably proposed the Paris trip in a last attempt to hold Margaret's affections. As Hutchins Hapgood remembered it:

> I met Margaret Sanger some years later in Province-town; a very pretty woman and at that time a friend of Emma Goldman and other anarchists, from whom she got her first ideas of birth control. . . . At that time, birth control was part of the whole revolutionary labor movement in France. And these ideas were later preached in America by the unpopular Anarchists, Emma Goldman *et al.* Margaret Sanger, being one of the converts here, received the inspiration. But this, as far as I knew, was not developed in her mind when I met her in Provincetown.[38]

35. See Chapter 7.

36. Richard Drinnon, *Rebel in Paradise: A Biography of Emma Goldman* (Chicago: University of Chicago Press, 1961), p. 67.

37. Sanger, *Autobiography*, p. 96.

38. Hapgood, *A Victorian in the Modern World*, p. 170.

Haywood's suggestion, then, was most likely after the fact, but he turned up in Paris soon after the Sangers' arrival and provided introductions to the leading syndicalists. While William Sanger spent his days studying art, occasionally meeting with Monet and Matisse, his wife talked with various French radicals about industrialism, labor unions, and contraception. They further agitated her itching restlessness. Soon it became obvious that all William Sanger's efforts could not contain her in a tame marriage. Burning with the ambition to take her part in what she saw as the impending revolution, she left her husband in Paris and with her children sailed for New York on December 31, 1913.

Margaret Sanger's radicalism grew from the profound sense of alienation from her environing culture which she had felt since childhood. It grew also from a temperament, inherited from her father, which was frustrated by orthodoxies and conventions, especially those supposed to govern the lives of women. " 'Virtue,' 'Marriage,' 'Respectability,' " she wrote in her journal in 1914, "they are all alike. How glorious too and how impudent the present society—which dares to shut up young girls or women in their 'homes' because that girl defies conventions and fills the longings of her nature. For this she is an outcast. The whole sickly business of society today is a sham," Mrs. Sanger concluded; "one feels like leaving it entirely or going about shocking it terribly." [39] She chose the second alternative. Discussions with the French radicals convinced Mrs. Sanger that her advocacy of contraception would both shock society and help prepare for the revolution.

In 1913 Rosa Luxemburg in Germany and Anatole France in France proposed that workers undertake a "birth-strike," a cessation of childbearing in order to stop the flow of exploited manpower into the industrial and military machines. Karl Kautsky and other orthodox Marxists rebutted

39. Margaret Sanger, "Journal," entry for November 3–4, 1914, MSP-SS.

those heretical proposals with the classic Marxist retort to
Malthusian ideas: that a reduction in the proletarian birthrate would harm socialism by dulling the revolutionary
fervor of the working class and weakening its numerical
strength. In the debate, the sympathies of the French syndicalists around Victor Dave were clear—they had been
advocating controlled fertility since at least 1900. They
persuaded Margaret Sanger. Control of conception, she
now perceived, would do more than alleviate suffering in
the slums and further the emancipation of women: it would
also serve as a weapon in the class struggle.[40]

When the *Woman Rebel* appeared in March 1914, it
aimed its incendiary message directly at the working class.
It lifted its banner slogan, "No Gods, No Masters," from
an IWW flyer distributed at the Lawrence strike in 1912.
The *Woman Rebel* circulated through IWW locals. Emma
Goldman distributed it at her lectures—fifty copies in
Minneapolis, five hundred in Los Angeles. Mrs. Sanger
filled the first issue with a paean to Mary Wollstonecraft,
an excerpt from an Emma Goldman lecture advocating
"free motherhood," and the IWW preamble. On the eighth
and last page appeared an article urging prevention of
conception in order to frighten the "capitalist class." The
article did not, however, give any specific contraceptive
advice.

In subsequent issues of the *Woman Rebel,* Mrs. Sanger
scattered her fire across a wide range of traditional radical
targets. After the Ludlow Massacre of April 1914, she
blasted John D. Rockefeller, Jr., as a "blackhearted pluto-
crat whose soft, flabby hands carry no standard but that of
greed." Philanthropists and social workers, she said, served
Rockefeller's purposes by trying to drug the laboring force
with "the vapid innocuities of religion" and the submissive
middle-class values of courtesy, obedience, and loyalty. The
workers could not be free of that tyrannical conspiracy,
she said, "while there is private property which prevents

40. See *Masses,* October and November 1913, for an account of the
debate on birth control among European radicals.

all men and women having free access to the means of life.
. . . All must possess together—in common that is." She
even condemned marriage as a form of property regulation
in which wives were sex-chattels. "The marriage bed," she
wrote, "is the most degenerating influence in the social
order." Along with political revolution must come the transformation of marriage into a "voluntary association." Only
then, said the *Woman Rebel,* paraphrasing Emma Goldman,
could there be a "new character, a new essence of personality, a new individuality." [41]

Though the *Woman Rebel* vibrated with the tones of
revolution and sexual liberation, it played a discordant
tune. Mrs. Sanger crudely counterpointed her commendable
assaults on worn sexual conventions and stupid censorship
with notes of intemperance, character vilification, and vir-
ulent class hatred. The result was a rather shrill squawk.
As Max Eastman commented in the *Masses,* "the *Woman
Rebel* has fallen into that most unfeminist of errors, the
tendency to cry out when a quiet and contained utterance is
indispensable." He added that since it was written "in a
style of overconscious extremism and blare of rebellion for
its own sake those who incline to the life of reason will be
the last to read it." [42]

The *Woman Rebel* discussed and advocated contraception—the June issue for the first time called it "birth
control," a term devised by Margaret Sanger and some
friends—though it never described contraceptive practices
in the detail Mrs. Sanger had led her readers to expect. But
the Post Office Department still found sufficient cause for
declaring the newspaper unmailable under the terms of
Section 211 of the Criminal Code of the United States.

Section 211 was part of the so-called Comstock law, a
group of statutes passed hastily in 1873 at the insistence of
Anthony Comstock and his Society for the Suppression of
Vice. To protect sexual purity and, allegedly, to suppress
quack medical advertisers, Congress had unreflectingly en-

41. *Woman Rebel,* March, May, June 1914, copies in MSP–LC.
42. *Masses,* May 1914, p. 5.

acted sweeping prohibitions against mailing, transporting, or importing "obscene, lewd, or lascivious" articles. Though the lawmakers offered no criteria by which to judge the obscenity of an article, they specifically included in the ban all devices and information pertaining to "preventing conception." [43] Margaret Sanger, however, had not yet violated that particular provision.

On April 2, 1914, the postmaster for New York City notified Mrs. Sanger that the March issue of the *Woman Rebel* could not be mailed, under the terms of Section 211. She tried to ascertain the specific basis of his complaint, but he would not stipulate what the censors found objectionable.[44] Since the government did not seem about to take immediate punitive action, Mrs. Sanger went ahead and published the April issue, with which the Post Office did not interfere. Subsequently, however, censors declared unmailable the issues for May, July, August, September, and October.

In August, two federal agents came to Mrs. Sanger's home and presented her with an indictment for violating the Comstock law on nine counts. The United States Attorney especially objected to an article in the *Woman Rebel* by Herbert A. Thorpe entitled "A Defense of Assassination," a description of which, read the indictment, "would defile the records of this Court." [45] With an apostolic fervor that was to become characteristic, Mrs. Sanger sat the two agents down and at the end of several hours had convinced them of the sense of birth control. But the law was less amenable than these two of its minions. On August 25, Margaret Sanger was arraigned in the United States District Court for Southern New York. She requested, and received, six weeks to prepare her case, and Judge John Hazel (who had

43. Now 18 U.S.C. 1461, 18 U.S.C. 1462, 19 U.S.C. 1305.

44. E. M. Morgan to Margaret Sanger, April 2, 1914, April 7, 1914, and Margaret Sanger to Morgan, June 5, 1914, MSP–LC.

45. A copy of the indictment is in the Federal Records Center, 641 Washington Street, New York, New York.

earned an historical parenthesis by swearing in Theodore
Roosevelt as President of the United States in a Buffalo
drawing room) released her on her own recognizance.

In her *Autobiography,* Mrs. Sanger claimed that the
court, several weeks later, suddenly called her case without
notice, rebuked her for failing to appear, and set her trial
for the following day, refusing to allow adequate time to
prepare her defense.[46] In fact, Mrs. Sanger had been ap-
prised of the date of the trial at her arraignment. She
deliberately neglected to go to court on the appointed day
though she had been duly notified a second time. Nor did
the court diabolically contrive to rob her of time to prepare
her case. She had, even by her own account, six weeks between the arraignment and the appointed trial; and when
she did not appear at the trial, the United States Attorney
gave her an extension of not one but eight days.[47] The in-
substantiality of Mrs. Sanger's own account revealed her
obsession with portraying herself as a battler against unscrupulous enemies. Her insistence on that posture not only,
as in this case, confused the historical record; it often con-
founded the progress of the birth control movement as well.

Mrs. Sanger's behavior in that fall of 1914 manifested
her continuing uncertainty of purpose. The *Woman Rebel,*
which had announced in the first issue its intention to give
contraceptive information, instead devoted its columns to
damning the Rockefellers, religion, and matrimony. In a
separate venture, however, Mrs. Sanger had had secretly
printed 100,000 copies of a small pamphlet entitled "Family
Limitation," in which she set out the various contraceptive
techniques she had allegedly learned in France.[48] She now

46. Sanger, *Autobiography,* p. 118.
47. H. Snowden Marshall to Margaret Sanger, October 7, 1914,
MSP–LC.
48. In that remarkable document Mrs. Sanger told women that "a
mutual and satisfied sexual act is of great benefit to the average
woman, the magnetism of it is health giving, and acts as a beautifier
and tonic." As contraceptives, she recommended douches, condoms,

had worked herself into a real imbroglio. She had supposedly set out to break the law prohibiting the dissemination
of contraceptive information and articles. But she had been
indicted under quite different provisions of the obscenity
statutes. There seemed little point in Mrs. Sanger's taking
her chances in court with the *Woman Rebel* charges when
they were, for her purposes, the wrong charges. "Family
Limitation," the one document that, if mailed, would
clearly violate the federal ban pertaining to "preventing
conception," still lay in the packing boxes in which it had
come from the printers. And the issue would only be confused if a test case involving "Family Limitation" came up
while Mrs. Sanger was already in jail on the *Woman Rebel*
charges. Her own stridency in the *Woman Rebel,* what Max
Eastman called "the blare of rebellion for its own sake," had
frustrated Margaret Sanger's desires to clarify the law on
contraception and disseminate contraceptive information.
Confused, discouraged, desperate, Mrs. Sanger decided she
could do but one thing. She left the country.

She went first to Montreal. Since she was charged with a
felony and was extraditable, she assumed the name "Bertha
Watson." About the first of November "Bertha Watson,"
without a passport, boarded the *R.M.S. Virginian* bound
for Liverpool. As the *Virginian* made its way down the St.
Lawrence, loaded with a cargo of munitions for the three-
month-old European war, Mrs. Sanger brooded about the
course her life was taking. Giving a clue, perhaps, to the
reasons for the disintegration of her marriage, she wrote in
her journal:

> The man who shouts loud about his liberal ideas and
> thinks himself advanced finds the servile submission
> of his wife charming and womanly. How he guards her
> lest she receive a word, inspire new thought, and re-

---

suppositories, and cervical cap pessaries. She most highly endorsed
the pessary and urged women to learn its use and then "teach each
other." Such statements as that were later to complicate Mrs. Sanger's
relations with the medical profession. See Chapter 7, p. 172 n.

bellion. How closely he keeps her within the boundary
of his own, like a priest who watches and weeds the
young ideas to keep them forever within the enclosure
of the church.[49]

Mrs. Sanger had broken out of the enclosure of a doll's-
house marriage but had bungled her first attempt at rebellion. Her *Woman Rebel* plan, whatever it might have been,
had backfired. Now, steaming across the gray North Atlantic
to wartime England, she paid the price. But, once she was
safely out of reach of the law, she cut her losses by sending
a cable releasing the 100,000 copies of "Family Limitation"
to prearranged distribution points. They went out principally through IWW locals to "comrades" all over the
country.[50]

Margaret Sanger arrived in Liverpool in the middle of
November, with vague plans and little money (what money
she had at this time and for the next several months came
chiefly through Leonard Abbott from the Free Speech
League, a libertarian organization closely associated with
the Liberal Club).[51] She wrote her sister that she looked
forward to meeting Edward Carpenter, to whom some
friends had given her a letter of introduction, and to calling on the offices of the Neo-Malthusian League in London.
At least the pattern of her personal life was becoming clear.
She understood now that William Sanger's year without her
in Paris (he had not returned until her indictment in
August) had prepared them both for "a parting of the ways
. . . it is always hard to live together after a long separation." Alone in Liverpool, she missed her children. She
especially pitied Stuart, now enrolled in a Christian Science

49. Margaret Sanger, "Journal," entry for November 3–4, 1914, MSP–
SS.

50. Sanger, *Autobiography*, p. 122; "Two comrades" to Margaret
Sanger, August 23, 1915, MSP–LC.

51. Somehow, with the aid of an influential shipboard acquaintance,
she fast-talked her way past the British immigration authorities, who
were, in wartime, understandably reluctant to admit anyone without
a passport.

School on Long Island. "Poor child," she wrote, "his father and mother anarchists and he in such a school." [52]

In her few weeks in Liverpool, Mrs. Sanger attended at least one meeting of the local Fabian Society. There she met Lorenzo Portet, an associate of the same Francisco Ferrer for whom the New York anarchists had named their school. He secured an interview for Mrs. Sanger with Mr. and Mrs. C. V. Drysdale, the leaders of the English Neo-Malthusian League. Accordingly, she proceeded to London to meet the people who at that time were the world's most prominent Malthusian propagandists. The Drysdales' secretary recalled that "on the appointed afternoon we awaited with curiosity, and also a little apprehension, the visit of the 'Woman Rebel,' but we were hardly prepared for the surprise given us by the soft-voiced, gentle-mannered, altogether charming 'rebel' who tapped at the door at four o'clock." The Drysdales, Dr. Binnie Dunlop, another prominent Malthusian, and F. W. Stella Browne, a noted feminist, listened to Mrs. Sanger's tale of her encounter with the notorious Comstock law. The little group applauded her enthusiastically. "That afternoon," Mrs. Sanger remembered, "was one of the most encouraging and delightful of my life." [53]

Her new friends comforted Margaret Sanger in her loneliness, and they furthered her education. They told her the story of English Malthusianism, of its roots in economic theory, its difficulties with the Socialists, its support from liberals like John Stuart Mill and Robert Owen, its victory in the Charles Bradlaugh-Annie Besant trial of 1877, and its propaganda activities since the trial. Encouraged by their support, Mrs. Sanger began to study regularly in the British Museum, eager to learn more of the history and rationale of birth control. At the museum, not entirely by chance, she met Edward Carpenter. Either through him or

52. Margaret Sanger to Mary Higgins, n.d., and November 20, 1914, MSP–SS.

53. Olive M. Johnson, typescript describing Margaret Sanger's visit to England, n.d., MSP–LC; Sanger, *Autobiography*, p. 130.

through Stella Browne, she received an invitation to tea with Havelock Ellis.

Havelock Ellis by 1914 had gained a worldwide reputation as one of the greatest living sexual psychologists. His seven-volume *Studies in the Psychology of Sex* had become the standard work on sexual abnormality. But he was more than a scientist. As a young man, Ellis had joined the Fellowship of the New Life, an organization formed in 1883 by a roving Scottish intellectual, Thomas Davidson, and James Hinton, an Englishman whom Ellis knew and revered. The New Life program shared the romantic philosophy preached by the New York anarchists. Whereas the English Fabians, like the American Socialists, believed "outer change would produce inner revolution," the members of the Fellowship, like the supporters of the Ferrer School, believed in creating "a kind of atmosphere in which it shall be possible for the outward life to be a true exponent of the inward life." Influenced by such ideas, Ellis informed his writing with an intuition, even an artistry, that gave his work an almost metaphysical character. Ellis's approach to sex, his biographer has observed, held out "the wonderful possibility of a mystical communion." [54] Clearly, Havelock Ellis stood with Edward Carpenter and Arnold Bennett in the same romantic tradition that appealed so strongly to Margaret Sanger.

To Ellis's flat in Brixton Mrs. Sanger came, timidly, in December 1914. Ellis, tall, lean, with long, wavy white hair and a beard like an Old Testament prophet's framing his large handsome features, was notoriously unable to make small talk. If there were no serious topics to be discussed, he would sit in calm, total quiet. So he did with Margaret Sanger, and she awkwardly struggled to break the long, painful silences. Eventually she worked her charm, and Ellis, always a generous soul, found his sense of chivalry aroused. He listened, "fascinated by the young woman's story, by her courage, her devotion to an ideal, her fire, her

54. Arthur Calder-Marshall, *The Sage of Sex: A Life of Havelock Ellis* (New York: G. P. Putnam's Sons, 1959), pp. 87, 113.

vitality and beauty." Then he began to offer some advice, which so impressed Margaret Sanger that she developed for him "a reverence, an affection, and a love which strengthened with the years." As for Ellis, "he had never been so quickly or completely drawn to a woman in the whole of his life." [55]

Margaret Sanger left Ellis's flat feeling as though she "had been exalted into a hitherto undreamed-of world." [56] New York radicalism had been too vague and unstructured to do more than further agitate her ambition. But in England she found world-famous personalities with a definite program for reform and more or less definite ideas about how to implement it. The Drysdales, and especially Havelock Ellis, insisted that she concentrate on one issue, birth control, and leave the denunciations of capitalism, churches, and matrimony aside. Ellis also tried to convince her of the value of caution and prudence. "I have been carefully reading the *Woman Rebel*," he wrote her. "You know I think you are splendid. I do not always agree with you when you attack, but I always agree when you define. . . . It is no use, however, being too reckless and smashing your head against a blank wall, for not one rebel, or even many rebels, can crush law by force." To change the law, Ellis pointed out, "needs *skill* even more than it needs strength." [57]

Skill demanded knowledge. Consequently, Ellis became Mrs. Sanger's tutor. Meeting her daily at the British Museum reading room, he advised her what to read, answered her questions, told her of the work of others in the field of contraception, and talked long hours with her about every phase of the subject of birth control. Under Ellis's tutelage, Margaret Sanger studied the early, crude population economics of Malthus, Mill, and Owen. She also read pamphlets on contraceptive technique, such as *Fruits of Philosophy*, published by a Boston doctor named Charles Knowl-

55. Sanger, *My Fight*, pp. 101–03; *Autobiography*, pp. 133–41; Calder-Marshall, *Sage of Sex*, pp. 197–98.

56. *Autobiography*, p. 136.

57. Havelock Ellis to Margaret Sanger, January 9, 1915, MSP–LC.

ton in 1832 but later suppressed in the United States. *Fruits of Philosophy* had enjoyed a wide circulation in England, and its distribution had been the immediate occasion of the Bradlaugh-Besant trial in 1877. Mrs. Sanger also read descriptions of contraceptive methods by the American R. T. Trall, by H. A. Albutt, and by Annie Besant herself.

Ellis introduced Mrs. Sanger to eugenic ideas with accounts of the supposedly scientific breeding practiced by the American Oneida Community under the leadership of John Humphrey Noyes. And Ellis showed her a book that had had a profound influence on his own life, and indirectly, on most twentieth-century thinking about sex: George Drysdale's *Elements of Social Science*. Drysdale, in a refinement of the classic Malthusian thesis, argued that mankind faced a choice between economic or amatory deprivation. Though Drysdale recognized the gravity of the former condition, he cared more about the latter. Only artificial contraception, he said, could increase the amount of love in the world. Drysdale was thus probably the first modern thinker to perceive the possibilities of applying the achievements of science to the enhancement of romantic love.[58]

With Havelock Ellis's guidance, Margaret Sanger began to shape the ideas she had assimilated into a systematic, even philosophic, justification for birth control. Her thought was finally acquiring the ideological structure it had so conspicuously and painfully lacked. More than anything else, Ellis and the Drysdales taught her that to be successful she would have to restrict and focus her energies. And they convinced her that birth control, not vague radical harangues, deserved her exclusive attention.

By January 1915, Ellis was urging Mrs. Sanger to go to Holland and visit the government-supported birth control clinic at The Hague. The Drysdales gave her a letter of introduction to Dr. Johannes Rutgers, who operated the clinic and had pioneered in the field of clinical contracep-

58. Havelock Ellis to Margaret Sanger, December 24, 1914, December 26, 1914, MSP–LC.

tion in the 1880s. In her own pamphlet "Family Limitation," Mrs. Sanger had recommended the Mispah cervical
cap pessary. Dr. Rutgers, however, showed her the superior
Mensinga diaphragm, invented by the German doctor Wilhelm Mensinga in the 1880s. Most significantly, Dr. Rutgers
dissuaded her from the view expressed in "Family Limitation" that women could "teach each other" contraceptive
methods or that they could learn from pamphlets such as
Mrs. Sanger's.[59] Every woman desiring birth control instruction, said Dr. Rutgers, must be medically examined and
individually fitted by a physician with the proper type and
size of pessary. Contraception, he insisted, was strictly a
medical matter. Margaret Sanger's acceptance of that lesson
determined the whole course of the subsequent birth control
movement.

After her visit to Holland, Mrs. Sanger returned briefly
to London and then set out for Spain. There she spent the
remainder of the winter as Lorenzo Portet's guest. The
warm weather was a welcome relief from the London damp-
ness which irritated her persistent tubercular condition.
But she missed her children more and more. She wrote her
sister: "Have you seen the kiddies? Write me about them
Nan, please do. . . . The poor dears—they are having a
rough time of it these days." [60]

The children were having an especially rough time of it.
Not only had their mother fled the country in the face of
criminal charges, but now their father faced jail too. Anthony Comstock in person had arrested William Sanger in
early 1915 for giving a copy of "Family Limitation" to a

59. While in England, Mrs. Sanger had written three more pamphlets
advocating birth control and describing contraceptive techniques.
They were "English Methods of Birth Control," "Dutch Methods of
Birth Control," and "Magnetation Methods of Birth Control." The
last described the Oneida technique, *amplexus reservatus*. Mrs. Sanger
sent copies of these, along with regular monthly newsletters, to her
"friends and comrades" in the United States. Many of the pamphlets,
however, went down with the *Arabic*. Copies are in MSP–SS.

60. Margaret Sanger to Nan [Higgins], n.d., and February 22, 1915,
MSP–LC.

Comstock agent in disguise. Mrs. Sanger wrote her "Comrades and Friends" that her husband's difficulties

> could be no more deeply burned in my soul than the sufferings and anguish of thousands of other women's loved ones, left alone in sorrow by death which has been caused by abortion. Nor could the loneliness of my children be any greater, or their orphanage more tragic, than those thousands of little ones left motherless through deaths caused by this same tricky government, through its ignorance and cruelty.

Though she deeply desired to return to her family in their time of trouble, she said, the cause of birth control demanded that she remain in Europe and continue her "education." [61]

Mrs. Sanger undoubtedly regretted the absence from her children. Nevertheless, she seemed in no hurry to return to the United States, and she had good reason not to. Leonard Abbott warned that on her return she would "almost surely have to go to prison." [62] By August 1915, she had nearly decided to accept Lorenzo Portet's offer of a three-year contract with a publishing house in Paris, where she would supervise the selection of English texts for translation. Then in September word came that William Sanger had been convicted on Comstock's obscenity charge and had elected to go to jail for thirty days rather than pay the fine. Mrs. Sanger expressed her resentment that "Bill had to get mixed up in my work after all, and of course make it harder for me and all of us!" [63] She apparently would have preferred

61. Margaret Sanger to "Comrades and Friends," February 4, 1915, MSP–LC.

62. Leonard Abbott to Margaret Sanger, May 1, 1915, June 1, 1915, MSP–LC.

63. Margaret Sanger to Nan [Higgins], n.d., from Barcelona, Spain, MSP–LC. In her *Autobiography* (p. 175) and in *My Fight* (pp. 117–18, 126), Mrs. Sanger explained that a mysterious psychic phenomenon also prevented her from concluding the arrangements with Portet. She had been conscious of the number "6," she said, for quite some time during her "exile." She could not understand the vision until

to carry on her work alone, from Paris, as a sort of propagandist in absentia, an American Christabel Pankhurst, remote and romantic in the glorious glow of martyrdom and exile. But her husband had spoiled that. Now she had to come home. By the end of September she had sailed from Bordeaux across the submarine-infested Atlantic.

As she gazed at the monotonous sea horizon on her lonely return voyage, Mrs. Sanger may have pondered how far from the obscurity of Corning her quest for experience had already brought her. And she may have wondered at the consequences of her decision, by now fairly well crystallized, to dedicate her life to a movement for the scientific control of human reproduction.

Margaret Sanger was, in many ways, an unlikely spokeswoman for a cause that so many at first considered so baleful. Mabel Dodge described her as "the Madonna type of woman." [64] One of her associates noted her difference from the conventional image of the feminine reformer:

> Those who, in the early days, not having seen her, pictured her as a massive, masculine, blustering creature, a sort of combination Carrie Nation and Mrs. Pankhurst, brandishing a hatchet in one hand and a contraceptive in the other, were amazed, if they had the good fortune to meet her, to find a rather slight woman, very beautiful, with wide-apart gray eyes and a crown of auburn hair, combining a radiant feminine appeal with an impression of serenity, calm, and graciousness of voice and manner. But woe to him who was misled by this calm exterior into ignoring the

finally it took the definite form "November 6." She did not know even then what was the significance of that date, but she was convinced it was something ominous. On November 6, 1915, just a few weeks after Margaret Sanger had returned to the United States, her daughter Peggy died of pneumonia.

64. Mabel Dodge Luhan, *Intimate Memories,* vol. 3. *Movers and Shakers* (New York: Harcourt, Brace, 1936), p. 69.

tremendous fighting spirit, the self-generating energy, and the relentless drive that lay beneath it.[65]

Similarly, Emma Goldman found that most women could not believe the editor of the brazen *Woman Rebel* was "a little, delicate woman, refined and shrinking." [66] Mrs. Sanger dressed conservatively, spoke softly and intelligently, but had a commanding presence. Few who met her failed to fall captive to her personal charm. Her charisma, fully as much as the persuasiveness of her arguments, made many converts to her cause.

Havelock Ellis did much to shape that charisma when he tempered the sharpness borne of Mrs. Sanger's alienation and embittered radicalism. To be sure, her father had taught her the value of charity when he told her to leave the world better than she found it. And her experiences in New York had awakened in her a strong humanitarian strain. But both her father and her New York comrades had also taught lessons of hatred. In Havelock Ellis's life and philosophy, there was no place for hatred. He had learned from James Hinton that he must "dedicate himself to what Christians called God but what he preferred with Hinton to call the Not-Self." [67] Margaret Sanger said of Ellis: "His philosophy, if it can be reduced to an essence, is that of life more abundant—attained through a more complete understanding of ourselves and an unruffled charity to all." [68] She tried to follow that philosophy, though frequently with imperfect results. Often, her old bitterness would assert itself, much to the detriment of her larger purposes. But Margaret Sanger stood ready, in 1915, to give her lifetime to charitable service to mankind.

65. Henry Pratt Fairchild, in *Nation*, May 7, 1955, p. 406.
66. Emma Goldman to Margaret Sanger, April 19, 1914, MSP–LC.
67. Calder-Marshall, *Sage of Sex*, p. 73.
68. Sanger, *Autobiography*, p. 141.

CHAPTER 2

The Nineteenth-Century Heritage: The Family, Feminism, and Sex

Margaret Sanger returned to a troubled country. By 1915, social, economic, and ideological forces were visibly transforming the most sacrosanct aspects of nineteenth-century life: the condition of the family, the status of women, and the nature of sexuality.

When Mrs. Sanger called contraception birth control and made it a public issue, she was not inventing a new social practice. But she did inject a new term and a new degree of frankness into the debate on what was coming to be called the sexual revolution. The place of birth control in that revolution, and the context within which it was debated, depended directly on its relation to the transformations affecting the family, woman, and sex.

The nineteenth-century American considered the family, Henry James, Sr. said, "the original germ-cell which lies at the base of all that we call society." That view drew support from the findings of American social scientists, who, in their Germanic search for the origins of all institutions, repeatedly demonstrated the initial formation of society in the microcosm of the family. And the sacredness of the idea of the family had more than an evolutionary derivation. In a country plagued by the divisive effects of civil war, territorial expansion, and the birth of modern industrialism, men put a high premium on the forces working for order and cohesion. The family, they thought, was such a force. Its significance, therefore, was less personal than social. The happiness of its members was well and good, but as James pointed out, "the true sanctity of marriage inheres at bottom in its social uses: It is the sole nursery of the social sentiment in the human bosom." [1] Since the family was both germ cell and nursery, any attempts to tamper with it contradicted nature and threatened the entire moral order. As a woman writer said in 1873: "Whatever tends to deteriorate the marriage relation and consequently the home, tends to deteriorate the whole machinery of life, whether social or political." [2]

By the beginning of the twentieth century, the very forces against which the home had been deemed the most effective defense appeared to many to be undermining the home itself. Critics blamed especially the recrudescence of primitive individualism, as evidenced by growing divorce rates, for the destruction of the traditional family. Several observers saw that ruinous spirit best typified in the dramas of Henrik Ibsen, whose philosophy was described as "bold and uncompromising selfishness." Many Americans agreed with the literary critic Chauncey Hawkins that in the face of such egotism, "the family, that institution which we have long regarded as the unit of civilization, the foundation of the state," could not long survive.[3]

The alarm had little substance. The nineteenth-century family, which the Victorians regarded as a contemporary embodiment of the primeval social unit, was in fact a relatively modern institution. As the French historian Phillipe Ariés has convincingly shown, the concept of the family did not emerge until the late Renaissance, and then only among the upper classes. The apparent disintegration of the family which the late Victorians decried in fact repre-

1. Henry James, "Is Marriage Holy?" *Atlantic Monthly*, March 1870, p. 363.

2. Abba Goold Woolson, *Woman in American Society* (Boston: Roberts Brothers, 1873), p. 82.

3. Chauncey J. Hawkins, *Will the Home Survive? A Study of Tendencies in Modern Literature* (New York: Thomas Whittaker, 1907), pp. 7, 56.

sented its adjustment to new living conditions brought
about by urbanization and industrialization. But those processes by no means spelled the death of the family.[4]

As Americans moved increasingly to cities in the nineteenth century, old patterns of family life had to change.
Separated in most instances from the protective and pre-
ceptive influences of kin groups and village culture, men
and women newly arrived in American cities began family
life without precedents and with only vague prospects. As
the sociologist Arthur W. Calhoun commented, America
was the first civilization that in any large way experimented
with "placing the entire burden of securing the success of
marriage and the family life upon the characters and capacities of two persons. . . . American marriage is a union
of two people and not an alliance between two families." In
that new atomistic union, marital partners took on new
roles and marriage itself assumed new character and functions. On the farm, the family had been an integral producing unit. In the city, families no longer worked together.
The factory or the office kept the father away from the home
most of the day. The urban economy forced the housewife out of the agricultural producing unit and, by emphasizing pecuniary rewards, tended to devalue household
labor. Moreover, industry itself usurped many of the functions the housewife had once been accustomed to perform-
ing. "The machine," wrote E. A. Ross, "has captured most
of the domestic processes." Thus the urban home by the
early twentieth century had lost nearly all its economic
cogency.[5]

4. Phillipe Ariés, *Centuries of Childhood* (New York: Alfred A.
Knopf, 1962); Christopher Lasch, "Divorce and the Family in America,"
Atlantic, November 1966, pp. 57–61; see also William L. O'Neill,
Divorce in the Progressive Era (New Haven: Yale University Press,
1967).

5. Arthur W. Calhoun, *A Social History of the American Family*,
vol. 3, *Since the Civil War* (Cleveland: Arthur H. Clark, 1919), p. 169;
E. A. Ross, "The Significance of Increasing Divorce," *Century Magazine,* May 1909, p. 151; see also Robert W. Smuts, *Women and Work
in America* (New York: Columbia University Press, 1959).

As industry deprived the family of many of its economic functions, the state took over many of its welfare functions by enacting laws creating compulsory education, maternal health programs, and juvenile court systems. Social critics from John Spargo to Theodore Roosevelt endorsed the Socialist idea of the state as an "over-parent" which should provide schools, housing, sanitation, and recreation in the crowded cities. "If this be Socialism," Roosevelt said, "make the most of it!" Thus with little dissent, the state substituted its services for the old self-sufficiency of the family.[6]

Paradoxically, many of the same critics who blamed "individualism" for the destruction of the Victorian family also observed a "new solidarity of the state" being built "at the expense of the old solidarity of the family." Somehow, the individualism that destroyed one institution was supposed to give birth to the collectivism that strengthened another.[7] The confusion reflected the Victorian failure to recognize the transformation of the family not as a collapse but as an adjustment. The family did not retreat before new social forces. Indeed, the late nineteenth century saw a continuation of the strengthening of the notion of the family, especially among the middle and upper classes. As Ariés has remarked, "the whole evolution of our contemporary manners is unintelligible if one neglects this astonishing growth of the concept of the family. It is not individualism which has triumphed, but the family." [8]

But in that triumph the family took on a new vital center. "The old economic framework of the family has largely fallen away," noted E. A. Ross in 1909, "leaving more of the strain on the personal tie." Ross did not mean that husbands and wives had never before loved each other or that personal relations had not always figured importantly in

6. John Spargo, *Socialism and Motherhood* (New York: B. W. Huebsch, 1914); Theodore Roosevelt, *The Foes of Our Own Household* (New York: George H. Doran, 1917), p. 183.

7. George Elliott Howard, "Changed Ideals and Status of the Family and the Public Activities of Women," *Annals of the American Academy of Political and Social Science* 56 (November 1914): 29.

8. Ariés, *Centuries of Childhood*, p. 406.

marriage. But when urban industrialism displaced economic
partnership from the matrix of marriage, such factors as
congeniality and affection assumed greater importance. "Essentially," said George Elliott Howard, a sociologist who
wrote frequently on the divorce problem, "the family society is becoming a psychic fact." The family, in other words,
had taken on increased, rather than diminished, emotional
significance. Husbands now had to be more than mere pro-
viders. And wives, having lost the role of economic partner,
had to assume several new ones. "In the old days," commented a woman in 1907, "a married woman was supposed
to be a frump and a bore and a physical wreck. Now you
are supposed to keep up intellectually, to look young and
well and be fresh and bright and entertaining." Rising divorce rates signaled more than the ease of separation in a
free and rich society. They also bespoke the difficulty of
adjustment to the intensified emotional demands of family
life.[9]

The new industrial economy also demanded a new work
discipline which denied emotion and encouraged exclusively cognitive behavior in the interests of production.
That compartmentalization of experience made the home
the exclusive arena for the play of emotion. And the growth
of the family's emotional exclusiveness made the home an
increasingly private place. As the urban family became less
self-sufficient, therefore, it simultaneously grew more committed to self-determination. Ariés has shown that "in the
18th century, the family began to hold society at a distance,
to push it back beyond a steadily extending zone of private
life." Nineteenth-century industrialism quickened that development, and by 1906 an American sociologist frankly
acknowledged "the manifest conflict of interests between
the individual family and the community at large." That
conflict was most marked, the writer said, when the family

9. Ross, "Increasing Divorce," p. 151; Howard, "Changed Ideals,"
p. 29; Lydia K. Commander, *The American Idea* (New York: A. S.
Barnes, 1907), p. 182.

refused to produce enough children for the service of the state.[10]

A new attitude toward childhood, along with the development of the family as a "psychic fact" and as a progressively more private institution, completed the list of characteristics that distinguished the modern family. Again, as Ariés has demonstrated, "the concept of the family, which thus emerges in the 16th and 17th centuries, is inseparable from the concept of childhood." Before the sixteenth century, children were considered "little adults," who were loved, to be sure, but whose primary value to the producing family was economic. After that time, in line with the general restructuring of the family, children took on a greater emotional value. Moreover, childhood came increasingly to be regarded as a special age of life, and the child as a special being with his own distinctive qualities. Foremost among those qualities was the child's capacity for formation and development. When that quality was recognized, as Christopher Lasch has said, "child-rearing ceased to be simply one of many activities and became the central concern—one is tempted to say the central obsession—of family life." The late nineteenth century made that concern explicit, as in the novelist Margaret Deland's proclamation of "the right of children *not* to be born." When parents, she said, "unable to support a child in physical and moral and intellectual well-being, bring such a child into the world . . . they are socially criminal." And when Charlotte Perkins Gilman said in 1911 that the duty of the family was to ensure children "an ever longer period of immaturity," by extending their education as long as possible, she was acknowledging the new status of the child not as an economic asset, but as an economic liability. In that way the oft-noted shift from a producing to a consuming psychology affected

10. Ariés, *Centuries of Childhood*, p. 398; American Sociological Society, *Papers and Proceedings* 1 (1906): 53. See also Kenneth Keniston, *The Uncommitted: Alienated Youth in American Society* (New York: Harcourt, Brace and World, 1965), pp. 241–81.

even the affairs of the family. Parents no longer produced children in the greatest quantity possible. They had fewer children in order to provide each with a better quality of upbringing.[11]

The shrinking size of the American family—especially among the genteel classes—caused at least as much alarm at the turn of the century as did the growing divorce rate. Benjamin Franklin had predicted in 1755 that the abundance of the New World would cause the American people to double their numbers every twenty years. At that rate, there should have been nearly 130 million Americans by 1900; in fact, there were scarcely 76 million. In Franklin's day, families commonly had eight or ten children. By 1900, the average number of children per family was closer to three. The birthrate of American women had been falling steadily since at least 1820. While 1,000 mothers in 1800 had 1,300 children under five years of age, the same number of mothers in 1900 had fewer than 700 such children. The trend indicated, said Theodore Roosevelt, that the American people were committing "race suicide." With that utterance in 1903, Roosevelt minted the phrase which for the next forty years was a frequent rallying cry for the opponents of birth control.[12]

President Roosevelt, in his annual message to Congress in 1905, described the transformation of family life "as one of the greatest sociological phenomena of our time; it is a social question of the first importance, of far greater importance than any merely political or economic question can be." Yet much of Roosevelt's concern for the condition of the family proceeded from his political assumptions. In his view, the family should be the servant of the state; it

11. Ariés, *Centuries of Childhood*, p. 353; Lasch, "Divorce and the Family," p. 59; Margaret Deland, "The Change in the Feminine Ideal," *Atlantic Monthly*, March 1910, p. 291; Charlotte Perkins Gilman, *The Man-Made World, or, Our Androcentric Culture* (New York: Charlton, 1911), p. 27.

12. *Historical Statistics of the United States* (Washington: Government Printing Office, 1961), pp. 23, 24, 180, 181; T. Roosevelt, *Foes*, p. 257.

should provide children to build national strength. Germany dominated Europe, Roosevelt wrote, because she had won "the warfare of the cradle . . . during the nineteenth century." If America aspired to ascendancy in world affairs, American parents must breed larger families.[13]

The race suicide alarm, however, fed more on ethnocentric fears than on nationalist ambition. Though Roosevelt complained because American population statistics did not keep pace with his jingoistic appetite, he considered the "worst evil" to be the greater infertility of "the old native American stock, especially in the North East," as compared with the immigrant population. In 1902 R. R. Kuczynski demonstrated what everyone had suspected for a long time—that the immigrant birthrate was 70 to 80 percent higher than the native birthrate. Worse, Kuczynski concluded, it was "probable that the native population cannot hold its own. It seems to be dying out." In a study a few years later, the United States Immigration Commission found that "the rate of childbearing on the part of women of foreign parentage is nearly twice as great as that of native American women." But significantly, the Immigration Commission reported another phenomenon: the average number of children borne by the second generation immigrant woman "was invariably smaller than the average for the first generation." Clearly, then, the determinants of fertility were not solely ethnic; they apparently had a great deal to do with economic status and the amorphous notion of class.[14]

13. *Messages and Papers of the Presidents* 16 (New York: Bureau of National Literature, n.d.): 6984; Theodore Roosevelt, "Race Decadence," *Outlook*, April 8, 1911, p. 765.

14. Theodore Roosevelt to Cecil Arthur Spring Rice, August 11, 1899, in *The Letters of Theodore Roosevelt*, Elting E. Morison, ed., 8 vols. (Cambridge: Harvard University Press, 1951–54), 2:1053; R. R. Kuczynski, "The Fecundity of the Native and Foreign Born Population in Massachusetts," *Quarterly Journal of Economics* 16 (1902): 141–86; U.S., Congress, Senate, *Report of the United States Immigration Commission*, 61st Cong., 2d sess. (Washington: Government Printing Office, 1911), 28:753, 749.

That perception added to ethnocentric fears the alarming prospect that not simply native Americans but in particular the upper classes, the highest products of evolution and natural selection, were failing to reproduce themselves. President Charles W. Eliot of Harvard confirmed the worst suspicions in 1902 when he reported that a typical group of Harvard graduates fell 28 percent short of replenishing its number. A later study revealed that only 75 percent of late nineteenth-century Harvard graduates married; of these, nearly a quarter had childless marriages, and the rest averaged scarcely two children per marriage. Yale graduates did little better. That was "gloomy enough," the report concluded, but it called the birthrate among college women "the most pathetic spectacle of all." In the average Wellesley class, for example, only one-half the graduates married, and those who did invariably had small families. A New York newspaper reporter in 1907 found only fifteen children in sixteen of the highest-rent residential blocks in New York. It seemed that the very class upon which many in the Progressive generation pinned their hopes for an orderly future was disappearing.[15]

Commentators cited a myriad of causes for the decline in the upper-class birthrate, ranging from the spread of venereal disease, to "physiological infertility" induced by "the high voltage of American civilization," to the inevitable consequences of spiritual degeneracy. But more disinterested observers recognized that the decline in the birthrate was voluntary. One writer noted that "outside our immigrant class, and a few native-born families scattered here and there, women have learned the art of preventing pregnancy."[16] Charles Knowlton's handbook of contraceptive

15. *Annual Reports of the President and the Treasurer of Harvard College, 1901–02* (Cambridge: Harvard University, 1903), pp. 31–32; John C. Phillips, "A Study of the Birth-Rate in Harvard and Yale Graduates," *Harvard Graduates Magazine*, September, 1916, p. 25; Commander, *American Idea*, p. 198.

16. Edward L. Thorndike, "The Decrease in the Size of American Families," *Popular Science Monthly* 63 (May 1903): 64–70.

techniques, *Fruits of Philosophy*, had only a small under-ground circulation in this country after its publication in 1832; but the declining birthrate indicated that the prac-tices he described—probably vaginal douching in particular —were increasingly employed in certain social classes. A doctor, as early as 1867, said that "there is scarcely a young lady in New England—and probably it is so throughout the land—whose marriage can be announced in the paper, without her being insulted within a week by receiving through the mail a printed circular, offering information and instrumentalities, and all needed facilities, by which the laws of heaven in regard to the increase of the human family may be thwarted." Anthony Comstock corroborated that statement in 1880 when he reported the confiscation, over the preceding seven years, of 64,094 "articles for im-moral use, of rubber, etc.," and 700 pounds of "lead moulds for making Obscene Matter." Despite scanty official medical attention, by the late 1800s certain sections of the public were well supplied with contraceptive information and de-vices. There was "hardly a single middle-class family" among his clients, said a doctor in 1906, that did not expect him to implement their "desire to prevent conception." [17] As Lydia Commander said in 1907, among the upper classes some kind of contraceptive knowledge was "practically uni-versal." [18]

But the availability of that knowledge did not in itself cause the general restriction in the size of native middle- and upper-class families. Many Americans manifested the modern consideration for the welfare of the child when they decided to limit their offspring to as many as could

17. Arthur W. Calhoun, *Social History of the American Family*, 3:228, 239; Anthony Comstock, *Frauds Exposed* (New York: J. Howard Brown, 1880), p. 435. Anthony Comstock, by his own account, also confiscated 202,679 "obscene pictures and photos," 4,185 "boxes of pills, powders, etc., used by abortionists," and 26 "obscene pictures, framed on walls of saloons"; See also E. A. Ross, "Western Civilization and the Birth Rate," American Sociological Society, *Papers and Pro-ceedings* 1 (1907): 29–54; and Hawkins, *Will the Home Survive?* p. 12.

18. Commander, *American Idea*, pp. 89–92.

be "given the necessary education to fit them for the best in life." [19] But that idea, though pervasively "modern" in its concern for children, took firmest hold among the middle class; and in its emphasis on the "best in life" it reflected more than enlightened theories of child-rearing. It also revealed an increasing concern for social mobility and the development of a middle-class definition of an acceptable standard of living. The *Nation,* in 1903, noted the apparent paradox that in America, contrary to all Malthusian predictions, the population was beginning to shrink in the face of an increasing food supply. But the paradox was easily explained, said the *Nation*: Malthus "did not, perhaps, give sufficient weight to the fact that the means of subsistence is a relative term, varying from age to age, and having different meanings to different peoples." [20] Similarly, Lydia Commander argued that the instinct of reproduction was subordinate to the instinct of self-preservation, which had taken on a new meaning in America. "The full dinner-pail," she said, did not mark the limits of the American's ambition. "It is only the bare beginning of his needs." [21] An article in the *North American Review* in 1903, by "Paterfamilias," frankly stated that the modern family limited its size in order to enjoy a certain "style of living." The author's "social position" was "very dear" to him, he said, and it would be threatened by additional children. Furthermore, more children would make a household drudge of his wife. Therefore he intended to have no more. "I presume," he said, "there are those who will think that this is an ignoble statement. But it is not only true, but it is true of about every family of which I have any personal acquaintance." [2]

19. Hawkins, *Will the Home Survive?* p. 12.

20. "The Question of the Birth Rate," *Nation,* June 11, 1903, p. 469.

21. Commander, *American Idea,* p. 96.

22. Paterfamilias, " 'Race Suicide' and Common Sense," *North American Review* 176 (1903): 897. The phenomenon of lower fertility associated with social mobility and class standing was by no means

The article by Paterfamilias elicited extensive comment in 1903, and though few disputed the accuracy of its thesis about the motives behind family limitation, many saw in those motives, as Theodore Roosevelt put it, "frightful and fundamental immorality." What Paterfamilias had defended as dedication to his "style of living," Roosevelt called submission "to coldness, to selfishness, to love of ease, to shrinking from risk, to an utter and pitiful failure in sense of perspective." [23]

Many observers agreed with Roosevelt that a new and destructive slavishness to the self was strangling the American family, but they went beyond his criticism when they branded the feminist movement as the principal vehicle of that egotism. In the simultaneous rise of the emancipated woman and decline of the family, they saw the fulfillment of a dark prophecy. Herbert Spencer had proclaimed in the mid-nineteenth century the iron biological law of antagonism between "Individuation and Genesis." Every higher degree of evolution, he said, was followed by a "lower degree of race-multiplication." As the New Woman, therefore, evolved to a greater individualism and self-sufficiency, she lost her capacity for reproduction. Specifically, Spencer said, "the overtaxing of their brains" through too much mental effort had "a serious reaction on the physique" of women and resulted in a "diminution of reproductive power." Spencer thus lent the prestige of evolutionary science to the argument that the women's movement bore a heavy responsibility for the shrinking family. In fact, Spencer provided only one of many points of contact between the criticisms of the modern family and the criticisms of the New

---

peculiarly American. The French demographer Jacques Bertillon found that as the Frenchman advanced from "prolétaire" to "propriétaire," he limited the size of his family. Bertillon concluded that "l'aisance entraine la stérilité." *La Depopulation de la France* (Paris: Felix Alcan, 1911). See also J. A. Banks, *Prosperity and Parenthood* (London: Routledge and Kegan Paul, 1954).

23. T. Roosevelt, "Race Decadence," p. 764.

Woman. From the time in the late nineteenth century when the condition of the family became a topic of general public discussion, it was rarely mentioned apart from the "woman question." [24]

Edward Alsworth Ross ascribed both the liberation of women and the transformation of the family to a "transition process in social evolution." At the heart of that process, said Ross, was a new sense of individuality which provided women with "a point of view of their own" and replaced the patriarchal with the "democratic" family. Though the process sometimes produced an "exaggerated self-will," Ross contended that it was rare and not to be held responsible for divorce and smaller families.[25]

But the individualism Ross thought salutary, conservative defenders of the family continued to damn as rank selfishness. They especially indicted women. A symposium in the *North American Review* in 1889 blamed women's self-indulgent romanticism for the divorce rate. Twenty years later Anna B. Rogers confidently explained "why American marriages fail": because women had become devoted to "the latter-day cult of individualism; the worship of the brazen calf of Self." [26]

Feminists admitted their role in changing the family, but they had a different explanation of their motives. In the feminists' view, the women's movement was redressing an ancient historical grievance. Social scientists such as Lewis Henry Morgan and Lester Ward, they said, had shown that the original family was a matriarchal institution. Somewhere along the line men had subverted that order and robbed women of their status and independence. As Thorstein Veblen wrote, the masculine ideal of marriage was "in point of derivation, a predatory institution." It

24. Herbert Spencer, *The Principles of Biology* 2 vols. (New York: D. Appleton, 1898–99), 2:430, 512–13.

25. Ross, "Significance of Increasing Divorce," pp. 151–52.

26. "Are Women to Blame?" *North American Review* 148 (1889). 622–42; Anna B. Rogers, *Why American Marriages Fail* (Boston: Houghton Mifflin, 1909), p. 16.

rested, said Veblen, on the mechanisms of ownership, coercion, and control. More than anything else, the feminists
objected to the coercion to which they said all married
women were expected to submit. In that protest they but
shared a general antipathy to authority deeply seated in
American traditions. The elder Henry James touched on that
tradition when he said that marriage came into "dishonor"
when it was not "*freely* honored, or honored exclusively
for its own sake." Prevailing opinion, on the other hand,
regarded marriage as "properly honored when it is enforced
by some external sanction." That element of force, said
James, had made marriage "the hotbed of fraud, adultery,
and cruelty." It could only become "holy" when it rested
not on constraint but on the sentiments of its members.[27]

The acrimony of the debate on the transformation of the
family and the role of women in that process often ob-
scured the common assumptions from which both sides
argued. Conservatives wished to preserve the sanctity of the
home, while reformers wanted to restore it to an ancient
dignity. Practically everyone agreed on the paramount importance of the family in human life. Both advocates and
adversaries of easier divorce invoked the sacredness of the
marital relation in support of their respective cases. Parti-
sans of women's suffrage and education justified their causes
with reference to the improvement of the home fully as
often as their opponents warned of its destruction. There
were really no radical opinions about the family. Even the
Socialist critics of marriage wanted only those changes that
would "make it possible for every mother to devote herself
to the care of her children." [28] From that goal, virtually
no one dissented. For all the noise surrounding the trans-

27. Lewis Henry Morgan, *Ancient Society* (Cambridge: Harvard University Press, Belknap Press, 1964; first published, 1877); Lester Ward,
Pure Sociology (New York: Macmillan, 1914), Ch. 14; Thorstein Veblen,
"The Barbarian Status of Women," *American Journal of Sociology* 4
(1899): 503–14; Henry James, letter to the editor, *Nation*, June 9,
1870, p. 366.

28. Spargo, *Socialism and Motherhood*, p. 32.

formation of the family in the late Victorian era, in the end the process simply strengthened the three distinctive characteristics that had been developing for two centuries. Beneath the confrontation of conservative and reformist views lay an undeniable consensus that the family had greater emotional importance than ever. With that growing importance had come the increasing privacy of the home. And within the segregated emotional center of the family, the child had come to be its greatest concern.

The divorce and race suicide alarm preoccupied, for a time, the debate on the "woman question," but that debate was an ancient one, and long after the height of the panic over the condition of the family had passed, Americans continued to disagree over the proper status of women. Indeed, that debate goes on, unresolved, in the present day. In the late nineteenth century, however, the age-old discussion of woman's place was just beginning to take on its modern urgency. No longer could that discussion be academic, as it had been earlier in the century: the New Woman was appearing on the scene and demanding to be taken seriously. The New Woman was in fact two different ladies, the self-sufficient working girl and the dependent, restless "parasite woman," the idle wife in a middle class with growing wealth and leisure. But each of these women was new, and each, in her own way, repudiated the nineteenth-century ideal of femininity.

The feminine ideal which the nineteenth century made an article of faith grew up as part of a reaction against older convictions of the sinfulness and depravity of humanity. That ideal was not so much Puritanical as it was anti-Puritan when it made woman symbolize the possibilities of perfection and benevolence. Man saw in woman, as Henry James, Sr. said, "a diviner self than his own," while his son enshrined such American goddesses as Daisy Miller and Milly Theale in the national imagination.[29]

29. James, "Is Marriage Holy?" p. 364. For the development of the symbolic view of women, see Leslie Fiedler, *Love and Death in the*

The idealized American woman was above all incorruptibly innocent. James made Daisy Miller's unreflecting innocence the quality that most puzzled Europeans. That innocence, said the biographer and muckraker Ida Tarbell, came easily to American girls who were "brought up as if wrongdoing were impossible to them." [30] Susan B. Anthony's mother had such a deeply bred fealty to the ideal of innocence that "before the birth of every child she was overwhelmed with embarrassment and humiliation, secluded herself from the outside world and would not speak of the expected little one." [31] High-minded men protected their wives and daughters from the outside world by making the home a citadel against threatening influences. Single-minded devotion to domestic duties, men preached, to "marriage and motherhood . . . the highest, indeed the only successful career for woman," was more than woman's duty; it was the only sure protection against the forces of corruption.[32]

A second characteristic of the feminine ideal was helplessness. In 1908 H. L. Mencken protested the "absurd" but nevertheless ubiquitous idea "that the civilization of a people is to be measured by the degree of dependence of its women." The idea of helplessness Veblen again traced to the predatory origins of marriage. But most Americans probably agreed with Theodore Roosevelt that "the woman has a harder time than the man, and must have, from the mere fact that she must bear and largely rear her children." Her dependence, in that view, proceeded from the "laws

American Novel (New York: Criterion Books, 1960); William Wasserstrom, Heiress of All the Ages: Sex and Sentiment in the Genteel Tradition (Minneapolis: University of Minnesota Press, 1959); and Barbara Welter, "The Cult of True Womanhood," American Quarterly 18 (1966): 151–74.

30. Ida M. Tarbell, The Business of Being a Woman (New York: Macmillan, 1912), p. 179.

31. Ida Husted Harper, The Life and Work of Susan B. Anthony (Indianapolis: Bowen-Merrill, 1899), pp. 12–13.

32. Mary Roberts Coolidge, Why Women Are So (New York: Henry Holt, 1912), pp. 44–45.

of nature," and it demanded of men, said Roosevelt, that they treat women with special respect, as they would treat "anything good and helpless." [33]

In a special way, the ideal American girl also embodied and symbolized goodness. Again, Henry James created the fictional archetype of the absolutely good woman in Milly Theale, the heroine of *The Wings of the Dove*. In Milly's unflinching purity of motive and action, James sought expression for an important part of the myth of the American woman. Milly's European acquaintances at first found her simply naïve; later, the terrible consistency of her conscience affected them all profoundly. "We shall never again be as we were," concluded Kate Croy after Milly's death, and she echoed James's own thoughts on the death of his cousin, Mary Temple. That death, he wrote, marked "the end of our youth." Somehow, James and other American men expressed their sense of lost youthful innocence, dependence, and goodness by creating an idealized picture of the American woman.[34]

Bronson Alcott pointed to another large component of the goodness the American woman was supposed to possess when he described his daughter as "duty's faithful child." [35] Louisa May Alcott earned that paternal praise by eschewing marriage and personal happiness and tending her father without complaint until his dying day. To pious believers in the feminine ideal, Miss Alcott revealed her true womanhood by that self-abnegating devotion to the service of another. So central was the belief in the generosity of the

33. H. L. Mencken, *The Philosophy of Friedrich Nietzsche* (Boston: Luce, 1908), p. 189; Veblen, "Barbarian Status of Women," pp. 504–07; Morison, *Letters of Theodore Roosevelt*, 2:904 (Roosevelt to Helen Kendrick Johnson, January 10, 1899), 3:520 (Roosevelt to Hamlin Garland, July 19, 1903).

34. Henry James, *Wings of the Dove* (New York: Dell, 1963), p. 512; Henry James, *Notes of a Son and Brother* (London: Macmillan, 1914), p. 47. See also Fiedler, *Love and Death in the American Novel*, and Wasserstrom, *Heiress of All the Ages*.

35. Thomas Beer, *The Mauve Decade* (Garden City, N.Y.: Garden City Publishing, 1926), pp. 19–21.

idealized woman that Americans found any contrary suggestion blasphemous or incomprehensible. When Henrik
Ibsen's *Doll's House* opened in Boston in 1889, a reviewer
remarked that the "ending can never be liked by American
audiences, who will be loath to believe that a woman owes
a higher duty to the development of her own nature than
to the young children she has brought into the world." In
New York, a reviewer confessed to "the difficulty an average
audience experiences to see what the playwright means—
what he is driving at." Another observer noted that when
Americans came across a (rare) woman like Nora Helmer,
who resolved to "do her duty to herself," they had "a dull
trick of suspecting mental disease." [36] The nineteenth-
century woman, said Mary Roberts Coolidge, a perceptive
and sympathetic critic of the feminist movement, was
raised to please men, not herself. Woman's personality had
come to resemble that of an actor, who, "like the woman,"
Mrs. Coolidge wrote, "makes his place in life chiefly by the
cultivation of manner and appearance. He, like her, depends for success upon pleasing rather than being admira-
ble. The 'matinee idol' is an extreme example of character
—or, rather, perversion of character—by the social necessity
of being charming and of trading in assumed emotions." [37]
Though "other-direction" has been called a characteristically twentieth-century component of personality, American
women obviously knew its meaning well before 1900. So
too, it could be argued, the "individualism" so highly
valued in the nineteenth century and ever since regarded
as a distinctive quality of American life in that epoch, was
apparently for men only.

By the end of the century, however, feminists had mounted
an active revolt against the burden of assumed emotions. The
picture of the idealized woman, they said, was false; and
certainly that picture of American women—as innocent, de-

36. *New York Daily Tribune*, October 31, 1889, p. 6; *New York
Times*, December 22, 1889, p. 11; *Belford's Magazine*, April 1890, p.
772.
37. Coolidge, *Why Women Are So*, p. 101.

pendent, good, and selfless—had always fitted masculine wishes better than it had the facts.

What men cherished as "innocence" was purchased at the price of often disastrous ignorance. Charlotte Perkins Gilman indicted the belief that innocence was a woman's chief charm. "What good does it do her?" she asked. "Her whole life's success is made to depend on her marrying; her health and happiness depends [sic] on her marrying the right man. The more 'innocent' she is, the less she knows, the easier it is for the wrong man to get her." Mary Roberts Coolidge noted ironically that though marriage and motherhood constituted a woman's only permitted career, "yet, nothing in her training had any direct relation to it, and the conventional standard of modesty required her to be wholly ignorant of its physical aspects." Certainly Susan B. Anthony learned little about the "physical aspects" of married life from a mother who took her confinement literally. An anonymous feminist in 1906 said that the average nineteenth-century girl "contemplated the sexual relation with the bitterest reluctance," because she had been "sedulously guarded from knowledge of the fundamental reasons of her being, cast suddenly and unprepared into marriage." Robert Latou Dickinson, probably America's most prominent gynecologist, corroborated those women's observations when he reported that his clinical practice had shown that "no single cause of mental strain in married women is as widespread as sex fears and maladjustments." He blamed the prevalence of those fears on the enforced sexual ignorance of women.[38]

The pathologic effects of the regimen of sheltered domesticity were not all psychological. The helplessness of the American woman—especially in the urban East and the upper-class South—owed at least as much to real physiological weakness as it did to compliance with a rigid moral

38. Gilman, *Man-Made World*, p. 167; Coolidge, pp. 44–45. Elizabeth B. Wetmore, *The Secret Life* (New York: John Lane, 1906), p. 93; Robert Latou Dickinson, "Marital Maladjustment—The Business of Preventive Gynecology," *Long Island Medical Journal* 2 (1908): 1–5.

ideal. "An American sculptor unhampered by the models of the past," said a woman writer in 1873, "would represent the Three Graces as lolling on sofa-cushions, with a bottle of salts in one hand and a fan in the other." To be ladylike, she said, was to be "lifeless, inane, and dawdling," and another woman later recalled a nineteenth-century rhyme which told that "the bride, *of course,* fainted, for, being acquainted with manners, she knew what was right." Robert Latou Dickinson insisted in the 1890s that the neurasthenic female was more than a caricature and that the causes of her condition were plain: lack of exercise and ridiculous standards of dress. "It is supposed to be sufficient exercise for the sister," he wrote, "to wave her handkerchief from the grand stand." Dickinson also suggested that the alleged "sexlessness" of American women owed at least in part to the relatively primitive state of gynecological medicine. Low-grade vaginal infections, later remedied routinely, could in the nineteenth century be an enduring and debilitating discomfort. And scores of other medical writers joined Dickinson in pointing out the harmful effects of the steel-ribbed corsets women wore to shrink their waists and expand their busts. The rigid "health waists" were especially damaging to working girls who leaned forward all day over a typewriter or a sewing machine. Still, in spite of almost daily evidence of the injury done to women by over-domestication and overdressing, the American male—whose house women kept and for whose eye they attired themselves—continued to pride himself on the manly protection he offered his delicate, dependent charges.[39]

Similarly, the myth of the ideal woman sanctified her generosity and selflessness by piously glorifying the sacrifices she was expected cheerfully to make. Men impressed upon

39. Woolson, *Woman in American Society,* p. 192; Deland, "Change in the Feminine Ideal," p. 293; R. L. Dickinson, "Simple and Practical Methods in Dress Reform," *Gynecological Transactions* 18 (1893): 411; R. L. Dickinson, "Bicycling for Women from the Standpoint of the Gynecologist," *American Journal of Obstetrics* 31 (1895): 25. See also Mark Sullivan, *Our Times,* vol. 1, *The Turn of the Century* (New York: Charles Scribner's Sons, 1926), pp. 385–95.

women, said Lydia Commander, the authoress of one of the most popular contemporary books on the family and feminism, "that it was a religious duty to suffer," especially to suffer the pains of childbirth and the exasperations of child-rearing. The duties of the American woman, said Theodore Roosevelt, exceeded those of the American fighting man and should receive far more adulation. Because of biology, he said, the woman "has a harder time than the man." A woman writer in 1916 perceived that in the nineteenth-century feminine ideal "the element of sacrifice is so obvious that it is even seized upon and treated as a virtue, an added glory for the crown of the wife and mother." [40]

Finally, the myth of the idealized American woman preserved her innocence and her goodness by denying her sexuality. In nineteenth-century fiction, said Thomas Beer, "the female principal is risen above romance and becomes an opalescent cloud, dripping odours which had nothing to do with the process of childbearing at all." The myth, therefore, not only kept women ignorant of what it simultaneously glorified as their chief honor and duty. It also insulated them from all passion and erotic desire. As Viola Klein has observed, in the whole Western world "during the nineteenth and at the beginning of the twentieth century it would have been not only scandalous to admit the existence of a strong sex urge in women, but it would have been contrary to all observation." H. L. Mencken called it a "good old sub-Potomac" idea that a woman "who loses her virtue is, *ipso facto*, a victim and not a criminal or *particeps criminis*, and that a 'lady,' by virtue of being a 'lady,' is necessarily a reluctant and helpless quarry in the hunt of love." But the idea held with nearly unassailable force above the Potomac as well. No genuinely passionate woman appeared in American fiction at least from the time of the Civil War to the naturalist outburst at the turn of the

40. Commander, *American Idea*, p. 235; Morison, *Letters of Theodore Roosevelt*, 3:520–21 (Roosevelt to Hamlin Garland, July 19, 1903); Jessie Taft, *The Woman Movement from the Point of View of Social Consciousness* (Chicago: University of Chicago Press, 1916), p. 55.

century. As late as 1908, Robert Latou Dickinson was urging the medical profession to tell nervous women patients there was no cause for alarm if they enjoyed sexual intercourse. And even such an otherwise perceptive man as E. A. Ross asserted confidently in 1906 that it was a "physiological fact that the sexual instinct is not only very much weaker in most women, but is altogether absent in a growing number of them." [41]

Feminists reacted against both the myth and the facts it so sanctimoniously concealed but could not change. By the end of the nineteenth century women were telling men that they wanted neither innocence nor ignorance, dependence nor disease, self-abnegation nor sacrifice, goodness nor sexlessness. The New Woman, Leslie Fiedler has said, refused to accept her prescribed function of "redemptive suffering," and with that refusal she "threatened to upset the whole Sentimental Love Religion" in which the myth of the ideal woman was enshrined. Independence became the religion of the New Woman, and Henrik Ibsen was one of its chief prophets. Ibsen showed, said one of his American admirers in 1890, "the necessity of a new life . . . a life divested of the conventional ideas of what is Woman's duty." In contrast to early feminist reformers who had sought to restructure legal forms in order to give women control over their own property and persons, by the late nineteenth century feminists more or less consciously sought to restructure the feminine personality itself. [42]

41. Beer, *Mauve Decade*, p. 54; Viola Klein, *The Feminine Character* (New York: International Universities Press, 1949), p. 85; Mencken, *Philosophy of Friedrich Nietzsche*, p. 186; Dickinson, "Marital Maladjustment"; Ross, "Western Civilization and the Birth Rate," p. 51. See Steven Marcus, *The Other Victorians: A Study of Sexuality and Pornography in Mid-Nineteenth Century England* (New York: Basic Books, 1964), pp. 28–32, for a most interesting discussion of a similar desexualizing of women in nineteenth-century England; for more on the phenomenon in the United States, see Fiedler, *Love and Death in the American Novel*, and Joseph Wood Krutch, *The Modern Temper* (New York: Harcourt, Brace, 1929).

42. Fiedler, p. 221; Annie Nathan Meyer, letter to the editor, *Critic*, March 22, 1890, p. 148.

Lydia Commander, describing the New Woman in 1907, noted the "radical alteration in her personality. Under the old regime," she said, "humility, self-sacrifice, and obedience were assiduously cultivated as the highest of womanly virtues." But now, she concluded, "self-sacrifice . . . is no longer in favor. Self-development is rapidly taking its place." For many American feminists in the last quarter of the century, an encounter with European ideas—in Ibsen, Friedrich Nietzsche, Henri Bergson, or George Bernard Shaw—finally broke the long-standing tension of trying to live up to the duties of the feminine ideal. After more than two generations of strictly legal progress, the women's movement began to turn inward to search for a definition of a new feminine personality. Later, the movement would again turn at least partly outward and justify itself with claims of the benefits it could bestow on society. But for a season its paramount concern was the development of a new sense of self. And in that development, society, and society's expectations, could only be enemies.[43]

The idea of antagonism between the feminine self and society coincided strikingly with a notion that underlay the very feminine ideal against which the reformers protested: the idea of woman's victimization. Men constantly regarded the innocent woman as a potential victim of sinister forces. They even sentimentalized the obviously corrupted woman, as H. L. Mencken noted, as an unwitting gull of evil persons. When the white slave panic reached its height around 1910, the image of the hapless prostitute as a victim of poverty or lechery found ready acceptance and frequent expression. And behind Theodore Roosevelt's idea that the woman achieved nobility by sacrifice stood the premise that biology—regrettably, but unavoidably—victimized women far more than it did men. A woman writer noted that society displayed its recognition of that victimization when it attempted to translate the experiences of women in marriage and motherhood "into a sort of fetish . . . exalted to

43. Commander, *American Idea*, pp. 144–45.

the point where they are assumed to be a sufficient compensation for any and all sacrifices." [44]

But though the New Woman was not to be so easily compensated, she herself nevertheless appealed to society's sense of her victimization when she did demand compensation in the shape of legal, economic, and social reforms. When the suffragists first shifted from a "natural rights" to an "expediency" argument for the vote, says Aileen Kraditor, they insisted "that women needed the ballot for self-protection." In other words, they asked for political power to combat the forces that victimized them. Similarly, protective labor legislation first came into being "in the name of defenseless women and children." And Christopher Lasch has noted perceptively that "it was not the image of women as equals that inspired the reform of the divorce laws, but the image of women as victims." In her search for equality, says Lasch, by appealing to the idea of victimization, "woman depended on a sentimentalization of womanhood which eroded the idea of equality as easily as it promoted it." [45]

Both feminists and antifeminists spoke of woman's victimization in terms of her sex. As Aileen Kraditor notes, "the antis regarded each woman's vocation as determined not by her individual capacities or wishes but by her sex. Men were expected to have a variety of ambitions and capabilities, but all women were destined from birth to be full-time wives and mothers. To dispute this eternal truth was to challenge theology, biology, or sociology." [46] Feminists flirted occasionally with the idea that their distinctive sexual characteristics made them superior. That idea proceeded

44. Taft, *The Woman Movement*, p. 55. See also Illinois, General Assembly, Senate, Vice Committee, *Report* (Chicago: State of Illinois, 1916); and Prince A. Morrow, *Social Diseases and Marriage* (New York: Lea Brothers, 1904).

45. Aileen Kraditor, *The Ideas of the Woman Suffrage Movement, 1890–1920* (New York: Columbia University Press, 1965), p. 54; Smuts, *Women and Work in America*, p. 107; Lasch, "Divorce and the Family," p. 59.

46. Kraditor, p. 15.

logically from the feminine myth which told women they
were purer, more generous, and morally better than men.
But more often women, in their quest for a new definition
of self, resented what Elsie Clews Parsons, a prominent
woman sociologist, called "the domination of personality
by sex." When the feminists talked about sex, they did not
intend the word as it is usually understood today. Today,
"sex" has an erotic meaning. It generally connotes instinct,
passion, emotion, stimulation, pleasure, often intercourse
itself. But the nineteenth-century feminists used "sex" almost exclusively to denote gender. For them, "sex" indicated all the special feminine characteristics men used to
differentiate and, said the feminists, to subjugate women.
Charlotte Perkins Gilman repeatedly condemned what she
called masculine oversexualization of the world; she was
speaking not of pornography or lechery but of a caste system which kept women in their place. Men saw "nothing in
the world *but* sex, either male or female," she argued, and
in such an atmosphere neither men nor women could develop the truly human qualities common to each. "Our
distinctions of sex," she said, "are carried to such a degree
as to be disadvantageous to our progress as individuals and as
a race." For women like Mrs. Gilman and Mrs. Parsons, the
new feminine personality could only emerge when sex became "a factor, not an obsession." Then "relations between
men and women will be primarily personal relations,
secondarily sexual." That was the dominant feminist position, though some other feminist sympathizers, such as
Ellen Key, and even, in his own way, Theodore Roosevelt,
promoted the alternative view that women had a separate
sexual identity but were nevertheless the equals of men.
In any case, all the theories about the relation of feminine
sex characteristics to personality manifested a conscious effort to define, or to redefine, woman's role.[47]

47. Elsie Clews Parsons, *Social Freedom* (New York: G. P. Putnam's
Sons, 1915), pp. 29, 36; Gilman, *Man-Made World*, p. 154; Charlotte
Perkins Gilman, *Women and Economics* (New York: Harper and Row,
1966; first published, 1898), p. 33.

The redefinition of woman's role encountered entrenched but confused opposition. Antifeminists argued on the one hand that woman's God-given, natural role was so immutable that the suggestion of change was ludicrous, and on the other that her sacred maternal and connubial functions were so susceptible to corruption that she must be protected from the forces of change. But the antifeminists' confusion did not temper the strenuousness of their objections. Indeed, the strength of the objections indicated anxieties that only indirectly touched the question of economic and educational equality for women. Those anxieties primarily concerned the male's own social role and his sexual identity.

"The study of the changes in sexual attitudes is the very first step, the *sine qua non,* of all coherent historical research," writes Gordon Rattray Taylor, because sex lies at the heart of personality. Though Taylor somewhat overstates his case the fact nevertheless remains, as Phillipe Ariés has said, that "society's consciousness of its behaviour in relation to age and sex" is still an "unexplored subject," and the historical imagination is poorer for the lack.[48] While it is undoubtedly difficult to trace events in the innermost lives of men, it is more difficult to imagine that the developments that moved nineteenth-century American life worked no changes on sexuality. And at no time did the effects of those changes come closer to the surface than when the nineteenth-century man confronted the New Woman.

Sex has always been central to the human condition, but Steven Marcus has found that only in the nineteenth century "did there emerge as part of the general educated consciousness the formulation that it might in fact be problematical—it is an idea that forms part of our inheritance." Nineteenth-century Americans first met the modern problem of sex by officially denying sexuality. In their minds, as William Wasserstrom has said, "manliness signified a state

48. G. Rattray Taylor, *Sex in History* (New York: Vanguard Press, 1954), p. 3; Ariés, *Centuries of Childhood,* p. 58.

of the soul which negated the claims of the body; womanliness resulted when the body was eliminated." Lester Ward complained that antagonism to the idea of sexuality was so pervasive that his fellow ethnologists even covered up the sex lives of former ages in an attempt "to palliate the supposed humiliation involved in such a state of things." [49]

In *Three Contributions to the Theory of Sex,* Freud noted that "the most pronounced difference between the love life of antiquity and our lies in the fact that the ancients placed the emphasis on the impulse itself, while we put it on the object. The ancients extolled the impulse and were ready to ennoble through it even an inferior object, while we disparage the activity of the impulse as such and only countenance it on account of the merits of the object." [50] Only in that context did the oft-noted nineteenth-century ideal of sexlessness have meaning. The Victorian man honored the ideal of sexlessness when he disparaged and even feared his own sexual instinct and denied the existence of the instinct in women. But, as the feminists often complained, he exaggerated sex—in the meaning of gender—when he emphasized and glorified the distinctly feminine qualities of his sexual object.

On the occasion of a sex murder in New York in 1870, the elder Henry James debated with the editor of *Nation* the character of the sexual instinct and its relation to marriage. Only in marriage, said James, could men's "baser nature"—their sexuality—be adequately contained. The purpose of wedlock, he said, "is to educate us out of our animal beginnings." The *Nation,* though more extreme, agreed. Sex, it said, was an "animal, brute passion, through which God, apparently in ignorance of the laws of 'moral progress,' has provided for the perpetuation of the species." But since "moral progress" was so desirable, some means had to be devised to regulate sex, and that means, adopted

49. Marcus, *The Other Victorians,* p. 2; Wasserstrom, *Heiress of All the Ages,* p. vii; Ward, *Pure Sociology,* p. 340.

50. Sigmund Freud, *Three Contributions to the Theory of Sex* (New York: Nervous and Mental Disease Monographs, 1948), p. 14 n.

in the infancy of the race, was marriage. "The first object of marriage," said the *Nation*, "still is to regulate [sex]." If the abstract entity, society, could somehow enunciate that Pauline doctrine, the *Nation* went on, it would say: "To keep down within [man] the animal love of change and attach him to his home, I excite in his mind extravagant notions of his authority and of the strength of the tie which unites his wife to him, and I confess that from this *some* women do suffer a great deal; but I am sure the whole female sex profits by it." In the *Nation*'s view, marriage, whatever its cost to the individual, was essential to the social order. Henry James hoped for a more spontaneous, humanitarian basis for marriage. But though James and the *Nation* disagreed over the proper sources of marital stability, they nevertheless shared a common appraisal of male sexuality as a bestial, egocentric, antisocial instinct that must somehow be regulated. And the *Nation*'s idea of marriage as the proper regulatory mechanism came closer than James's to the current popular view.[51]

Just as women were sentimentally venerated partly as compensation for their victimization, men, the *Nation* implied, were granted all the prerogatives of the patriarchal family to compensate for the difficulty with which they held their sexual instinct in check. In both cases, the denial of sexuality, in its modern sense of instinct, was closely tied to the nineteenth-century idea of sexual role. And in both cases, for themselves and for women, men defined the proper roles. Men saw themselves as patriarchal and authoritarian because they suppressed a sexual nature that was aggressive, even potentially brutal. And they saw woman as innocent, dependent, good, and generous because she was— ideally—sexless.

By the end of the nineteenth century, it was becoming increasingly difficult to contain real women within the myth of the feminine ideal. The emergence of the New Woman necessitated adjustments in man's role, and, less demon-

51. James, "Is Marriage Holy?" p. 364; "Society and Marriage," *Nation*, May 26, 1870, pp. 332–33.

strably but no less importantly, in his sexuality. Women
entered the work force by the hundreds of thousands. Men
showed their sensitivity to role when, often without economic logic, they allowed many newly emerging forms of
employment to become exclusively women's. While women
felt free to attempt almost any traditionally male job, men
usually abandoned any occupation that became identified
with women. G. Stanley Hall, the psychologist who brought
Freud to Clark University, touched on that phenomenon in
1906 when he reported that several "independent statistical
studies" showed that girls often held masculine "ideals,"
but that "boys almost never choose feminine ideals." In the
transvaluation of sexual roles, the movement seemed to be
all in one direction. Women took on traditionally masculine
functions with apparently little stress; men, by contrast,
feared the impairment of the very masculinity they had
previously characterized as nearly beyond restraint. The
"feminization" of education, Hall complained, rather than
producing a desirable refinement in boys, instead unnaturally stifled their most virile traits—their "brutish elements." The fault with the women's movement, said Hall,
lay in its exaggerated notion of sexual equality. The time
had come, he insisted, for a "new movement . . . based
upon sexual differences, not identities." He urged that
course—which was in fact reactionary—not, as conservatives
had previously done, for the sake of preserving a delicate
femininity, but in defense of a beleaguered masculinity.[52]

Steven Marcus found in investigating the sex life of
Victorian England that masculine fear of sexuality was
ambivalent—men feared both impotence and potency, impulse and loss, attraction and repulsion. So too in America;
ambivalence was built in. The furor over the changes in
men's and women's roles showed that while he had made the
feminine principle symbolize goodness, the prospect of his
"feminization" evoked profound anxieties in the nineteenth-
century American man. And though he invested his sexual

52. G. Stanley Hall, "The Question of Co-Education," *Munsey's
Magazine*, February 1906, pp. 588–92.

object with qualities which, according to Freud, should have justified the gratification of a supposedly despicable instinct, he often found that the glorified object, instead of elevating the instinct, precluded it. The figure of woman in American fiction, as Leslie Fiedler has said, became "refined to the point where copulation with her seems blasphemous." Further, however much the American man had denigrated his latent bestiality and bemoaned the difficulty of keeping it in check, that view of his sexual nature had lain at the heart of his self-image. By the 1890s it appeared that his purportedly primeval, almost irrepressible instinct was in fact propped up by an elaborate but fragile system of role definition based on exaggerated sexual differentiation. When women rebelled against that system, the illusion of man's aggressiveness—which seemed so indispensable to his sexual identity—grew more difficult to maintain. And in such laments as G. Stanley Hall's for the stifling of the "brutish elements," it became clear that the American man had feared more than the unleashing of his aggressive sexual instinct; he had also feared its loss.[53]

Male sexual ambivalence had underlain the notorious "double standard" against which femininists and moralists railed. "As a result of this double standard," said Dr. Prince Morrow, "society practically separates its women into two classes: from the one it demands chastity, the other is set apart for the gratification of the sexual caprices of its men. It thus proclaims the doctrine, immoral as it is unhygienic, that debauchery is a necessity for its men." [54] In either case, men made objects of women. Both the Fair Maiden and the Dark Lady served man's needs—one the needs of his conscience, the other the needs of his body. But the New Woman who came to self-consciousness toward the end of the century was no longer content to serve as a mere object. In a few years the double standard, and with it the traditional nineteenth-century idea of masculine sexuality, was

53. Marcus, *The Other Victorians*, p. 29; Fiedler, *Love and Death in the American Novel*, p. 276.

54. Morrow, *Social Diseases and Marriage*, p. 342.

under severe attack. It drew its heaviest fire in the hysteria about prostitution during the Progressive period.

The new form of male sexuality that began to emerge in the late nineteenth century was forced to abandon "full aggressive potency, demonic genitality," as Steven Marcus has said, because such a definition of personality was "permanently at odds with that elaborately developed life of the emotions which is our civilized heritage—and our burden." [55] That heritage proceeded primarily from the romantic movement of the late eighteenth and early nineteenth centuries. The feminists—indeed nearly all Progressives— spoke often about the "social consciousness" they wished to inaugurate. Under that regime, they thought, the self would no longer be the first referent for experience but would "appear and develop as the *result* of its relation to other selves." The new, socially conscious self would be the basic building unit in a society founded on cooperation and harmony rather than the pursuit of self-interest. That vision looked forward to the character style later called "other-directed." It also looked backward to the romantic philosophers' notion that sympathy should form the basis of all moral decision and human interaction.[56] Lester Ward considered it one of the nineteenth century's greatest tragedies that it had submerged the romantic heritage and allowed the "rational faculty" to outstrip the "moral sentiments." Even Spencer, he said, had recognized "that the abuse of women by men is due in the main to the feeble development of sympathy." But by the early twentieth century, said Elsie Clews Parsons, "sympathy and insight [were] called upon in measure undreamed of by the antique moralist whose sole anxiety is to preserve his reassuring social categories intact." And with the growth of the sympathetic faculty, men grew less able to objectify women. That did not mean that they afforded women full equality. But with

55. Marcus, *The Other Victorians,* p. 180.
56. Taft, *The Woman Movement,* pp. 37–49.

sympathy the touchstone for sexual relationships, men no longer could entrap women so easily in myths and ignore their individual personalities.[57]

The romantic influence also modified that ambivalent fear of the emotions so evident in the nineteenth century. "There has been an increasing tendency," said Mary Roberts Coolidge, "to believe that imagination and intuition were effecting quite as much progress as the logical understanding." And, she implied, the system of masculine values was becoming "feminized" in a subtle way not usually perceived by the antifeminists: modern psychologists were "placing higher value upon the very mental quality [intuition] which was not long ago held to establish woman's inferiority." In America, William James contributed much to the development of a new regard for sensibility and the validity of emotional experience. And the increasing emphasis on the emotions sanctioned a new sense of subjectivism. That subjectivism harked back to Emerson, but it grew especially strong in the late nineteenth century because it went hand in hand with the relativism engendered by new researches in the biological and social sciences. And with the liberation of women, the transformation of masculine sexuality, the destruction of the double standard, the sanctioning of emotional experience, and the encouragement of a new sense of subjectivism, the nineteenth century had set the scene for the revolution in morals of the twentieth.[58]

The new notion of morality shared the endemic contempt for formalism characteristic of the early twentieth century. The old morality, as exemplified by Theodore Roosevelt, had been founded on the concept of duty; and as Roosevelt

57. Ward, *Pure Sociology*, pp. 346–47; Parsons, *Social Freedom*, p. 32.
58. Coolidge, *Why Women Are So*, p. 299; see also Henry May, *The End of American Innocence* (Chicago: Quadrangle Books, 1964); and for a good account of the elements of romanticism, see Walter Jackson Bate, *From Classic to Romantic: Premises of Taste in Eighteenth Century England* (New York: Harper and Row, 1961), especially Chs. 4 and 5.

said, "The doing of duty generally means pain, hardship, self-mastery, self-denial." [59] But as the emotions grew less fearsome, they no longer needed to be so strenuously mastered and denied. As a sociologist said in 1908, "Virtue no longer consists in literal obedience to arbitrary standards set by community or church but rather in conduct consistent with the demands of a growing personality." [60] The new morality no less than the old sprang from a sense of inwardness common to the Puritans, the proper Victorians, and the romantics; but the romantic appraisal of the inner self was by far the most sanguine. That optimistic view of the self, for example, revolutionized the function of the school, which had been one of the principal agencies of moral indoctrination. In the new view the school should no longer mold the child to make his behavior conform with rigid social rules. The popularity of the ideas of Maria Montessori and John Dewey reflected a new confidence in the goodness of the unfettered personality. Education should not discipline; it should liberate. And in its emphasis on the liberation of the individual personality, the new morality legitimized subjectiveness. Just as the family grew more and more private as it became increasingly an emotional center, so too did the new approval of emotionalism and subjectivism in the life of the individual reinforce the view that his conduct was his private concern.

The romantic ideas of sympathy, emotion, and subjectivism took more than one hundred years noticeably to affect sexual relationships. Nevertheless, by the early twentieth century the influence of those ideas could not be doubted. Then came Sigmund Freud. Freud did not so much start a revolution as rechannel one already in progress. William James and others in the nineteenth century had identified the inner self with the emotions. Freud superimposed on that view the idea that all emotion—indeed all

59. Morison, *Letters of Theodore Roosevelt*, 3: 521 (Roosevelt to Hamlin Garland, July 19, 1903).

60. American Sociological Society, *Papers and Proceedings* 3 (1908): 171.

psychic life—sprang from sexuality, and therefore that the self was defined by sexuality. Freud also provided the discussion of sex with a new, scientific vocabulary.

Unquestionably, Freud did much to further the liberation of sexual behavior, but in many ways Freud's influence was reactionary. For the old belief that woman was victimized by biology or by selfish men, Freud substituted the view that penis envy and a peculiar Oedipal situation made women the victims of their own psychic natures. The maternal impulse, according to the Freudians, proceeded not so much from biological and evolutionary laws as from inner psychological needs. That new thesis was scarcely less deterministic than the old. Thus Freud furnished scientific support for the old Victorian view that Nature victimized women and that they should seek compensation in wifehood and maternity. Moreover, just as sympathy was beginning at last to inform sexual relationships, Freud reemphasized sexual differences and reinstated, in a new form, the old notion of necessary sexual inequality. For Freud, the essence of masculinity was action; of femininity, passiveness. The only currency of sexual interaction, therefore, must consist of power and domination. Finally, Freud's insistence that the primary component of the emotional life was sexual, irrational, and morally uncommitted both undermined the romantic confidence in the goodness of the emotions and made them seem more important than ever. Freud diverted a romantic revolution, or emotional revolution, at its very beginning and made it a sexual revolution. The sexual revolution, though carried forward under the banner of Freudian science, would continue to show its romantic beginnings. And the women's movement, with which the revolution, by whatever name, was intimately bound up, found in Freud a false liberation. Freudian ideas proved a diversion and an obstacle which women have not yet overcome.[61]

61. See R. V. Sampson, *Equality and Power* (London: Heinemann Educational Books, 1965) and Hendrik M. Ruitenbeek, *Freud and America* (New York: Macmillan, 1966) for the influence of Freudian ideas.

Mrs. Sanger in 1915 was about to learn the nature of the recent changes affecting the family, woman, and sex. By that time it was apparent that the new condition of the family was not so different after all. The most radical criticisms of the family had only defined the boundaries of an expanding consensus. Indeed, said Floyd Dell, in light of what many had expected to happen to the family, the supposedly subversive Ellen Key "comes into the lives of many in this country as a conservative force, holding up a spiritual ideal, the ideal of monogamy." The feminists, too, by 1915, counted themselves and their cause well on the way to success if not already there. As early as 1906 a woman had noted that the "Woman Question . . . has lost all its interrogation point." The New Woman, though she was still considered new and still drew considerable criticism, had nevertheless arrived to stay. Similarly, the debate over the new sexual ideas showed that while Americans disagreed over their implications, virtually no one was content any longer to ignore the fact of sexuality. It had struck "Sex O'Clock in America," said *Current Opinion* in 1913, pointing to the fact that prostitution, once a shadowy subject discussed only in locker rooms, had become "the chief topic of polite conversation." [62]

Beneath the surface of those sanguine developments lurked some disturbing shadows not without significance to the future of birth control. By the time Margaret Sanger decided to make birth control a public issue, it was already very much a private one. Upper-class families had long since accepted the idea of family limitation. Those families at first had to defend their right to restrict their size against exhortations, such as Theodore Roosevelt's, to breed more. In their defense they were supported by a growing sense of privacy and self-determination in family life. Ironically, the same isolation of the family that contributed to the early upper-class defense of contraception would later make

62. Floyd Dell, *Women as World-Builders* (Chicago: Forbes, 1913), p. 80; Wetmore, *The Secret Life*, p. 81; "Sex O'Clock in America," *Current Opinion*, August 1913, pp. 113–14.

lower-class families impervious to Margaret Sanger's pleas to breed less. The factors of class and privacy which in the one case promoted birth control proved, in the other, the greatest obstacles to its further spread.

With regard to women, the new Freudian ideas shifted the sense of woman's victimization to a different plane, but they reinforced that sense nevertheless. Just at the moment when feminists had nearly triumphed over the nineteenth-century notion of women's biological inferiority, Freud supplied a biopsychological definition of feminine inferiority which was even more difficult to combat. To that definition Margaret Sanger easily adjusted her arguments for birth control.

Finally, the new ideas about sexuality had captured the budding emotional revolution, but they had not completely supplanted the romantic currents from which the revolution had originally sprung. In the years to come sexuality would be invested with much of the semimystical and spiritual ideology which was a large part of romanticism. The Freudians unwillingly inherited that ideology when they grafted their supposedly scientific theories onto the emotional changes of the late nineteenth century. But that union of science and romanticism created a context of attitudes toward sex that eventually helped make birth control acceptable to many Americans.

The modern family, the New Woman, and the sexual revolution had, by the time of World War I, ceased to seem quite so modern, or new, or revolutionary. They roughly defined, rather, a pattern of American social life that most articulate Americans endorsed. To Margaret Sanger fell the tasks of making birth control a consciously accepted part of that pattern and of extending it to the less articulate. But before she could begin her work in earnest, she had to find her audience and her own voice.

CHAPTER 3

The Organization of
a Social Movement

While Margaret Sanger was studying and traveling in England and Europe in 1915, the birth control movement in America had begun to take on organization and direction. Undoubtedly inspired by the dramatic example of Mrs. Sanger's self-imposed exile, supporters of birth control began to form groups for the public advocacy of contraception. In that process of increasing publicity and consolidation, Mrs. Sanger's pamphlet "Family Limitation" also played an important role. Its circulation throughout the country by IWWs and other radicals acquainted thousands for the first time with practical contraceptive techniques. And the pamphlet occasioned the arrest of William Sanger, whose case, a *cause célèbre* among radicals and free-speech advocates, proved a powerful magnet which drew many hundreds into active participation in the birth control movement.

In late 1914, a man who gave his name as Heller appeared at William Sanger's studio and asked for a copy of "Family Limitation." Professing to sympathize with Margaret Sanger's work, he said he would like to have her pamphlet translated into different languages, "to distribute amongst the poor people he worked with." Sanger innocently gave him a copy. Heller turned out to be a decoy. A month later, in early 1915, Anthony Comstock came in person to Sanger's studio and arrested him for violating the New York law which forbade "obscene, lewd, lascivious, filthy, indecent and disgusting" literature. Comstock's real purpose, although he relished the arrest, was to flush Margaret Sanger from hiding. This his action ultimately accomplished; but

in the meantime William Sanger's trial generated considerable support for birth control as a free-speech issue—so
much so that, when Mrs. Sanger returned to the United
States in October 1915, she found that a good many people
had done a great deal of work for the cause she would have
liked to consider exclusively hers. As for Comstock, death, in
September, cheated him of a last attempt to get Margaret
Sanger in the clutches of the law.

From all over the country came support for William
Sanger against the much-hated Comstock. The *Masses,*
which had long printed irreverent cartoons caricaturing
the portly head of the Society for the Suppression of Vice,
carried several articles on the case and collected money for
Sanger's defense. From Portland, Oregon, came a petition
with 127 signatures protesting the arrest. The novelist
Robert Herrick contributed to the Sanger defense fund.
When Sanger finally came to trial in September 1915, his
case had become so notorious that subpoenas, issued in
excess of the number of intended witnesses, were sold to
those desiring admission to the courtroom.

Sanger conducted his own defense. "The law is on trial
here, not I," he said. The presiding judge thought differ-
ently. He called Sanger a "menace to society" and cautioned
that "if some of the women who are going around and advocating equal suffrage would go around and advocate
women having children they would do a greater service."
Pronouncing Sanger guilty, the judge gave him a choice of
a $150 fine or thirty days in jail. Sanger replied: "I would
rather be in jail with my conviction than be free at a loss
of my manhood and my self-respect." Sanger served his
thirty days, but the apparently persecutive tactics of Comstock and the acerbity of the magistrate's wanton jabs at the
New Woman gave strength to the birth control movement.[1]

1. The fullest account of the William Sanger trial and the events
surrounding it is in James Waldo Fawcett's pamphlet, *The Trial of
William Sanger* (New York: Birth Control Review, 1917), a copy of
which is in MSP–SS. See also the scrapbooks in MSP–LC; *New York
Times,* September 5, 1915, sec. 2, p. 8, and September 11, 1915, p. 7;

Emma Goldman, emboldened by Margaret and William Sanger's dramatization of the birth control issue, began to speak much more frankly and explicitly on birth control. From coast to coast, throughout 1915, she lectured on such topics as "Birth Control" and "The Right of the Child Not To Be Born." Following the channels through which "Family Limitation" had circulated, she spoke to predominantly radical audiences and collected money for both the Sangers. She and her cohort, Ben Reitman, a medical doctor devoted to her and to radicalism, were arrested in Portland, Oregon, in August 1915 for distributing birth control literature.[2]

Other radicals were equally hard at work. Eugene Debs had written "Comrade" Margaret Sanger in December 1914 that if her "capitalist persecutors" attempted to "railroad" her, "we now have some means of defense and we can call a pretty good-sized bunch of revolutionists to arms." Such extreme methods did not prove necessary. Elizabeth Gurley Flynn, an IWW organizer, wrote to Margaret Sanger in Paris that on her return she should imitate Emma Goldman's speaking tour. "I am sure," she wrote, "the IWW locals would gladly arrange meetings wherever they exist and supplemented by Anarchist groups, woman's clubs, etc., a splendid trip is possible." Caroline Nelson, a San Francisco IWW worker, told of a birth control group she had organized in San Francisco, and of another in Portland, Oregon.[3]

and *Masses,* March, May, June, September, and November 1915. The information about the sale of subpoenas is in a letter from Harry Weinberger to his client, Emma Goldman, December 30, 1916, Harry A. Weinberger Memorial Collection, Sterling Library, Yale University, New Haven, Connecticut.

2. Richard Drinnon, *Rebel in Paradise: A Biography of Emma Goldman* (Chicago: University of Chicago Press, 1961), pp. 167, 168; see also Francis McLennon Vreeland, "The Process of Reform with Especial Reference to Reform Groups in the Field of Population" (Ph.D. diss., University of Michigan, 1929), pp. 74, 75. A complete record of Emma Goldman's several arrests for birth control activity is in the Harry A. Weinberger Memorial Collection, Yale University.

3. Eugene Debs to Margaret Sanger, December 16, 1914, Elizabeth Gurley Flynn to Margaret Sanger, August 16, 1915, and Caroline Nelson to Margaret Sanger, June 12, 1915, all in MSP–LC.

The support that American radicals gave to the birth control movement provided further proof, if proof were needed, that they were not doctrinaire Marxists. In Europe, Malthusian ideas were anathema among Marxists, who claimed that family limitation both reduced the numerical strength of the workers, and, by alleviating their suffering, blunted their class consciousness and revolutionary fervor. In America, although the radicals appreciated Marx, they did not trifle over doctrine. They considered birth control a humanitarian reform which fit well with their own theory of revolution. That theory did not hold with the European view that grinding misery would finally produce class war. New World assumptions of social mobility and aspiration colored the American radicals' program. Poverty, they claimed, cowed the spirit of the worker. But, "in a community . . . where birth control is consciously practiced and where the scarcity of labor results in good wages for all, the worker begins to measure his resources against those of the capitalist." [4] The comparison goaded his ambition; he resented his inequality, his stalled mobility. Only then could the revolution come. That non-Marxist viewpoint gained wide currency among American radicals between 1915 and 1920.

For all the support the radicals gave to birth control, the movement was not destined to serve their ambitions. Caroline Nelson perceived that irony in 1915. Although there was much interest in birth control, she said, "it is almost impossible to interest the workers," the very people about whom Mrs. Sanger was most concerned. The workers and "our very learned radical men" could not discuss the subject without "giggling and blushing." Consequently "our League here consists mostly of professional people . . . but no real working people. . . . This outfit will simply keep it as a semi-fashionable league. They are the people who don't need the information and never did, and how we

4. *Birth Control Review*, June 1917, p. 7. See also *Birth Control Review*, April 1920, p. 13.

are going to get it to the workers is the problem that I constantly harp on." [5]

The reluctance of the working class and the eagerness of the middle class to take up the cause of birth control became clearer as the movement progressed. As early as March 1915, a group had come together in New York City to form the first American birth control organization. The Birth Control League of America, which Margaret Sanger had prematurely announced in the *Woman Rebel,* "never had more than a nominal existence," according to one of Mrs. Sanger's associates.[6] But in Mrs. Sanger's absence in 1915 the National Birth Control League took on definite shape. Its director was Mary Ware Dennett, an artist by training, mother of two, and secretary, for a time, of the National Suffrage Association. Among the organizers were Jessie Ashley, Clara Gruening Stillman, Bolton Hall, and Lincoln Steffens—all liberals, not radicals. Many members had upper-middle-class backgrounds. Significantly, they purposely excluded from their ranks the extreme radicals associated with birth control, notably Emma Goldman. They directed their appeal to the conservative and the wealthy. Eschewing Margaret Sanger's spectacular law-breaking, the league pursued the more genteel strategy of trying to repeal restrictive statutes. Maintaining that birth control was a "purely scientific topic," the league worked for the Amendment of state and federal laws that treated birth control as obscene.[7]

5. Caroline Nelson to Margaret Sanger, June 12, 1915, MSP–LC.

6. Otto Bobsien to Mabel Dodge, November 17, 1914, Mabel Dodge Luhan papers, Beinecke Library, Yale University, New Haven, Connecticut. Mabel Dodge sent this letter to Walter Lippmann, who returned it with the notation: "I do not know this man, but I am convinced that if he is like Margaret Sanger he will not help the cause. This propaganda will [not] be successful in the hands of the people who are bent on the business of 'épater le bourgeois.'" Lippmann was essentially correct. What he could not know, in 1914, was that within a few years Mrs. Sanger would be conscientiously wooing "le bourgeois."

7. Vreeland, "The Process of Reform," pp. 68–70. Since the records of the NBCL were not preserved, and since the early records of the

Although Margaret Sanger shared the league's view that birth control should be removed from the category of obscenity, so strongly did she differ with regard to tactics, and so deeply did she resent the rivalry to her eminence as the sole birth control "pioneer," that her relations with the NBCL often verged on open hostility. She did, however, take some cheer from the increasing public discussion of birth control. Symbolically, one of the first things she saw on Manhattan when she disembarked on October 10, 1915, was a headline on the cover of the *Pictorial Review* with the very words—birth control—she had coined eighteen months before.[8]

But that was small compensation for the torrent of troubles that rushed upon her. Her husband was still serving his thirty-day sentence. Worse, less than four weeks after Margaret Sanger's arrival, her young daughter Peggy died, on November 6, of pneumonia. The death shattered the young mother, who soon suffered a nervous breakdown. As she wrote later:

> The joy in the fullness of life went out of it then and has never quite returned. Deep in the hidden realm of my consciousness my little girl has continued to live, and in that strange, mysterious place where reality and imagination meet, she has grown up to womanhood. There she leads an ideal existence untouched by harsh actuality and illusion.[9]

Perhaps, as she sifted through the dozens of consoling letters from "comrades" all over the country, Margaret Sanger brooded on the possibility that her year's absence in Europe

later American Birth Control League were lost in the late 1920s, Vreeland, who knew and worked with many of the birth control advocates in the '20s, is the best source for the organizational history of the birth control movement through 1928. See also Mary Ware Dennett, *Birth Control Laws: Shall We Keep Them or Abolish Them?* (New York: Frederick H. Hitchcock, 1926), pp. 67–69.

8. *Margaret Sanger: An Autobiography* (New York: Norton, 1938), p. 180.

9. *Autobiography*, p. 182.

had somehow been responsible for Peggy's death. But the death seemed to clarify her sense of purpose and renew her resolve. "Blessed be work!" one friend wrote. "That is all that is left for you, dear. And of that you will be able to find more than enough to fill your waking hours. You will be able to make sweet little Peggy's sacrifice worthwhile."

Mrs. Sanger heeded that advice. She had written the United States Attorney for Southern New York on her arrival in October, gently suggesting that the indictments against her be dropped, given the publicity and discussion birth control had received in her absence. He replied that the indictments still stood. After November 6, Margaret Sanger rejected any easy way out. She determined to vindicate her exile and her daughter's death. She would face the charges, conduct her own defense as her husband had done, as Annie Besant and Charles Bradlaugh had done, and make herself a martyr whose sacrifices would inspire others to take up the cause.

Some of her friends, including Leonard Abbott, Theodore Schroeder, and Gilbert Roe, lawyers, liberals, and free-speech advocates all, advised her to plead guilty and to take the undoubtedly light sentence that would be given her. She could then go on with educational work. But Mrs. Sanger refused to plead guilty, because, she said, "the whole issue is not one of a mistake, whereby getting into jail or keeping out of jail is of importance, but the issue is to raise . . . birth control out of the gutter of obscenity and into the light of human understanding." [10] Max Eastman correctly observed that Mrs. Sanger's statement had "absolutely no meaning." He and others pointed out that the indictments against Margaret Sanger made no mention of contraception, but dealt with *Woman Rebel* articles concerning assassination, marriage, and feminine hygiene. Even a favorable decision in court would not touch the laws prohibiting the dissemination of contraceptive information. A decision against Mrs. Sanger, on the other hand, would

10. Margaret Sanger to "Friends and Comrades," January 5, 1916, MSP–LC.

penalize her for what was, for her purposes, the wrong crime. In her troubled state of mind, Mrs. Sanger only imperfectly grasped the situation. Eastman, irritated, commented on her "pride, or your feeling that you ought to be brave enought to stand up for what you think, or whatever it is that is making you refuse the advice of counsel." He could not help remarking, he said, "that you are not facing clearly in your mind the motive of your action, whatever it is." [11]

Whatever the peculiar blend of self-justification, stubbornness, ambition, naïveté and dedication that constituted Margaret Sanger's motive, she was undeniably wide of the mark when she chose to take her stand on the nine counts against her *Woman Rebel* publications. Her friends rightly demonstrated the irrelevance of those counts, before the law, to the issue of contraception. As for the publicity value of the trial, the government would only improbably take dramatic action against Mrs. Sanger. Even if the court did give her a stiff sentence, the war in Europe was crowding all other news from the headlines. The *Masses,* for example, preoccupied by the war, had not bothered to announce Margaret Sanger's return to the United States.

Mrs. Sanger's lawyer, Leonard Abbott, realized the futility of his client's gestures. He tried to put the case clearly on the grounds of contraception by asking the United States Attorney to drop the *Woman Rebel* indictments and instead bring an indictment against Mrs. Sanger for mailing "Family Limitation." But the government attorney would not cooperate. If, he said, Mrs. Sanger should post a copy of her pamphlet, he would bring the matter before a grand jury. In the meantime, he would not drop what he—and Leonard Abbott—considered an airtight case against Mrs. Sanger on the *Woman Rebel* charges.[12] But he apparently

11. Max Eastman to Margaret Sanger, January 11, 1916; see also Bolton Hall to Leonard Abbott, December 13, 1915, Gilbert Roe to Leonard Abbott, December 15, 1915, and Emma Goldman to Margaret Sanger, December 8, 1915; all in MSP–LC.

12. H. Snowden Marshall (U.S. Attorney for Southern New York) to Leonard Abbott, December 15, 1915, MSP–LC. That Marshall blithely

assured Abbott that Mrs. Sanger would get off lightly if
she pleaded guilty. On those accounts Abbott all the more
strongly urged his client to get out of the imbroglio as
quickly and easily as possible.

Margaret Sanger rejected the hint of a "deal" with the
forces of reaction. Disgusted at what she considered the
supine compromising of Abbott and the liberal lawyers,
she announced her intention to appear without counsel in
court, where she would deny the validity of the statutes
under which she was indicted. Abbott, though convinced of
her clear guilt and the futility of her position, could do
nothing but give his approval. "Go ahead," he wrote her,
"each of us will do what we can to help you." [13]

Whether Abbott's or Margaret Sanger's approach was
correct was never resolved. On February 18, 1916, much to
everyone's surprise, the government entered a *nolle prose-
qui*. Possibly, though not demonstrably, Woodrow Wilson
himself intervened in Mrs. Sanger's behalf, after he had received scores of letters pleading her case, among them one
signed by Marie Stopes, H. G. Wells, and other prominent
Englishmen. More likely, the government's attorney simply
decided that the prosecution was not worth the effort and
might backfire. As the Assistant United States Attorney commented, "We were determined that Mrs. Sanger shouldn't
be a martyr if we could help it." [14]

The denial of her martyrdom in no way silenced Margaret Sanger. In a speech at the Hotel Brevoort in January,
she had argued that her role in the birth control movement was primarily agitational, that, as she told her audience, "all of you are better able to cope with the subject
than I am. I know that physicians and scientists have a

ignored the 100,000 copies of *Family Limitation* already distributed
indicated both his certainty of conviction on the original indictments
and his unwillingness to pursue the matter any more vigorously than
he already had.

13. Leonard Abbott to Margaret Sanger, n.d., MSP–LC.
14. U.S. District Court for Southern New York, Criminal Docket, 7:
152–54, "United States v. Margaret Sanger"; also, *New York World*,
February 19, 1916, clipping, MSP–LC.

greater technical fund of knowledge than I had on the subject of family limitation." But the scientists, she said, did nothing. She hoped, therefore, to be able "to dramatize the situation—to focus attention upon obsolete laws. . . . Then, others more experienced in constructive organization can gather together all this sympathy and interest which has been aroused, and direct it. . . . This is the next most important step and only in this way can I be vindicated." [15] Accordingly, she set out on a speaking tour in the spring of 1916 to "dramatize the situation" to audiences all over the country.

Mrs. Sanger's route followed the paths Alexander Berkman, Elizabeth Gurley Flynn, and especially Emma Goldman had blazed for her in 1915. In Chicago, St. Louis, Detroit, Portland, Oregon, Los Angeles, and San Francisco, radical audiences had been prepared for Margaret Sanger's message. But they could not have been prepared for Margaret Sanger. Unlike the stout, pugilistic Emma Goldman, or the violent Alexander Berkman, she was small, pretty, quietly dressed, and soft-spoken. Her forensic technique was not to harass and harangue, in the manner to which her radical auditors were accustomed. In the speech she delivered again and again in the spring and summer of 1916, she recounted the experience with Sadie Sachs which, she said, provided the emotional impetus to her work; she pleaded for new moral standards allowing free discussion of sexual knowledge; she decried the dangers of abortion and the proliferation of the defective; she demanded the emancipation of women and an end to charity as the answer to social problems. Mixing a captivating potion of charm, logic, statistics, often maudlin sentiment, and high idealism, Mrs. Sanger enchanted her audiences. She communicated an energy and a dedication that attracted a devoted band of personal followers.

She also inspired opposition. In Portland, Oregon, she

15. Margaret Sanger, speech, January 17, 1916, copy, MSP–LC. A version is also in *My Fight for Birth Control* (New York: Farrar and Rinehart, 1931), pp. 132–34.

was arrested, though immediately released. In St. Louis, she found the theater where she was to speak locked and barred—allegedly the result of a threatened Catholic boycott.[16] But Mrs. Sanger knew the value of those incidents. She protested long and loudly whenever the opposition was foolish enough to take public action against her. "As a propagandist," she said later, "I see immense advantages in being gagged. It silences me, but it makes millions of others talk about me, and the cause in which I live." [17]

By the spring of 1916, Mrs. Sanger's activities had surely made thousands, and perhaps millions, talk about her. When she returned to New York in the summer she began laying plans for a still more ambitious project. She determined to open a clinic. She had written from England of her intention to implement the lessons learned from Dr. Rutgers in Holland; now, she wrote, " 'clinics' is the watchword." [18]

16. For accounts of the speaking tour in 1916, see Vreeland, "The Process of Reform," app., p. 528; Alexander Berkman to Margaret Sanger, December 19, 1915, MSP–SS; scrapbooks, typescript of Mrs. Sanger's speech, and a letter from Marie Equi to Margaret Sanger, October 20, 1916, all in MSP–LC; also Sanger, *Autobiography*, pp. 192–209.

17. Margaret Sanger, speech at Ford Hall Forum, Boston, April 16, 1929, copy, MSP–LC. (Since the Boston authorities had threatened to close any meeting at which Mrs. Sanger spoke, she appeared on stage gagged, and Arthur M. Schlesinger, Sr., read her prepared text to the bemused audience.) Mrs. Sanger was not the only birth control advocate arrested in 1916. Emma Goldman went to jail several times for birth control activity. Some of the New York liberals were also arrested, including Bolton Hall, Ida Rauh Eastman, and Jessie Ashley. In Boston, a young man named Van Kleek Allison was arrested in July. The district attorney made the modest claim that Allison's case involved "the welfare and decency of society more than any prosecution that has ever been brought within the written history of the Commonwealth." Allison received the immodest sentence of three years. The sentence was later reduced, but the outrageous incident precipitated the organization of the Massachusetts Birth Control League. See Vreeland, "The Process of Reform," pp. 74–78; and scrapbooks, MSP–LC.

18. Quoted in Keith Briant, *Marie Stopes: A Biography* (London: Hogarth Press, 1962), p. 118.

In October 1916, Margaret Sanger, with her sister Mrs. Ethel Byrne, who was also a trained nurse, and a third woman, Fania Mindell, opened a clinic in the Brownsville section of Brooklyn, on Amboy Street near the corner of Pitkin Avenue. The three women distributed a flyer in English, Yiddish, and Italian advertising the service they offered:

> Mothers! Can you afford to have a large family?
> Do you want any more children?
> If not, why do you have them?
> Do not kill, do not take life, but prevent.
> Safe, harmless information can be obtained of trained nurses. . . . Tell your friends and neighbors. All mothers welcome. A registration fee of 10 cents entitles mothers to this information.[19]

Dozens of neighborhood women crowded the clinic daily.

Mrs. Sanger and her co-workers fully expected police interference. They were not disappointed. Police officers, on October 26, confiscated many of the articles (condoms and Mizpah pessaries) which Mrs. Sanger was prescribing. On November 14, officers again visited the clinic and heard Mrs. Sanger give a lecture to some of the neighborhood mothers. The district attorney then brought suits, under Section 1142 of the New York State Penal Code, against Mrs. Sanger and Mrs. Byrne for selling contraceptive devices, and against Fania Mindell for distributing "obscene" literature.[20]

Section 1142 made it a misdemeanor for anyone to "sell, lend, or give away," or to advertise, loan, or distribute, "any recipe, drug or medicine for the prevention of con-

19. A copy of the flyer is in MSP–LC; see also Sanger, *Autobiography*, p. 216.

20. Brief for Respondents, before Court of Appeals, State of New York, 1917, pp. 3–5; and Brief for Defendant-in-Error, before Supreme Court of the United States, 1919, pp. 3–5, copies of both, MSP–SS. The briefs give a slightly different and more reliable account of the arrests than does Mrs. Sanger's *Autobiography*, pp. 219–23.

ception." Section 1145, however, provided an exception,
stating that "an article or instrument, used or applied by
physicians lawfully practicing, or by their direction or prescription, for the cure or prevention of disease, is not an
article of indecent or immoral nature to use, within this
article." [21] Since no one in Mrs. Sanger's clinic was a physician, she could not take advantage of the exception Section
1145 allowed. Although a few physicians had already come
forward to support birth control by 1916, Margaret Sanger
claimed she could find none willing to serve in the Brownsville clinic. That circumstance may have been due as much
to the haste resulting from Mrs. Sanger's impetuous desire
for "direct action" as to timidity within the medical profession. At all events, the operation and now the legal defense of the clinic fell exclusively to Margaret Sanger.

For Mrs. Sanger, the Brownsville clinic served several
purposes. It implemented the program she had seen in
Holland. The clinic also afforded her a weapon with which
to challenge the National Birth Control League for leadership in the birth control movement. It offered the chance
for a test of the constitutionality of the prohibitive New
York law. Finally, the clinic and her expected arrest provided an opportunity for the publicity so vitally necessary
to all Mrs. Sanger's other goals.

Mrs. Byrne's case came up first. Her counsel, moving for
a jury trial, noted that impoverished women should be
spared the burdens of too numerous children. But, auguring
much later birth control propaganda, he argued most forcefully that Section 1142 was unconstitutional because it
denied a woman "her absolute right of enjoyment of intercourse unless the act be so conducted that pregnancy be
the result of the exercise. This clearly is an infringement
upon her free exercise of conscience and pursuit of happiness." Counsel made clear that this logic applied to "married persons, or even single persons." To such an argument
the court was predictably unreceptive; Mrs. Byrne's case, the

21. *Laws Relating to Birth Control in the United States and its
Territories,* pamphlet (New York: Clinical Research Bureau, 1938).

court declared, would come before the Court of Special Sessions in Brooklyn on January 4, 1917.[22]

However bleak the legal outlook, the juridical proceedings generated the publicity Margaret Sanger desired. Mrs. Amos Pinchot organized a "Committee of 100" notable women to aid in the legal battle and work for the reform of the New York State law. The day of Mrs. Byrne's trial, fifty women, many of them, according to the *New York Times,* "prominent socially," called for Mrs. Sanger, took her to breakfast at the Vanderbilt Hotel and escorted her to the courtroom. But even that formidable gallery of matrons could not impress the judges of the Court of Special Sessions. Mrs. Byrne's counsel, Jonah J. Goldstein, intended to bring "high medical testimony" (principally Mrs. Sanger's own physician, Morris Kahn), to show that Section 1142 contravened the purpose of the state's police power in that it actually worked for "the detriment of the health of the people." Kahn's testimony, Goldstein said, would show the high infant and maternal mortality rates in large families, the damage of overbreeding to maternal health, the effects of uncontrolled fertility in transmitting defects, and the "insanity, nervousness, sex perversion and homosexuality" resulting from celibacy. The court, less amenable to sociological argument than the Supreme Court of the United States had been in accepting the famous "Brandeis brief" in 1908, barred the witness from testifying and on January 22, 1917, sentenced Mrs. Byrne to thirty days on Blackwell's Island.[23]

Mrs. Byrne, after the example of the English suffragettes, declared her intention neither to eat, drink, bathe, nor work while she was in jail. The tactic commanded tre-

22. "Opinion of Kelby, J." clipping from *New York Law Journal,* December 5, 1916, p. 847, MSP–LC.

23. *New York Times,* January 5, 1917, p. 4; *New York Call,* January 9, 1917, p. 1. In 1908, in Muller v. Oregon (208 U.S. 412), Louis D. Brandeis had supported his successful argument for the constitutionality of an Oregon maximum hours law with a brief that relied heavily on statistical and sociological data. The brief gained wide notoriety for its departure from exclusively legal arguments.

mendous public notice. Amidst all the clamor of European war and American diplomatic maneuverings in late January 1917, Mrs. Byrne's hunger strike and the grim accounts of her forced feeding (brandy, warm milk, and eggs through a tube inserted in the esophagus) made front-page news from January 26 to January 29. By the end of the month, the Pless decision announcing the German resumption of unrestricted submarine warfare had driven birth control from the spotlight. But the point had been made. The birth control advocates had succeeded in convincing the public that insensitive judges and cruel jailers had wantonly persecuted a dedicated woman. While Margaret Sanger, with an unfailing instinct for showmanship and newsmaking, issued dark statements about Mrs. Byrne's fast-failing health, Mrs. Amos Pinchot, with public opinion mounting behind her, prevailed on Governor Charles Seymour Whitman to release the prisoner. "It will be hard," commented the outraged *New York Tribune*, "to make the youth of 1967 believe that in 1917 a woman was imprisoned for doing what Mrs. Byrne did." [24]

Margaret Sanger's own trial came up on January 29. In the face of the furor Mrs. Byrne's sentence had created, the judges desired to deal leniently with Mrs. Sanger. They offered her her freedom if she would promise not to repeat her offense. Mrs. Sanger replied that she had broken the law deliberately, that she regarded hers as a test case, and that she could "not respect the law as it exists today." Declining an opportunity to pay a fine, she was sentenced to thirty days.

She went on no hunger strike, probably realizing that the news value of such action had diminished. She did, however, release to the press a photograph showing her seated with her sons, radiating maternal pride and affection. Thus she shrewdly maintained the picture of victimized innocence the public had been made to see in the case of Mrs. Byrne.

24. *New York Times*, January 23, 26, 27, 28, 29, 1917; Sanger, *Autobiography*, pp. 226–34; *New York Tribune* comment quoted in *Birth Control Review*, April–May, 1917, p. 9.

Her only acts of defiance were her refusal to be finger-printed and her newspaper blasts against the commissioner of corrections, Katherine B. Davis, for the allegedly atrocious conditions of prison life. From her own account, however, her "stretch" was something of a lark. She wrote in her diary that it was "tragic, to see human beings forced to so low a level" as the drug addicts and prostitutes she encountered in jail.[25] But she enjoyed the exotic experience and her status as a heroine among the other female prisoners. The romantic glow of her long-awaited martyrdom must have brightened even more when she emerged through the prison gates on March 6 to find her comrades greeting her with the "Marseillaise." [26]

Mrs. Sanger appealed her conviction to the New York State Supreme Court and to the New York Court of Appeals. Each unanimously affirmed the original judgment against her. The Supreme Court of the United States dismissed a final writ of error in 1918. But though Mrs. Sanger's guilt was affirmed, she advanced her cause. On January 8, 1918, Judge J. Crane, writing for the unanimous Court of Appeals upholding Mrs. Sanger's conviction, broadened the definition of the circumstances in which the exception provided by Section 1145 applied. Most physicians had regarded the statute's phrase "for the cure or prevention of disease" as applicable only to venereal disease. Judge Crane said:

> This exception in behalf of physicians does not permit . . . promiscuous advice to patients irrespective of their condition, but it is broad enough to protect the physician who in good faith gives such help or advice to a married person to cure or prevent disease. "Disease," by Webster's International Dictionary, is defined to be "an alteration in the state of the body or of some

25. *New York Times*, February 16, 1917, p. 20; Margaret Sanger, Diary, entry for February 8, 1917, MSP–LC.

26. Sanger, *Autobiography*, pp. 238–50; *New York Times*, March 7, 1917, p. 20.

of its organs interrupting or disturbing the performance of the vital functions and causing or threatening
pain and sickness; illness; sickness; disorder." [27]

That construction allowed physicians a wide latitude in
judging the conditions that warranted contraception—
either as a preventive or a therapeutic device. But the
doctors did not seem eager to take advantage of their new
discretion; nor did Mrs. Sanger immediately urge them to
do so. She concentrated instead on a broad educational
campaign aimed at the general public.

The chief instrumentality in this campaign, besides Mrs.
Sanger's personal appearances, was a magazine, the *Birth
Control Review*.[28] Frederick A. Blossom, former head of
the Cleveland Associated Charities, whom Margaret Sanger
had met at the National Conference of Social Work in Indianapolis, came to New York from the newly organized Ohio
Birth Control League in late 1916. As one of his first
projects, he joined with Mrs. Sanger to launch the *Birth
Control Review*. Blossom, a Socialist, later a Wobbly, en-
listed considerable radical support behind the *Review*. He
personally distributed the first issue at a mass meeting for
Mrs. Sanger at Carnegie Hall on January 29, 1917.[29]

27. People v. Sanger, 222 N.Y. 102 (1918).

28. Mrs. Sanger added a novel note to her speaking appearances in
1917 when she showed audiences a moving picture entitled "Birth
Control." (Advertisements for the film called it an "Illuminating
Drama for the Ages . . . A Cheerup Photoplay for the Universe.")
The film depicted Mrs. Sanger working in the slums and contrasted
misery there with scenes of obviously well-to-do families with few
children. The scenario showed the opening of the clinic and "a
movement undertaken by persons of means" to suppress it. The film
concluded with Margaret Sanger behind bars and the title "no matter
what happens, the work shall go on." The commissioner of licenses
for the city of New York, however, enjoined Mrs. Sanger from showing
the film in the city, on the grounds that it promoted immorality, was
against the public welfare "in view of the pending war," and had "a
tendency to arouse class hatred." Mrs. Sanger appealed the Commissioner's decision, but he was upheld. See Message Photoplay Corp.,
Inc. v. Bell, 179 App. Div. 13; 166 N.Y. Supp 338 (1917).

29. *New York Times*, January 30, 1917, p. 4.

Throughout the war, the *Review* occupied most of Mrs. Sanger's time. She wrote articles, edited, raised money, and even hawked copies on street corners.[30]

The *Review*, both a propaganda sheet and a house organ, publicized birth control activities and kept the developing local leagues in communication. Its propaganda marked a significant change from the ill-tempered broadsides of the *Woman Rebel*. Although the *Review* did not entirely avoid mawkishness, it printed factual, statistical articles on such subjects as child labor, eugenics, demography, and the legal status of birth control. The *Review* became less hortatory and more objective through the years.[31] Olive Schreiner, Havelock Ellis, Eugene Debs, William J. Robinson, M.D., and David Starr Jordan were among its contributors. Although many probably purchased the *Review* on the mistaken assumption that it contained contraceptive information, for a good number of subscribers it served as a forum for the promulgation and discussion of scientific and quasi-scientific ideas relating to birth control.

Mrs. Sanger further publicized her ideas in two books, *Woman and the New Race*, published in 1920, and *The Pivot of Civilization*, which appeared two years later.[32] Describing these works as her "heart" and "head" books, respectively, she assembled in them every conceivable argument, emotional, rational, and polemical, in support of birth control. Her books, as well as her dramatic activities, soon established Mrs. Sanger as an international personality.

30. See Sanger, *Autobiography*, pp. 252–62.

31. Vreeland, "The Process of Reform," pp. 234–35. Vreeland did a survey of articles contributed to the *Review* from 1917 to 1926 and found that the percentage of articles that could be called "emotional" decreased from 31 percent in 1917 to 4 percent in 1922 and 0 percent thereafter. While admittedly a subjective impression, the survey reflected the tone of the *Review* over the years.

32. *Woman and the New Race* sold over 200,000 copies, many, again, to readers who hoped for practical contraceptive advice. They were of course disappointed. Mrs. Sanger did, however, send information or the name of a friendly physician to countless thousands of women who asked her help.

By 1922, she had made her fourth trip to Europe, had been received with honors in Japan, and had won worldwide recognition as the foremost leader in the birth control movement.

Her ascendancy in the movement had its costs. She had been separated from William Sanger since 1913. Finally, in 1920, she divorced him. And not without struggle did Mrs. Sanger win the hegemony she ultimately enjoyed in the birth control movement.

The struggle had begun immediately on her return to the United States in 1915. At that time, she declined an offer to be on the executive committee of the NBCL. She was likely to go to jail soon, she said, and "she did not want her mishaps to involve the activity of others." The excuse was, perhaps, disingenuous, since the purpose of all her activities had been to involve as many others as possible with birth control. But at the time, Mrs. Sanger did object to the character of the NBCL, which emphasized legislative change. Her function, she said, expressing her continuing commitment to the tactic of direct action, was "to break the laws rather than . . . to change them." [33] (Both groups, of course, wished the laws to be changed—the NBCL by statutory amendment, Mrs. Sanger by judicial interpretation.) Further, she wanted little to do with any organization she could not effectively control.

To counter the influence of the National Birth Control League, some of Margaret Sanger's friends—notably Frederick Blossom—organized the New York Birth Control League in December 1916. The members, said an early student of the movement, were "of a more radical stripe than those in the older organization." [34] The new league announced a threefold purpose: to help Margaret Sanger in her legal fight; to amend the state and federal laws to allow physicians to give scientific instruction in birth control; and to advocate birth control as a means of protecting maternal and infant health and promoting the social welfare.

33. Dennett, *Birth Control Laws*, p. 67.
34. Vreeland, "The Process of Reform," p. 88.

This platform differed significantly from that of the NBCL. Though Mrs. Sanger, by 1917, had come to agree with Mary Ware Dennett that legislative lobbying, not direct action, offered greater hope of success for the birth control movement, she disagreed on the form legislative amendment should take. From 1917 to 1919 the NBCL promoted at Albany a draft version of a bill written by John Dewey which simply struck "for the prevention of conception" from the list of illegal uses of drugs and devices given in Sections 1142 and 1145. That amendment would have made contraceptives as freely available as aspirin. The NYBCL bill, in contrast, written by the Columbia University Legislative Drafting Bureau, deleted the words "for the cure and prevention of disease" from Section 1145 only. That change allowed contraception for any reason whatsoever, but only under a doctor's supervision. Ironically, the more "radical" NYBCL, showing the influence of Dr. Johannes Rutgers's conversion of Mrs. Sanger to the belief that contraception was primarily a medical matter, had taken a more conservative position, while the middle-class reformers of the NBCL demanded radical changes in the name of free speech. Furthermore, Mrs. Sanger's group, intent on founding clinics, regarded the state law as the primary obstacle. Mrs. Dennett's National League, however, on the model of the Woman's Party, gave a higher priority to reforming the federal law.[35]

Throughout the years of the First World War, there were three centers of birth control activity—the NBCL, the NYBCL, and the group associated with the *Birth Control Review*. Individuals contested between and within these groups for title to leadership of the movement. The discord that had appeared when Mrs. Sanger refused to join the NBCL increased after the sensation of her trial and imprisonment. When the National League slackened its financial support of Mrs. Sanger in early 1917, she complained of the lack of harmony. She wished, she said, that there

35. NBCL newsletter, January 11, 1917, MSP–LC; *New York Times*, February 1, 1917, p. 22; Dennett, pp. 69, 73; Vreeland, pp. 89–90.

could be "one office, one staff, one bill to be presented to the legislature, one aim and one ideal to be fought for." The league's officers agreed that discord was "most unfortunate." They were sorry, they said, but "the N.B.C.L was of course organized for one purpose only—the change in the law," and therefore could not join with Mrs. Sanger.[36]

Within the office of the *Birth Control Review*, an even more serious conflict was brewing. Sometime in the spring of 1917, Frederick Blossom, the managing editor of the *Birth Control Review*, suddenly quit, taking with him lists of subscribers, account books, funds, and even the office furniture. He so disorganized the operation that no issues of the *Review* appeared between June and December 1917. Blossom's only apparent motive was his ambitious desire to dominate the movement, a psychological disposition Mrs. Sanger could well understand but hardly tolerate in another. When direct appeals to Blossom failed to return the missing items, Mrs. Sanger went to the district attorney. That was a fateful move.

Margaret Sanger's birth control agitation had begun as a radical, even revolutionary, phenomenon. Although Mrs. Sanger accepted the financial support of the middle-class reformers who organized the NBCL in 1915, she had shunned association with them. She had maintained her affiliations with the radicals whom Blossom had drawn together to form the NYBCL and support the *Birth Control Review*. These radicals viewed an appeal to the district attorney as high treason. They persuaded Mrs. Sanger to drop her public charges against Blossom and instead to accept an investigation by the Socialist Aldermanic Committee. But the damage had been done. The radicals in the NYBCL, "very much incensed" at Mrs. Sanger, drubbed her out of the league. Although it developed that the Socialist investigating committee regretted the whitewash they gave Blossom, one of the investigators said later: "The undisputed fact . . . remained that Mrs. Sanger had gone to an outside

36. Margaret Sanger to Mrs. Amos Pinchot, April 16, 1917, and reply, April 17, 1917, MSP–LC.

agency—the capitalist district attorney—to involve and perhaps imprison a comrade. In this respect she was guilty.
We prepared for and actually succeeded in ousting her."
This incident marked the final and irreparable rupture between Margaret Sanger and the radicals.[37]

Although the appeal to the district attorney had finally
precipitated the break, Mrs. Sanger had been moving away
from the radicals and from radicalism for some time. In
Margaret Sanger's early years, Mary Ware Dennett noted,
she had regarded organization as a "bourgeois, pink tea,
lady-like" affair and considered only "direct action" worthwhile.[38] Certainly the *Woman Rebel* was an example of
direct action, just as the Brownsville clinic was "propaganda by the deed," both typical anarchist tactics. But the
clinic episode had also demonstrated the value of organized
support. After early 1917, Mrs. Sanger experienced that
ambivalence toward organization which Richard Hofstadter
has found to be characteristic of so many reformers in the
early twentieth century. As she said in her *Autobiography,*
she had a "dread" of organization, yet she appreciated the
"advantages of strength and stolidity which would enable
[the organization] to function when the individual was
gone." [39] Reluctantly, Mrs. Sanger decided to seek those
advantages through organization.

Margaret Sanger perceived that any successful organi-

37. Statement of Henry Fruchter to Elizabeth Gurley Flynn, in a
report on Blossom commissioned by John Grady, general secretary
of the IWW, September 16, 1922, MSP–SS. Blossom went on to work
for the Rand School and the IWW, but both these groups later dis-
credited him. Mrs. Sanger's ouster produced a schism in the NYBCL.
Both pro-Sanger and anti-Sanger factions claimed legitimacy as the
"true" league. The contest faded, however, as both wings of the
league soon became moribund. As for the *Birth Control Review*, Mrs.
Sanger reorganized it in 1918, raising capital by forming a stock company and selling shares for $10 (Sanger, *Autobiography*, p. 260).

38. Mary Ware Dennett, statement issued November 18, 1921, copy,
MSP–LC.

39. Compare Richard Hofstadter, *The Age of Reform* (New York:
Vintage, 1955), pp. 215–27, with Margaret Sanger's *Autobiography*, pp.
299–300.

zation needed influence, money, and manpower. The radicals had been able to provide only the last in sufficient quantities, and the war was decimating and dividing the radical ranks. The leisured, wealthy wives of the middle class possessed all three resources in abundance. Mrs. Sanger, more than a year before her final break with the radicals, had written her sister from jail: "It is true that the fashionable seem far removed from the cause, and its necessity— but we cannot doubt that they and they alone dominate when they get an interest in a thing. So little can be done without them." [40] The Blossom incident gave Mrs. Sanger a final push into the arms of the "fashionable." She began to court the NBCL, which she had once scorned. But that organization had its own difficulties. Congress, absorbed by the war, had little time to consider the repeal of the federal Comstock law. Financial difficulties forced the resignation of the league's director, Mrs. Dennett. The league sponsored an Eastern States Birth Control Conference in 1918, but by the end of 1919 the NBCL had ceased to exist.

Almost immediately after the NBCL's demise, Mrs. Dennett organized the Voluntary Parenthood League, whose sole aim was repeal of the federal statutes. Mrs. Sanger would join no group with such a limited focus, nor one she had no hope of controlling. She had, however, rejuvenated the *Birth Control Review,* and with the *Review* staff as a nucleus she began to build an organization to compete with the troublesome Mrs. Dennett. Financed by Mrs. George Rublee, Mrs. Paul D. Cravath, Mrs. Dwight Morrow, and other prominent New Yorkers, she worked throughout 1920 and 1921 organizing the First American Birth Control Conference, held in New York, November 11–13, 1921. On the eve of the conference Mrs. Sanger met with her backers and formally established the American Birth Control League. The president of the new league, Margaret Sanger, announced its existence at the opening of the conference.

40. Margaret Sanger to Ethyl Byrne, February 14, 1917, MSP–LC.

The conference gave notice that the new league was a far more ambitious enterprise than anything yet undertaken in the birth control movement. Purposely scheduled to coincide with the international naval conference in Washington, D.C., and with the meeting of the trustees of the American Medical Association in Chicago, the conference underscored Mrs. Sanger's awakening to widening implications of birth control. While the diplomats haggled over capital ships and Pacific insular possessions, and while the AMA's trustees made sober pronouncements on pay clinics and the tax problems of their profession, the delegates at the Birth Control Conference discussed the relation of birth control to individual and public health, to eugenics, to the problems of delinquency and labor, to the chronic world famine, and to the very issues of disarmament and war under such intensive debate in Washington. The conference program also included a contraceptive "clinic" for doctors only and a final mass meeting at Town Hall on the subject "Birth Control: Is It Moral?" The conference, with its elaborate program, planning, and recruitment of delegates from two continents, indicated the energy and sophistication with which the ABCL was to pursue its goals in the 1920s.

The conference stirred little general notice until the mass meeting to discuss morality on November 13. On that evening, when Mrs. Sanger arrived at Town Hall with her featured speaker, Harold Cox, editor of the *Edinburgh Review,* she found a crowd gathered outside. One hundred policemen, obviously intending to prevent the meeting, ringed the locked doors of the hall. When the police opened the doors to let people already inside exit, those outside rushed in, carrying Mrs. Sanger and Cox before them. Once inside, Mrs. Sanger tried several times to speak, but policemen forcibly removed her from the platform. While shouts of "defy them" came from the crowd, Cox managed only to blurt, "I have come across the Atlantic to address you," before two policemen hauled him from the stage. The police arrested Mrs. Sanger and led her out of the hall while the

audience sang "My Country 'Tis of Thee." Outside, the
drama continued as Mrs. Sanger strode haughtily up Eighth
Avenue to the Forty-Seventh Street Police Station in the
van of a procession of police, hundreds of supporters, and
more hundreds of the curious. Police reserves had to be
called to keep the crowd at a safe distance from the station
house. Mrs. Sanger's connections and attorneys swiftly arranged her release on her own recognizance.[41]

Even bigger news broke the next day. The *New York
Times* headlined: "Birth Control Raid Made by Police on
Archbishop's Order." Monsignor Joseph P. Dineen, secretary to Roman Catholic Archbishop Patrick J. Hayes, had
apparently telephoned Captain Donahue of the West Forty-
Seventh Street Station "some time before the meeting" and
requested the captain to meet him at Town Hall. When the
captain arrived, Dineen told him to prevent the meeting.
Dineen never explicitly admitted his role in this affair, but
there could be little doubt that the chancery had a hand in
the raid. Such, at least, was the popular impression when
Dineen told the press that he and the Archbishop were
"delighted and pleased" at the police action. "Decent and
clean minded people," he said, "would not discuss a subject
such as birth control in public." Though the police acted
before a word had been spoken at the meeting, Dineen implied that the topic itself justified the disruption.[42]

The suppressed discussion was held five days later at the
Park Theatre. This time the police provided protection—
and stenographers to record any "obscenities." Mrs. Sanger
invited Archbishop Hayes to send representatives to the
Park Theatre to debate her spokesmen. The clergyman declined, but he kept the issue boiling when he gave to the
press on November 21 a lengthy statement against birth
control.

When the publicity began to flag in early December, the
corporation counsel's office gave it an inadvertent boost by

41. *New York Times,* November 14, 1921, p. 1; Sanger, *Autobiography,* pp. 298–305.
42. *New York Times,* November 15, 1921, p. 1.

arresting Mrs. George Rublee while she was in the act of testifying at an investigation into the charges of church influence behind the raid of November 13. The arrest, an incredible blunder, had absolutely no foundation. Further, George Rublee was one of New York's most prominent citizens. Henry Morgenthau, Lewis L. Delafield, Charles C. Burlingham, Paul M. Warburg, and other notables protested the treatment given Mrs. Rublee.[43]

The city soon dropped the charges against her, and the investigating commission finally evaded the issue of church interference and laid sole responsibility for the raid on the hapless Captain Donahue. But the controversy served several purposes. As a friend told Margaret Sanger: "It is the very best thing that could have happened." [44] The police raid generated tremendous publicity for Mrs. Sanger and for the newly formed ABCL. It consolidated her support among the well-to-do, many of whom were ardent libertarians and especially resented the attack on Mrs. Rublee, one of their own. Finally, the raid raised the specter of a militant Catholic conspiracy to block birth control.

Although Dineen's complicity in the raid was never proved, no one doubted the Catholic church's vigorous opposition to Mrs. Sanger's idea. Regrettably, here and in the years that followed the raid, the troubled currents surrounding the issue of birth control swept both adversaries to extremes. The church confused its moral obligations to its members with its political obligations in a democracy. Mrs. Sanger, remembering her childhood ostracism and the radicals' hatred for all ecclesiastical authority, could never regard the church with equanimity. Remembering also the radical maxim that a visible enemy was an indispensable source of inspiration for a social movement, she used the Catholic church—as she had previously used the

43. *New York Times,* November 21, 1921, p. 1; December 3, 1921, p. 9; December 18, 1921, p. 18; February 21, 1922, p. 13; Sanger, *Autobiography,* pp. 309–15.

44. Telegram, Florence Whitney to Margaret Sanger, November 14, 1921, MSP–LC.

"plutocrats" and Anthony Comstock—as a goad to energize her supporters and as a foil to dramatize her cause. Catholic opposition was real enough and often irresponsible. But to advance her cause, Mrs. Sanger confronted that opposition with a deliberately high-pitched emotionalism. Her attitude created an atmosphere that poisoned dispassionate dialogue with liberal Catholic elements and stifled whatever slim chance there might have been for peaceful coexistence between the Catholic church and the birth control movement.

While Mrs. Sanger's emotional fervor hindered a rapprochement with the Catholic church, it served the movement well in other regards. Noting the spirit and loyalty of the ABCL's staff, one observer ascribed it to "hero-worship of Mrs. Sanger." Nearly all of the staff workers were women; they spoke without embarrassment of "our beloved leader," and "our guiding light." Her secretary described Margaret Sanger as a "singing symbol" and wrote her that no one could look at her "without a stirring of the pulse and quickening of the spirit at the realization that in your person is [sic] embodied the triumph of the human spirit and the power of integrity over the forces of circumstance." [45]

Mrs. Sanger's forceful spirit and charm also got her a second husband. She had written her sister from jail in 1917: "I'll have to go west and find a widower with money and settle down for life." In 1922 she did just that.[46] J. Noah H. Slee was president of the Three-In-One Oil Company, a wealthy patron of birth control, and a widower more than twenty years Mrs. Sanger's senior. Though she finally capitulated to his importuning (he followed her everywhere, incessantly, in pursuit of her hand), she insisted on a unique

[45]. Vreeland, "The Process of Reform," p. 147; Florence Rose to Gladys Smith, May 16, 1935, MSP–LC; Florence Rose to Margaret Sanger, January 15, 1939, MSP–SS.

[46]. Margaret Sanger to Mary Higgins, March 1, 1917, MSP–SS. Actually, Mrs. Sanger reversed the order. She found her wealthy widower, and later moved with him to a winter home in Tucson, Arizona. The Slees also maintained an estate, Willow Lake, in Dutchess County above New York. *New York Times,* February 18, 1924, p. 4.

marital arrangement. Mrs. Sanger was probably innocent of the perversities that had lain behind Edith and Havelock Ellis's domestic arrangement; however, in her admiration for Ellis she decreed that her marriage should be modeled on his: the Slees would have separate domiciles, or, later, separate quarters within the same house.[47] Neither was to have the slightest influence over the business of the other. Moreover, when both were busy, communications would be exchanged through their secretaries. Mrs. Sanger would keep her first married name, because of the celebrity attached to it. She even kept the marriage secret for nearly two years.

Mr. Slee must have been content with these bizarre arrangements, if donations to the American Birth Control League accurately gauged his marital felicity. Between 1921 and 1926, Slee gave the league over $56,000, a considerable amount for an organization whose largest budget, in 1926, was $38,000. Slee was certainly the birth control movement's principal source of funds. One investigator concluded that the nature of ABCL financing made the league more of a private philanthropy than a national social movement.[48]

In spite of her new husband's generosity, Mrs. Sanger complained in 1923: "We have no definite and dependable financial resources. Without this foundation we cannot continue our fight. Our workers should . . . be relieved of the ignoble task of collecting penny by penny." [49] Later, the ABCL would try to systematize financial support by

47. Havelock Ellis was for years functionally impotent. His wife, Edith, long maintained a separate residence at least partly to facilitate her lesbian liaisons.

48. Vreeland, "The Process of Reform," p. 359; see also *Birth Control Review*, January 1923, p. 3; report of the John Price Jones Corporation, 1930, MSP–LC; Minutes of Board of Managers of the Clinical Research Bureau, September 19, 1929 (at this meeting Slee pledged $100,000 toward an endowment fund for the Bureau if $400,000 could be raised elsewhere), MSP–LC; *Time*, March 18, 1929, p. 36.

49. Margaret Sanger to Mrs. Dexter Blagden, August 1, 1928, MSP–LC.

appealing to other nonprofit organizations—foundations—
for regular contributions. As early as 1922 Mrs. Sanger ne-
gotiated with one of the leading medical philanthropies,
and one of the first to be organized as a foundation, the
Milbank Memorial Fund. She apparently had no success.
In the early 1920s, individual solicitation, especially from
League members, remained the ABCL's principal fund-
raising technique.

By 1926 the league had a membership of over 37,000.
The typical member was Protestant, native white born of
native parents, better educated than most other Americans,
Republican, married, under 35 years of age, and the parent
of fewer than 3 children. The average member's family income, $3,000 a year, was higher than the national average.
The northern states furnished more members, both pro-
portionately and absolutely, than did the southern, and the
thickest concentration of membership was naturally around
New York City. (Illinois, Ohio, California, Michigan, and
Texas also had sizable memberships.) Eighty-eight percent
of the members were women; and because they were of the
upper middle class, most were able to escape the urban
centers in the warm months. The result was a perennial
summer slump in birth control activity. As one worker put
it: "Reform is a winter pastime for the clubwoman, and
everything fluctuates with her." [50]

The league recruited its membership in several ways. It
absorbed many of the local leagues that had been affiliated
with the NBCL (although some, notably the quite active
Chicago group, remained in closer contact with the Voluntary Parenthood League, which was more nearly the NBCL's
successor). It actively recruited prominent people to give
their names to a "National Council," which had no function
other than lending prestige and respectability to the cause.
Mrs. Sanger's personality itself attracted many individuals
to the movement. Finally, the league employed fieldworkers

50. Vreeland, p. 359. On pages 157–210 Vreeland gives a detailed
profile of ABCL membership, based on league records and on nearly
1,000 responses he received to a questionnaire in 1927.

who canvassed the country organizing affiliated local leagues and soliciting the support of such groups as women's clubs and social work organizations.

The ABCL carried out an ambitious and varied program in the 1920s. In its declaration of "Principles and Aims," in 1921, the league defined a broadly based platform of education, research, legislative reform, and national and international organization.[51] The use of spectacular, publicity-generating events gave way as an educational technique to lecture tours and especially conferences. The ABCL employed a Cornell professor in 1926 to speak on the West Coast. Slee paid James F. Cooper, M.D., $10,000 a year to speak under the league's aegis before county medical societies all over the United States.[52] The league sponsored the Sixth International Birth Control and Neo-Malthusian Conference in New York in 1925, the most impressive symposium on sexual, eugenic, and demographic problems that had ever been held.[53] In addition, the league organized

51. See Margaret Sanger, *The Pivot of Civilization* (New York: Brentano's, 1922), app., pp. 279–84; and *Birth Control Review*, December 1921, p. 18.

52. Margaret Sanger to J. Noah H. Slee, February 22, 1925, MSP–LC.

53. Five earlier Neo-Malthusian conferences had discussed population problems: Paris, 1900, Liege, 1905, The Hague, 1910, Dresden, 1911, London, 1922. The Conferences brought together representatives of the British Neo-Malthusian League, the French *Ligue de la Régénération Humaine,* and other European Malthusian organizations formed since about 1880. The early conferences were sparsely attended, underground affairs, usually taken up with tedious debates about the relation of Malthusian principles to Marxism. By 1922 however, the topic had gained enough in respectability that such a reputable speaker as John Maynard Keynes graced the London program, and over one hundred physicians attended a session devoted to contraceptive techniques. A few Americans, notably Emma Goldman, had attended one or another of the earlier conferences, and Margaret Sanger was in London in 1922. But the location of the sixth conference in New York indicated that American money and American organizational talent would in the future dominate international Malthusianism. And the revised title of the conference, to include the words "birth control," which Margaret Sanger had coined, symbolized her growing leadership in the world movement.

numerous local and regional conferences throughout the 1920s.

The ABCL delegated its medical service functions to the Clinical Research Department, formed in 1923, which was in reality a birth control clinic adjoining the league's offices at 104 Fifth Avenue in New York. The clinic was not allowed to advertise, and its resident physician-director could prescribe only for a "health reason" under the New York statutes. Although the clinic was affiliated with the league, Mrs. Sanger incorporated it separately to comply with New York State medical licensing regulations. Nevertheless, it was ABCL policy simply to refer patients down the hall to the clinic for specific contraceptive information.[54]

The league's several attempts at legislative reform were uniformly unsuccessful. Mrs. Sanger and her associates made futile assaults on the New York, Connecticut, and Pennsylvania anticontraception statutes. In early 1926, after the model of the VPL, Anne Kennedy, one of Mrs. Sanger's closest associates, set up a lobby in Washington, D.C., from which to mount an attack on the federal Comstock law. But after extensive interviewing, and without even drafting a bill, the league closed its Washington office late in the year. Mrs. Kennedy's report noted that "the amendment of all laws opposing the dissemination of Birth Control information by physicians seems unimportant in comparison to the educational work to be done among the women of the country." [55]

Mrs. Sanger determined to carry the educational work beyond the "women of the country." She went to Europe

54. The league also maintained a "Mother Department," which consisted of one secretary to answer the considerable number of letters requesting birth control information from Mrs. Sanger. The league generally referred inquiring women to local physicians known to be sympathetic to birth control or sent the address of local clinics where they existed. Occasionally, the league mailed a copy of "Family Limitation." The use of the mails to transmit this information was of dubious legality, but it went on without interference.

55. Anne Kennedy, report on 1926 "federal work," n.d., MSP–LC.

in 1926 to organize a World Population Conference. The conference assembled scientists of international renown in order to impress the world, and especially the League of Nations, with the importance of population questions and the geopolitical relevance of birth control. When the conference materialized in Geneva in 1927, a dispute arose over placing Mrs. Sanger's controversial name on the program. Finally, though Margaret Sanger had been primarily responsible for organizing the conference, and though her husband had financed much of it, the nervous, perhaps simply stodgy, delegates granted her no official recognition and barred the topic of contraception from the agenda.

Other defeats soon followed at home. Mrs. Sanger was gone from the United States for eighteen months in 1926 and 1927, preparing for the conference and vacationing with her husband on the Cote d'Azur, in St. Moritz and Nassau. In her absence, Mrs. Ellen Dwight Jones, a member of the ABCL's board of directors, had been acting president of the league. Margaret Sanger found on her return to the United States that Mrs. Jones had made changes in the ABCL's institutional structure. She had regularized fundraising and diffused the power of the president, giving the board of directors a greater voice in league affairs. Mrs. Sanger should have welcomed the first of these changes, but she predictably resented the latter. In June 1928, amidst a storm of name-calling, accusations, and ill will she resigned as president of the American Birth Control League.

In her *Autobiography*, Mrs. Sanger curiously attributed her resignation from the league presidency to Mrs. Jones's efforts to establish a stable and permanent source of income for the ABCL. She knew, she said, "the apathy which came from a fat bank balance." She had always believed, she claimed, "that offerings should be voluntarily measured by the individual's desire. In this way you could appeal whenever a special occasion warranted and receive anywhere from one dollar to three hundred." [56] That explanation

56. Sanger, *Autobiography*, p. 393.

ignored her own complaint in 1923—"We have no definite and dependable financial resources"—and conveniently
overlooked her bitterness at the challenge to her authority.

Mrs. Sanger made a brave attempt to keep up appearances
in 1928. She wrote a friend:

> I hope you understand that the reason for my resig-
> nation is that we have been so successful in the growth
> of the League that there is already too much for me
> to do, and we have divided the work so the Board of
> Directors will now do the legislation and organization
> part. I have taken on the clinic and the extension and
> expansion of the research work. It is great fun and I
> know it is a big field to explore.[57]

But the "great fun" did not last long. The "conservatives,"
as Mrs. Sanger chose to call those who challenged her
spirited but autocratic and often chaotic leadership, made
another power play. Success in the contest for the ABCL
presidency inspired Mrs. Jones to seek even greater changes.
Late in 1928, she proposed that the *Birth Control Review,*
the official organ of the ABCL since 1922, be placed under permanent professional management, superseding Mrs.
Sanger's editorship. With this, Mrs. Sanger quit the league
entirely (until this point she had remained on the board
of directors), and also quit the *Review.* Her husband termi-
nated his financial support of the league in January 1929, a
blow from which it never fully recovered. He objected most
strongly, he wrote the directors, to "the attempt to place
a subordinate and paid employee above the woman whose
inspiration and knowledge has [sic] made the Movement
respected throughout the world." [58] Mrs. Sanger now wrote
more candidly to the same friend she had addressed
earlier: "My leaving the *Review* and the League was not
because I wished to leave but because there was created
inside the Board an influence and an atmosphere which

57. Margaret Sanger to S. Adolphus Knopf, September 22, 1928,
MSP–LC.

58. J. Noah H. Slee to ABCL, January 12, 1929, MSP–LC.

caused such pettiness and criticism that one could do nothing but get out." [59]

Contrary to her previously announced intention to "divide the work" and to leave legislative reform to the ABCL, Mrs. Sanger in 1929 stole a march on the league and organized the National Committee on Federal Legislation for Birth Control. The ABCL gave her a brief fight over control of the clinic, but the league, either sated with its success in the matters of the presidency and the *Review,* or alarmed at Mrs. Sanger's aroused wrath, finally backed down. By the end of 1929, Mrs. Sanger had exclusive control of the clinic and had set up the rival National Committee, with headquarters in Washington, D.C., to compete with the ABCL on the national level. The ABCL, having lost at one stroke Mrs. Sanger's notoriety and Mr. Slee's money, was only a feeble institution in the 1930s.

By the time the Big Bull Market had collapsed and the New Era come to an inglorious end, birth control had emerged from tabooed obscurity to become the basis of an organized international social movement. The development of that movement had, of course, depended on the evolution of public attitudes toward contraception and several related issues such as sex, feminism, and the condition of the family. But the pace and pattern of the movement's organizational development proceeded from the competition between groups and individuals for the personal and public satisfactions that came with leadership in the movement. As Mrs. Sanger contested with her rivals for the attention of various publics and for the support of a limited number of financial backers, she necessarily made birth control a different issue from what it had been when she began her efforts in 1914.

Most notably, as Caroline Nelson had gloomily foreseen in 1915, birth control ceased to be a radical cause and was taken up by the "fashionable"—the respectable matrons

59. Margaret Sanger to S. Adolphus Knopf, March 6, 1929, MSP–LC.

of the middle class. It was predominantly these "New Women"—and not the daughters of the working class—who supported Margaret Sanger and effectively practiced her precepts. Indeed, they and their forebears had been acquainted with contraception long before Margaret Sanger called it birth control and made it a social cause. In this sense, Margaret Sanger did not make the New Woman possible; it was the other way around.

Those middle-class women brought to the birth control movement the techniques of organization and propaganda they had learned in other women's reform efforts, such as the temperance movement and especially the women's suffrage movement. The struggle for the Nineteenth Amendment provided training for many women who held administrative positions in the ABCL and later in the National Committee for Federal Legislation for Birth Control. When the ABCL replaced Mrs. Sanger's episodic sensationalism with a systematic educational program of conferences, salaried speakers, and fieldworkers, it showed the influence of an educated class of women familiar with relatively sophisticated techniques of opinion formation.

Over all the organizational history of the birth control movement, however, Margaret Sanger cast her shadow. Her daring activities between 1914 and 1921 gave her a public image that enabled her to dramatize birth control in a way none of her rivals could approach. Her reputation commanded access to the media and ensured the success of any publicity associated with her name. Finally, her marriage to J. Noah H. Slee gave her great financial leverage with which to pursue her goals.

For all her altruism and humanitarianism, one of Mrs. Sanger's goals was complete and exclusive control of the birth control movement. However hard others might work for the cause, she nevertheless insisted on the major part of the glory. She spurned any organization she could not dominate; she relentlessly maneuvered to displace her rivals within the movement. And for her enemies outside the movement, however useful she knew them to be for her ultimate purposes, she had irreconcilable scorn.

The organization of the birth control movement, then, and the tactics it employed, were shaped by the movement's changing sources of support, its responses to opposition, its intramural rivalries, and above all by the imposing personality of the movement's principal figure, Margaret Sanger.

As she turned from radicalism to respectability in both her private and public lives, Mrs. Sanger changed not only the organizational structure of the movement; the rationale—or, as she liked to call it, the "philosophy"—of birth control underwent changes equally profound.

CHAPTER 4

Revolution and Repression: The Changing Ideology of Birth Control

Margaret Sanger proposed an idea that many at first considered preposterous, even insidious. To legitimize her aims, she had to develop a body of arguments that demonstrated the desirability and practicability of contraception. Havelock Ellis had perceived that necessity when he guided Mrs. Sanger through a more or less systematic study of birth control at the British Museum. There she began to build a complex rationale for her reform. With the passage of time, her case for birth control took on different emphases; eventually it underwent changes in substance as well. By the end of the 1920s birth control propaganda bore little resemblance to Mrs. Sanger's prewar pronouncements.

Drawing on the lessons of her study with Ellis, Mrs. Sanger argued first of all that birth control in some form was inevitable. Citing the Finnish anthropologist E. A. Westermarck, she wrote that from time immemorial woman "has sought some form of family limitation. When she has not employed such measures consciously, she has done so instinctively. Where laws, customs and religious persecutions do not prevent, she has recourse to contraceptives. Otherwise, she resorts to child abandonment, abortion and infanticide, or resigns herself hopelessly to enforced maternity." [1] Officialdom, said Mrs. Sanger, could not resist the spontaneous demand for contraceptive information.

1. Margaret Sanger, *Woman and the New Race* (New York: Brentano's, 1920), p. 11.

That "spontaneity theory" had a special appeal for Mrs. Sanger, whose radical training led her to sympathize with the historical resentments of the masses against church and state. She had also taken from radicalism the notion that any successful social movement must have a visible enemy, and the "spontaneity theory" provided one in the form of the conspiratorial, repressive ecclesiastical and political establishment.

Since some form of family limitation was inevitable, said Mrs. Sanger, society should endorse the practice of artificial contraception. The scientific regulation of reproduction would prevent the social waste of abortion and infanticide and would reduce maternal mortality by preventing pregnancy among women with tubercular, coronary, or renal disorders. Birth control would also check the debilitating effects of hereditary afflictions, especially, Mrs. Sanger said, those stemming from venereal disease.

Mrs. Sanger made a powerful propaganda appeal when she pointed out the relation of birth control to the health and welfare of children. Drawing on statistical reports by the Federal Children's Bureau, she said that most infant deaths were due to "malnutrition, or to other diseased conditions resulting from poverty, or to excessive childbearing by the mother." And her slogan "every child a wanted child" embraced more than the physical condition of the infant. "No child," she said, "can be what it should be, physically, mentally, or spiritually, if it is conceived and carried by a mother to whom the embraces of her husband are repugnant." Because birth control promoted connubial affection, said Mrs. Sanger, it enhanced the child's psychological welfare by creating an environment of love in the home.[2]

Margaret Sanger also argued that birth control would eradicate poverty and its consequences. If the individual family and the nation achieved abundance by restricting their numbers, she said, all manner of social evils—insanity, crime, unemployment, slums, and prostitution—would

2. *Birth Control Review*, April 1919, p. 5.

disappear. Implicitly invoking the classical wage-fund theory, usually the refuge of conservatives and the nemesis of
reformers, Mrs. Sanger portrayed birth control as a one-
stroke solution to several of the problems that had plagued
the progressive generation.

Margaret Sanger's early advocacy of birth control on di-
verse grounds, while manifesting the pragmatic character of
all propaganda, showed especially the influence of her own
eclectic nature. But though she appealed to various arguments, even occasionally touching a curiously conservative
theme like the wage-fund theory, in the years before World
War I the teachings of the Ferrer School anarchists and the
French syndicalists gave her propaganda a certain unity.

Sexual reform, because it offended the most sacrosanct
features of the established order, had a particular emotional appeal to radicals, and especially to Mrs. Sanger, who
considered society "sickly" and wanted to "go about shocking it terribly." Her sense of alienation and her contempt
for "respectability" accounted for both the vigor and the
venom in her depiction of contraception as a means to destroy the existing social structure. The American birth control movement, said Mrs. Sanger in 1915, was "intense with
indignation, anger, and contempt." [3]

As she had in the *Woman Rebel*, Mrs. Sanger continued
to direct her anger at capitalists, and she found the best
justification for birth control in its usefulness as a weapon
in the class struggle. She damned "welfare societies" with
their bourgeois lady reformers who preached the capitalist
values of docility and submission. Only birth control, she
said, could help the laboring class. Working women, she
argued repeatedly, echoing Rosa Luxemburg, should not
"produce children who will become slaves to feed, fight,
and toil for the enemy—Capitalism." [4] Mrs. Sanger remained faithful, in 1915, to the lessons of her radical ap-
prenticeship in New York. But her fidelity was fragile.

3. Margaret Sanger, speech to Fabian Society Meeting, July 5, 1915,
copy in MSP–LC.

4. Margaret Sanger, "English Methods of Birth Control," pamphlet,
1915, copy in MSP–LC.

Margaret Sanger had been totally, but not deeply, attached to radicalism. It absorbed all her energies but did not evoke an abiding inner commitment, probably because she had no taste for its ideological complexities, and because her practical sense suggested that the political program of the American radicals was futile. Nevertheless, radicalism served for a time to express Mrs. Sanger's brooding dissatisfaction as well as her humanitarianism and to give structure to her early thought on birth control.

Havelock Ellis, however, had convinced her of the pragmatic value of confining her activity to birth control alone. And she was both solipsistic and perceptive enough to appraise birth control as of greater social importance than the vague proposals of the radicals. When the New York Birth Control League read her out of the radical movement in 1917, therefore, she shed no tears. She had already recogized that the radicals were a small and ineffective group and that to make the birth control movement successful she would have to appeal to a broader base of support. She turned both her organizational loyalties and her propagandistic arguments to those whose interests lay not with revolution but with middle-class reform. Mrs. Sanger gave one of the first specific indications of her new outlook in 1920, when she explicitly drew on the wage-fund theory and said that "the basic principle of craft unionism is limitation of the number of workers in a given trade. . . . Every unionist knows, as a matter of course, that if the number is kept small enough, his organization can compel increases of wages, steady employment and decent working conditions." [5] No longer did she speak boldly of blows at the profits of bloated capitalists; no longer did she preach class war and allude darkly to revolution. She now recited the elitist principles of trade unionism and the relatively conservative labor program long promoted by Samuel Gompers—better wages and hours and job security.

Mrs. Sanger had already revealed a subtle though significant shift in her attitude when she wrote in 1918 that "all

5. Sanger, *Woman and the New Race,* p. 138.

our problems are the result of overbreeding among the working class." [6] The detachment, the sense of "we against them" connoted by the separation of "our problems" and the working class, measured the distance Margaret Sanger had traveled from the strike lines at Lawrence. Two years later, she renounced her indictments of "Welfare Societies" and called on women of the "wealthy and upper classes" to come to the aid of the workers. [7] By 1922 she had explicitly repudiated Marxism as "purely masculine reasoning," which perpetuated the melodramatic fiction of class antagonism and which, because of its "superficial, emotional and religious character," had a "deleterious effect upon the life of reason." Marx relied too much, she concluded, on "moral fervor and enthusiasm. To build any social program upon the shifting sands of sentiment and feeling, of indignation or enthusiasm, is a dangerous and foolish task." [8]

To Emma Goldman, to Big Bill Haywood, to the readers of the *Woman Rebel*, to Mrs. Sanger's auditors at radical gatherings on her 1916 speaking tour, those last words must have seemed strange indeed. Margaret Sanger had been the paragon of the very qualities she now rejected as dangerous and foolish. Now her indignation, her contempt, even much of her old alienation were gone, and so, too, was her sympathetic identification with the lower class, which had become a "problem."

Mrs. Sanger had come full circle to the very Malthusian idea that European Marxists, and Margaret Sanger herself, in her early days, had strenuously resisted: that working-class misery was attributable not to economic and political dislocation, but to the fecundity of the working class itself. In that view, birth control was not intended as a weapon for the lower classes to use against the system that oppressed them. On the contrary, the artificial restriction of

6. *Birth Control Review*, February–March 1918, p. 14.

7. Sanger, *Woman and the New Race*, p. 70.

8. Margaret Sanger, *The Pivot of Civilization* (New York: Brentano's, 1922), pp. 8, 167.

fertility was seen as an instrument with which the dominant classes could check threatened social disruption. Perhaps it was only to be expected that in history's most bourgeois nation any social reform, to be successful, had to be
administered by and for the "fashionable" middle class
Mrs. Sanger now found so indispensable.

Radicals had seen in the suppression of contraceptive information and birth control propaganda an aspect of the
class struggle. Capitalists, the radicals believed, conspired
with clerics and politicians to withhold knowledge of contraception from the working class. The real logic of the
divine command "increase and multiply," said the radicals,
lay in "the selfish glorification of conquering war-lords"
and robber barons who needed large armies and labor
pools. Capitalist hypocrisy, the argument ran, was clearly
manifest in the small families of the well-to-do.[9] Margaret
Sanger had agreed with that argument when she insisted
that upper-class women had knowledge of contraceptives
but for purposes of class subjection refused to give it to
others.

After 1920 Mrs. Sanger found a different significance in
the obvious disparity between upper- and lower-class family
size. She capitalized on the alarm many Americans had felt
for a generation over the drastically declining birthrate of
the white, native, Anglo-Saxon, Protestant stock and the
high fertility of immigrants. Mrs. Sanger still demanded
birth control for the lower classes—but not in order to free
them from exploitation. Now she described how birth control would protect the rest of society from the prolific alien
poor and "unfit."

When Margaret Sanger spoke of controlling the birthrate
of the "unfit," she did not abandon her humanitarianism,
but she certainly set it in a different perspective. To her
depiction of birth control as a device to alleviate the suffering of the poor, she now added the persuasive argument
that contraception could be an effective means of social

9. *Birth Control Review*, February 1920, p. 17.

control. That notion, she soon found, attracted to her camp a large number of middle-class reformers fascinated with the idea of biologically regulating society according to the principles of eugenics.

Eugenics had begun, writes Mark H. Haller, as "a scientific reform in an age of reform," arising from the characteristically progressive concern for the application of scientific solutions to social problems. Francis Galton in England and August Weissman in Germany had enunciated the first principle of eugenics in the late nineteenth century when they rejected the Lamarckian idea that acquired characteristics could be inherited. Not environment, they emphasized, but heredity principally determined the quality of life and was the key to social change. The rediscovery of Mendel's laws of genetic selection in 1900 lent further scientific weight to the ideas of Galton and Weissman." [10]

In America, eugenic thinking appealed strongly to men who cherished the elitist social theories of the late nineteenth century but felt uncomfortable with the smug moralism nineteenth-century apologists had invoked to support their views. Eugenics provided antimajoritarian thinking with scientific sanctions to replace the antiquated religious ones of the Gospel of Wealth.

By the 1920s American eugenicists were well organized. Their leading spokesman, Charles B. Davenport, had established the Eugenics Record Office in 1910 at Cold Spring Harbor on Long Island. With the financial backing of Mrs. E. H. Harriman, Cold Spring Harbor became the holy city of American eugenicists—a cult which numbered among its faithful such men as David Starr Jordan, Alexander Graham Bell, Henry Fairchild Osborne, Lothrop Stoddard, Madison Grant, Ellsworth Huntington, Edward A. Ross, and E. M. East. The eugenics movement drew its greatest support from people who saw daily the tragic consequences of hereditary disease—social workers, public health officers, charity workers, and supervisors of institu-

10. Mark H. Haller, *Eugenics: Hereditarian Attitudes in American Thought* (New Brunswick, N.J.: Rutgers University Press, 1963), p. 5.

tions for the defective. Other groups, alarmed at the growing problems attendant on immigration, composed another
large wing of the movement.

Eugenics held out to such people the enticing possibility
of social control through application of principles of
"biological efficiency." The concept of efficiency had a
strong hold on the minds of Americans in the early twentieth century, especially among those men who called
themselves progressives and were attempting to adjust
American life and institutions to the facts of modern industrialism. But efficiency connoted more, to the progressives, than social harmony. It also meant, as Samuel Haber
has written, "the leadership of the 'competent.' . . . Efficiency provided a standpoint from which those who had
declared allegiance to democracy could resist the levelling
tendencies of the principle of equality." [11] Eugenics furnished those who believed in efficiency with a specific
biological program which included a concern for the general welfare but was heavily freighted with notions of elitism
and even racism.

Margaret Sanger had learned of eugenics from Havelock
Ellis. She first acknowledged the place of birth control in
the eugenicists' program when she announced in 1919:
"More children from the fit, less from the unfit—that is the
chief issue of birth control." [12] Mrs. Sanger usually used
the word "unfit" to refer to the mentally retarded and
physically deformed. "Birth control," she said in 1920, "is
nothing more or less than the facilitation of the process of
weeding out the unfit, or preventing the birth of defectives
or of those who will become defectives." [13] Increasingly,
she saw feeblemindedness, the bogey of all the heredi-
tarians, as antecedent to poverty or social organization in
the genesis of social problems. "The philosophy of birth
control," she said in 1922,

11. Samuel Haber, *Efficiency and Uplift: Scientific Management in
the Progressive Era* (Chicago: University of Chicago Press, 1964), p.
viii.

12. *Birth Control Review*, May 1919, p. 12.

13. Sanger, *Woman and the New Race*, p. 229.

points out that as long as civilized communities encourage unrestrained fecundity in the "normal" members of the population—always of course under the
guise of decency and morality—and penalize every attempt to introduce the principle of discrimination and
responsibility in parenthood, they will be faced with
the ever-increasing problem of feeble-mindedness, that
fertile parent of degeneracy, crime, and pauperism.

As did all the eugenicists, Mrs. Sanger quoted the evidence
of the army intelligence tests administered to millions of
American men during the First World War. The striking
incidence of substandard scores, she said, proved the reality of the "menace of the feebleminded." [14]

Margaret Sanger and others considered the most menac-
ing aspect of proliferating unfitness to be the growth of the
custodial welfare state. "Protective and paternalistic laws,"
said a speaker at the Sixth International Neo-Malthusian
and Birth Control Conference in 1925, benefited "the least
desirable elements of society." Such laws, he said, "are
usually put forward upon moral or humane or altruistic
grounds and in nearly all cases by professional agitators
and stupid busybodies. . . . What they actually accom-
plish is the preservation of the misfit, the degenerate, the
low, the unworthy and the more or less defective elements
at the expense of the strong and exceptional." If practiced
by the right people, he suggested, birth control could wipe
out those evils for which welfare legislation gave at best
merely symptomatic relief.[15]

That Spencerian attitude, embracing the familiar tenets

14. Sanger, *Pivot of Civilization*, pp. 81, 91, 240; Mrs. Sanger apparently believed that "70% of this country's population has an intel-
lect of less than 15 years" (Margaret Sanger to Isabelle Keating, January 13, 1932, MSP–LC).

15. Max G. Schlapp, M.D. (Professor of Neuropathology, New York
Post-Graduate Medical School; Director, New York Children's Court
Clinic), "The Survival of the Unfit," in Margaret Sanger, ed., *The
Sixth International Neo-Malthusian and Birth Control Conference*,
vol. 3, *Medical and Eugenic Aspects of Birth Control* (New York:
American Birth Control League, 1926), pp. 129–50.

of individualism, elitism, and antistatism, provided one base for the eugenic program. In 1922 Mrs. Sanger registered her acceptance of such ideas when she said that if society applied to reproduction the techniques of efficiency employed by "modern stockbreeders," there would be no need for measures that were "fostering the good-for-nothing at the expense of the good." [16] In the 1930s, Mrs. Sanger found that argument especially well received among those who opposed New Deal welfare legislation.

Mrs. Sanger pointed out other dangers presented by an allegedly degenerate populace. "In a democracy," she said, "it is the representatives of this grade of intelligence who may destroy our liberties, and who may thus be the most far-reaching peril to the future of civilization." She condemned the initiative, the direct primary, and other progressive majoritarian reforms as "pathological worship of mere number." [17] She insisted that only the scientific regulation of fertility could save democracy from the threatening hordes of the unfit. Parents, she suggested, should have to "apply" for babies, just as immigrants had to apply for visas to enter the country.[18]

Racism provided another base for eugenics. Many eugenicists did not confine the description of "unfit" to those with hereditary afflictions. They saw in Mrs. Sanger's reference to immigration more than a convenient rhetorical analogy. Although Mrs. Sanger usually strove to avoid an ethnic definition of "unfit," she herself occasionally pandered to the rankest nativist sentiment. In 1920 she decried the rising proportion of immigrants from southern and eastern Europe, and their greater relative fertility once they arrived here. Those "foreigners," she complained, were ignorant of hygiene and the conditions of modern life. They filled the slums and made the cities wretched. They threatened to replace native workers in many industries.

16. Sanger, *Pivot of Civilization*, pp. 262, 105.
17. Sanger, *Pivot of Civilization*, pp. 177–78.
18. Margaret Sanger, speech in Hartford, Connecticut, February 11, 1923, copy in MSP–LC.

But having mentioned those repulsive features of the "new immigration," Mrs. Sanger was quick to add that the receiving American society had been less than fair in its treatment of the immigrants; it had "bustled and kicked them . . . animalized" them.[19]

In spite of that attempt to even the balance, when Margaret Sanger linked the issues of immigration and birth control she struck a deep vein of anti-alien sentiment, just as her talk of eugenics had touched a strong current of antidemocratic feeling. Increasingly, sometimes embarrassingly for Mrs. Sanger, support for birth control came from the most tory and bigoted quarters. As late as 1934, she had to go out of her way to clarify her definition of unfit, emphasizing that she "deplored" the use of the term in reference to "races or religions." But the very necessity for clarification, at that late date, showed how prevalent was the nativist application of birth control.[20]

The *Birth Control Review* had since 1917 carried articles by such leading eugenicists as Paul Popenoe, editor of the *Journal of Heredity*. By 1920 the eugenicists were specifically advocating the adoption of birth control by the slumdwellers and impoverished, who had always been Margaret Sanger's chief concern. In that year, Warren S. Thompson noted that the real "race suicide" threat was not Anglo-Saxon biological extinction, but the loss of Anglo-Saxon political and economic hegemony to numerically superior "Slavs, Latins and Hebrews." Those who read between Thompson's lines could easily find nativist justification for such programs as the Brownsville clinic.[21]

Other birth control supporters did not leave the implications unsaid. Clarence C. Little, a biologist, for a time president of the University of Maine, later of the University of Michigan, and for many years on the council of the

19. Sanger, *Woman and the New Race,* pp. 36–37.

20. Margaret Sanger, reply to questionnaire from *Yale Daily News,* February 13, 1934, MSP–LC.

21. Warren S. Thompson, "Race Suicide in the United States," *Birth Control Review,* August 1920, p. 9.

American Birth Control League, justified birth control in 1926 as an influence counter to the process of the melting pot. In a singular analogy he likened the mixing of races and nationalities in America to the blending of "cherry, pineapple, chocolate, coffee, vanilla, strawberry, raspberry, lemon and orange" syrups in a soda fountain. Little spoke fondly of Maine where

> the proportion of the old New England stock is very, very high. That . . . I consider an anchor, one of those places in the soda fountain where the label reads for instance, "Yankee Stock." I don't want to see that particular element in the situation mixed up, or marked up. I want to keep it the way a chemist would prize a store of chemically pure substance that he wants to use for testing, that he wants to use for definite purposes when a certain element is needed. But it is very difficult to bring that about. The whole tendency is to grow, to grow in size, to import foreign labor.

Birth control, he concluded, by restricting the rate of growth and the numbers of "foreign labor," "makes the situation simpler; it magnifies the chance of survival of this civilization." [22]

Guy Irving Burch, for a time legislative secretary of the National Committee on Federal Legislation for Birth Control, a director of the American Eugenics Society, and a leader in the American Coalition of Patriotic Societies, was even more frankly racist than Little. He supported birth control, he said, because "my family on both sides were early colonial and pioneer stock and I have long worked with the American Coalition of Patriotic Societies to prevent the American people from being replaced by alien or Negro stock, whether it be by immigration or by overly high birth rates among others in this country." [23]

22. *Birth Control Review*, August 1926, pp. 244, 257.
23. Guy Irving Burch to Arthur J. Barton, January 23, 1934, MSP–LC.

But despite the optimism with which many eugenicists and nativists embraced Mrs. Sanger's cause, the more perceptive among them had always recognized an unresolved dilemma inherent in the relationship of birth control to eugenics. Arthur J. Barton, the chairman of the Southern Baptist Convention, identified that dilemma when he wrote to Guy Irving Burch:

> You have a very wrong estimate as to what effect birth control would have both on the population and on the morals of our people. My observation leads me to believe that the Negroes and the poorer element of the white population are not interested in birth control and would not be materially affected by it. My judgment is that if there should be a general dissemination of information about birth control such information would be used mainly by white people in better circumstances, among whom the birth rate is already too low, and that the poorer white element and the Negroes would continue to have large families which would increase the disproportion in the increase of population as among the different classes of our people.[24]

In other words, the spread of contraceptive practice in the absence of coercive application to certain classes would have not a eugenic but a dysgenic effect. When it became obvious that Mrs. Sanger's "spontaneity theory" had been in error, that the "unfit" were not clamoring for birth control information, most eugenicists reversed their attitude toward the birth control movement.

Mrs. Sanger had characteristically claimed too much for the union of birth control and eugenics. Not only did birth control in fact undermine the purposes of the eugenicists, but the eugenicists themselves could never satisfy the more reasonable advocates of contraception that there was any feasible way to determine standards for the judgment of

24. Arthur J. Barton to Guy Irving Burch, January 31, 1934, MSP–LC.

"fitness." The question of standards did not trouble some of the more intrepid eugenicists, such as a speaker at the Sixth International Conference, who included among the inferior "the dullard, the gawk, the numbskull, the simpleton, the weakling, and the scatterbrain." The viciousness of such a categorization of the unfit revealed the perils inherent in any system of social control that necessitated a decision as to standards of superiority. Even Clarence C. Little wondered at the appropriateness of the current popular standard, which equated upper-class status with fitness. The wealthy, he said, had become slaves of their environment in their lust for Rolls Royces, Southern winter homes, and pet Pomeranians. "Why encourage that type of person to have enormous families?" he asked. "It simply would degenerate into a benevolent society for pug dogs or something of that kind." Some eugenicists, such as the prominent birth control advocate Ira S. Wile, M.D., called for statistical studies "to establish the criteria of racial controls," but Margaret Sanger and others eventually realized the danger and futility of any such effort.[25]

Nevertheless, for all their incompatibility, eugenics and birth control made an effective propaganda combination throughout the 1920s. Mrs. Sanger had first embraced eugenic rhetoric as just another addition to her grab-bag of arguments for contraception. Soon, however, eugenics dominated birth control propaganda and underscored the conversion of the birth control movement from a radical program of social disruption to a conservative program of social control. Ironically, Margaret Sanger's earliest attempts to shift the justification for birth control from emotional to rational grounds had ended in the temporary capture of the movement's ideology by a philosophy that masked prejudice in the guise of efficiency. In Mrs. Sanger's continuing war between her "head Me" and "heart Me," the forces of reason seemed capable of only hollow victories.

25. *Sixth International Conference,* 3:146; *Birth Control Review,* January 1926, p. 34.

Radicals, perhaps, found further irony in the fact that class-consciousness in the United States had taken firmest hold not among the proletariat but among the middle class. The self-consciousness of the prosperous bourgeoisie produced the hope that it would be possible in America to create a wholly middle-class society. In the early twentieth century, it seemed for a time that the middle class sought to implement that vision by absorbing lower-class elements. By the 1920s, however, many middle-class reformers sought through eugenic reform simply to eliminate the alien and the poor. They modified the Spencerian description of society as an organism to allow for some surgical removals without damage to the vital parts.

The attitude that identified the middle class with society itself rendered possible birth control appeals of a certain level of abstraction—notably in terms of the "population problem." The accelerating increase in the number of the planet's people figured only slightly in the earliest American birth control propaganda. Indeed, Mrs. Sanger felt that she had improved on the bland English Neo-Malthusian program by avoiding such relatively impersonal issues as population economics. Because the United States was new and uncrowded, she said in 1917, the American birth control movement had "less direct interest in this phase of the matter than have the advocates of the same doctrine in the tightly packed United Kingdom." [26] The World War, however, awakened Margaret Sanger and her associates to the relation between war and population pressure. Before long birth control advocates were applying the regulatory principles of eugenics to geopolitics. Will Durant, for example, told the Sixth International Conference in 1925 that "to offset the so-called 'yellow peril'" the United States should "spread Birth Control knowledge abroad so as to decrease the quantity of peoples whose unchecked reproduction threatens international peace." [27]

26. *Birth Control Review*, July 1919, p. 3.

27. Will Durant, "Message to Sixth International Neo-Malthusian and Birth Control Conference," 1925, copy in MSP–LC.

Mrs. Sanger eventually appealed more directly to middle-class self-consciousness when she spoke not of the pressure of population on international boundaries or the means of subsistence, but, in a modification of classic Malthusian arguments, of the relation of population levels to standards of living. Overpopulation, she said, was not a quantitative matter; quite possibly the world could support a sizable population increase. "But any such rapid increase of population could be maintained," she added, "only by lowering the standard of living both physically and spiritually." Birth control, on the other hand, could "elevate standards of living for the family and the children of the responsible —and possibly more selfish—sections of the community." [28]

Margaret Sanger here touched, but appeared only imperfectly to comprehend, an important truth. Though Malthus had argued that only the food supply provided an economic check on fertility, the behavior of the middle class in the Western world during the nineteenth century had disproved that aspect of his theory. Birthrates did not drop nearly so dramatically among the lower class, struggling to obtain the means of subsistence, as they did among the "selfish" middle class, striving to protect and elevate its economic position. Many reformers recognized that only when the standard of living had *already* improved, when people took on the complex of attitudes toward self, sex, society, and status that came with entry into the amorphous middle class, only then did people effectively practice contraception. When Mrs. Sanger urged the poor to achieve prosperity by limiting the number of their children, she was engaged, critics charged, in the futile exercise of putting the cart before the horse.

The birth control movement under the leadership of Margaret Sanger did little to alter the fact that the fertility of the lower classes has almost always exceeded that of the upper classes. Indeed, the peculiar orientation she gave to the movement may have helped perpetuate the differential

28. *Birth Control Review*, August 1928, p. 277; Sanger, *Pivot of Civilization*, pp. 179–80.

in the birthrate. For when she assumed that the principal obstacle to the effective practice of contraception by poor people was their ignorance of contraceptive techniques and inferred, therefore, that her own chief enemy was repressive officialdom, she committed a grave tactical error, albeit one for which she cannot be too seriously indicted. Only in recent years have demographers come to appreciate the stubborn fact that family planning is not so much a technological problem as an attitudinal one. In other words, it was not simply the inaccessibility of birth control information that inhibited lower-class family planning; nor was it, as Mrs. Sanger later claimed, the absence of a simple, inexpensive contraceptive suitable to the uneducated poor. Lee Rainwater, noting the persistent inability of the very poor to control the size of their families, lays those myths to rest. After more than four hundred interviews, Rainwater concludes that "very few couples of any class do not know of one or two methods they could use to control the size of their families. At the simplest level of knowledge, even the lower-class respondents seem at least as well equipped as were the highest status persons in Europe and England at the time these latter groups began limiting their families." [29] Yet the lower classes continue to have families markedly larger than middle-class families. As Rainwater observes elsewhere, "In the working class ineffective contraceptive practice has relatively little to do with the technical excellence of the method and much to do with the ways in which people approach the task." [30] It has to do, in other words, with attitudes.

Rainwater suggests that one explanation for the inability of members of the lower classes effectively to practice contraception lies in their attitude toward time, especially the future. Neither the upbringing nor the employment of the

29. Lee Rainwater, *Family Design: Marital Sexuality, Family Size, and Contraception* (Chicago: Aldine, 1965), p. 211.

30. Lee Rainwater, *And the Poor Get Children: Sex, Contraception, and Family Planning in the Working Class* (Chicago: Quadrangle Books, 1960), p. 142.

poor equips them to think systematically about the future and to plan on the basis of long-term consequences of present acts. (The poor, for example, have jobs, not careers.) Hence, says Rainwater, among the working class, "trust in a predictable and reasonably gratifying future is not common, nor is a belief in one's personal efficacy in relation to that future." [31] The incompatibility of such an attitude with effective family planning is obvious.

Rainwater further suggests that the lower-class woman, contrary to what Margaret Sanger long insisted, is reluctant to restrict the number of her children because she has a much greater emotional investment in motherhood than does the middle-class woman. "Motherhood is much more completely her reason for being than it is for the middle class woman, who is taught the value of outside interests for establishing her validity as a person." [32]

Finally, Rainwater argues that there is a high correlation between ineffective contraceptive practice and what he calls "segregated conjugal-role relationships," that is, marriages in which masculine and feminine functions are the most clearly delimited, in which husband and wife have separate interests and activities, rarely plan anything together, and still more rarely discuss the intimate details of sexual behavior that must be agreed upon if contraception is to work. Such familial arrangements, in turn, occur most frequently in the lower classes. [33]

Such facts indicate that the changes the early twentieth century witnessed in middle-class attitudes toward the family, woman, and sex had little if any relevance to the lower classes. Had Margaret Sanger recognized that, had she escaped the middle-class outlook she so exclusively embraced after World War I, she might have adopted a different and more effective strategy. Instead of attacking officialdom and preaching the benefits of a liberated sexual instinct to the

31. Rainwater, *And the Poor Get Children*, p. 52.

32. Rainwater, *And the Poor Get Children*, pp. 82–83.

33. Rainwater, *Family Design*, ch. 2, pp. 28–60; *And the Poor Get Children*, ch. 5, pp. 69–91.

ladies of the middle class, she might have engaged in a massive educational effort directed at the lower classes, who were her original concern.

To Margaret Sanger, birth control was a panacea that made all other reforms irrelevant. She invoked nearly every imaginable argument in its support, and made extravagant claims for its benefits. One writer in 1927 noted the tendency to advocate birth control as a nostrum that "makes the eyes shine and hair curl, perfumes the breath, [and] prevents the trousers from bagging at the knees." [34] Still, for all the catholicity of Mrs. Sanger's propaganda, after about 1920 she spoke almost exclusively to the middle class. All her persuasiveness did little to increase appreciably the practice of contraception among the poor and disadvantaged, who, in her phrase, needed it the most.

34. Thomas D. Eliot, "The Policies of the Neo-Malthusian Movement: Criticisms and Appraisals," *Journal of Social Hygiene* 13 (1927): 134.

CHAPTER 5

Margaret Sanger, Sexuality,
and Feminism

Margaret Sanger, wrote Mabel Dodge Luhan, "was the first person I ever knew who was openly an ardent propagandist for the joys of the flesh." One evening at dinner, while Mrs. Luhan and a companion listened attentively, Mrs. Sanger "sat there, serene and quiet, and unfolded the mysteries and mightiness of physical love [and] it seemed to us we had never known it before as a sacred and at the same time a scientific reality." Margaret Sanger believed, Mrs. Luhan wrote, "that the attitude towards sex in the past of the race was infantile, archaic, and ignorant, and that mature manhood meant accepting the life in the cells, developing it, experiencing it, and enjoying it with a conscious attainment of its possibilities." [1] Mrs. Luhan, whatever the peculiarities of her personal approach to sexual matters, had nevertheless touched on an important aspect of Margaret Sanger's advocacy of birth control.

Mrs. Sanger intended birth control not simply to reduce the suffering of the poor and the number of the unfit, but also to increase the quantity and quality of sexual relationships. The birth control movement, she said, freed the mind from "sexual prejudice and taboo, by demanding the frankest and most unflinching re-examination of sex in its relation to human nature and the bases of human society." That function of the movement, she pointed out, was the "most important of all." [2]

1. Mabel Dodge Luhan, *Intimate Memories,* vol. 3, *Movers and Shakers* (New York: Harcourt, Brace, 1936): 69–71.
2. Margaret Sanger, *The Pivot of Civilization* (New York: Brentano's, 1922) p. 244.

In addition, Mrs. Sanger felt that much of the opposition to birth control stemmed not necessarily from nice calculations of differential birthrates and projected class and ethnic strengths but from a "loathing, disgust or indifference to the sex relationship." [3] Overcoming those attitudes, therefore, was a tactical necessity as well as a substantive goal.

As perhaps the foremost propagandist for sexual reform in twentieth-century America, Margaret Sanger exemplified a critical shift in sexual attitudes from those of the nineteenth century. Though she had never regarded sex as a "dirty" or an obscene subject, she preached a corollary of the Victorian fear of sex when she treated it as a dangerous instinct whose propagative effects had to be suppressed, especially among the lower classes. But as time went on, Mrs. Sanger supplemented her argument that contraception facilitated social control of the sexual instinct. Increasingly, she emphasized the function of birth control not only in the scientific regulation of propagation, but also in the scientific liberation of the "feminine spirit" by enhancing the amative aspects of intercourse.

Margaret Sanger, of course, was not solely responsible for the romanticization of sex in the twentieth century. At least since the days of the troubadors in Languedoc and Acquitane in the late Middle Ages, courtly love had been a literary theme, though not a widespread social practice. The romantic ideal, with its separation of love and marriage, its glorification of the amative and derogation of the generative purposes of sexual intercourse, had come under massive interdiction from institutional moralists at least since the time of the scholastics. By the beginning of the twentieth century, the force of those interdictions still swayed most people; but new sanctions were developing to support the legitimacy of romantic sexual love. The early-nineteenth-century romantics had initiated that develop-

3. Margaret Sanger, *Woman and the New Race* (New York: Brentano's, 1920), p. 111.

ment, and such figures as William James and Sigmund Freud had continued to shape it. By the time Margaret Sanger began her career, the "cult of the irrational," as Henry Steele Commager has called it, was beginning to represent a consensus. Part of that consensus, in Commager's words, involved "an obsession with sex, especially in its abnormal manifestations, as the most powerful of all the instincts and the interpretation of all conduct in terms of sex." [4] The new conception of the centrality of sex in human life encouraged the diffusion, the democratization, of the ideal of courtly love.

Margaret Sanger had absorbed romantic ideas about sex from an early age. She had read and approved Edward Carpenter's declaration that the prime object of sexual relations was not propagation but "a more complete *soul-union,* a strange and intoxicating exchange of life, and transmutation of elements." [5] Havelock Ellis's attribution of semimystical qualities to sex also fostered Mrs. Sanger's appraisal of sexuality as a powerful spiritual force. And in the British Museum she had absorbed George Drysdale's argument that the "great law of population" pressed upon the middle class "in a different, but scarcely less fearful manner, than upon the poor. It produces among us the want of *love,* just as it does the want of food among the poor." That deprivation, said Drysdale, was especially hard on women, "whose sexual hopes have been blighted by want of love." [6] In the 1920s, Mrs. Sanger found an eager audience for romantic sexual propaganda among the supposedly sexually blighted middle-class women whom Drysdale had described.

Mrs. Sanger did not advocate artificial contraception for those who wished to avoid pregnancy simply because she

4. Henry Steele Commager, *The American Mind: An Interpretation of American Thought and Character Since the 1880's* (New Haven: Yale University Press, 1950), p. 122.

5. Edward Carpenter, *Love's Coming-of-Age* (New York: Mitchell Kennerly, 1911), pp. 179–80.

6. George Drysdale, *The Elements of Social Science* (9th ed. London: E. Truelove, 1871), pp. 334–35.

felt that the alternative method, abstinence from sexual intercourse, was inefficient. She also indicted abstinence because, she said, it implied "that there is something bestial and reprehensible about the normal expression of affection between husband and wife." [7] Of course it did not necessarily imply anything of the kind, but Mrs. Sanger's claim showed Drysdale's influence in her greater devotion to the promotion of sexual happiness in marriage than to the simple prevention of births. "Especially in the case of women," she said, "may the damage entailed by too long continued sexual abstinence bring about deep disturbances." [8]

Why she thought abstinence to be more damaging to women than to men Mrs. Sanger never explained. But she invoked a similar argument in condemning the oldest known contraceptive practice, *coitus interruptus*. Mrs. Sanger disapproved of that method not, significantly, because of its impracticality or inefficacy, but because of its damaging neurological and psychological effects on women. In "Family Limitation" Mrs. Sanger mentioned the uncertain utility of *coitus interruptus,* but claimed that the "greatest objection" to it was "the evil effect upon the woman's nervous condition. She has not completed her desire, she is under a highly nervous tension, her whole being is perhaps on the verge of satisfaction. She is then left in this dissatisfied state, which is far from humane. . . . Withdrawal on the part of the man should be substituted by some other means that does not injure the woman." In another pamphlet in 1915, Mrs. Sanger discussed at length the "nervous disturbances and other serious conditions of the generative organs in woman" occasioned by *coitus interruptus,* without even bothering to add that it was an ineffective contraceptive measure. Along the same lines, Mrs. Sanger recommended the use of the condom, not simply as a contraceptive, but to help avoid premature ejaculation and achieve

7. *Birth Control Review,* April–May 1917, p. 4.
8. Sanger, *Woman and the New Race* p. 104.

the perfect mating when "the climax of the act is reached together." [9]

Mrs. Sanger characteristically sought a scientific rationale for her sexual theories. She found it, she thought, in the ideas of Sigmund Freud. Margaret Sanger, with so many others, misread Freud to mean that he endorsed virtually unlimited sexual indulgence. Repression, which Freud had designated as the process by which subconscious phenomena are kept from the attention of the conscious, Mrs. Sanger interpreted as a system of social and psychological, but in either case tyrannical, constraints on the free exercise of sexual instincts. Women, Mrs. Sanger urged, should overcome "repression" and substitute "the greatest possible expression and fulfillment of their desires upon the highest possible plane. . . . This is one of the great functions of contraceptives." [10]

Mrs. Sanger agreed with the legions of observers who noted that many American women had "an ideal of frigidity." She had a specific explanation: "Back of that frigidity is often the fear of pregnancy." [11] Birth control, therefore, by eliminating the anxieties that attended the expectation of pregnancy, would do away with repression and promote happiness, even ecstasy. That naïve prescription manifested both a pervasive faith in the miraculous possibilities of science and Mrs. Sanger's persistent tendency to exaggerate her claims for birth control. As William L. O'Neill has said of the divorce reformers in the same era: "Almost half a century of experience with the new sexual canons suggests that the pioneers' most crucial error was their exaggerated sense of the ease with which sexual gratification could be obtained. They assumed that if the old taboos were repealed and a modicum of technical infor-

9. Margaret Sanger, "Family Limitation," pamphlet, 1914, and "English Methods of Birth Control," pamphlet, 1915, copies in MSP–LC.

10. Sanger, *Woman and the New Race*, p. 117.

11. Margaret Sanger, speech at Hartford, Connecticut, February 11, 1923, copy in MSP–LC.

mation made generally available, almost anyone could have a sane and satisfying sex life." [12]

Margaret Sanger aspired to more than mere sanity and satisfaction in sex life. Intercourse, she said, was not simply a propagative act, and science should be applied to more than its reproductive aspects. Scientific birth control, she insisted, following George Drysdale, Edward Carpenter, and Havelock Ellis, could make sex "a psychic and spiritual avenue of expression." Especially women, she wrote, would find that birth control made sex "the energy enhancing their lives and increasing self-expression and self-development." [13]

With other feminists, Margaret Sanger resented the sexual objectification of woman which either denied her sexuality or relegated "the sacred function of her body" to the category of pornography. Perhaps reflecting her lingering resentment of her father, she indicted men for employing "brute force" to obtain sexual satisfaction. She subscribed to the nineteenth-century view of masculine sexuality as bestial, selfish, and dangerous.

Mrs. Sanger made a quite different appraisal of feminine sexuality. Unlike such feminists as Charlotte Perkins Gilman and Elsie Clews Parsons, who wanted to free women *from* sex, Mrs. Sanger called upon women to develop their sexual natures. Mrs. Gilman, continually denying the primacy of sex in human relations, claimed that women could be free only when an inclusive concept of humanity replaced the restrictive categories of masculine and feminine which stunted all human interaction. Ironically, by the feminists' own admission, centuries of masculine domination had given all the definitions of "humanity" a masculine cast. That produced the paradox Christopher Lasch has noted: "The determination to be a 'true woman' forced one in effect to lead a man's life." [14] Margaret Sanger

12. William L. O'Neill, *Divorce in the Progressive Era* (New Haven: Yale University Press, 1967), p. 156.

13. Sanger, *Pivot of Civilization*, pp. 140, 258.

14. Christopher Lasch, *The New Radicalism in America, 1889–1963* (New York: Alfred A. Knopf, 1965), p. 68.

avoided that paradox by stressing woman's unique sexual nature and the unique possibilities of its development.

Mrs. Sanger demanded that feminism be nonemulative. Woman's "self-realization," she wrote, "will come through a gradual assertion of her power in her own sphere rather than in that of men." [15] Women were too much inclined, she said,

> to follow in the footsteps of men, to try to think as men think, to try to solve the general problems of life as men solve them. If after attaining their freedom, women accept conditions in the spheres of government, industry, art, morals, and religion as they find them, they will be but taking a leaf out of man's book. The woman is not needed to do man's work. She is not needed to think man's thoughts. She need not fear that the masculine mind, almost universally dominant, will fail to take care of its own. Her mission is not to enhance the masculine spirit, but to express the feminine; hers is not to preserve a man-made world, but to create a human world by the infusion of feminine element into all of its activities. [16]

Margaret Sanger never precisely defined the unique "feminine element," though it seemed for her, as for Freud, to have a great deal to do with motherhood. Perhaps to avoid the charge that birth control would make every woman a sterile virago, Mrs. Sanger had to insist on the power and constancy of the maternal impulse. More likely, her fascination with maternity reflected her allegiance to the ideas of the Edwardian romantics about the psychological implications of primal biological functions. At all events, Mrs. Sanger claimed that birth control would liberate something she variously called the "absolute, elemental, inner urge of womanhood," the "feminine spirit," or the "intuitive forward urge within." That liberation, in turn,

15. Margaret Sanger, "New Woman of Japan," unpublished article, 1923, copy in MSP–LC.
16. Sanger, *Woman and the New Race,* pp. 98–9.

would produce a "free womanhood" which, having achieved "fullness of expression and experience in life," would become the "race mother" and create a "new race." [17] Whatever the specific content of those semimystical propositions, Mrs. Sanger intended to implement them by freeing intercourse from its propagative consequences. That intention marked again Mrs. Sanger's attachment to the general antirationalism of the twentieth century. "Emotion," she had written in 1914, "urges from within, without consciousness of fear or consequences." [18] Now, she said, "scientific" birth control not only facilitated rational family planning, but had even greater utility in fostering a life of spontaneous emotion.

Though here, and occasionally elsewhere, Margaret Sanger lapsed into some rather opaque metaphysics, she defined a unique position on sex and womanhood. Her position was at marked variance with that of the more orthodox feminists such as Charlotte Perkins Gilman. By dwelling not on the similarities between men and women, but on their differences, in aspiring not to simple economic or legal equality for women, but to such abstract goals as the development of the "intuitive forward urge within," and by associating that "intuitive forward urge" with an immutable maternal impulse that lay at the center of woman's nature, Margaret Sanger more nearly paraphrased the lessons of Freud than those of other feminists and of her beloved Havelock Ellis. She stood in the Freudian tradition, too, when she emphasized the aggressiveness of male sexuality; and when she called upon women to develop their own sexual aggression, she implicitly accepted Freud's belief in power as the indispensable currency of sexual relationships.

Those arguments Mrs. Gilman might well have challenged. How free were women who could seek satisfaction only in maternity and the cultivation of their sexuality?

17. Sanger, *Woman and the New Race*, pp. 231–32.
18. Margaret Sanger, "Journal," entry for November 3–4, 1914, MSP–SS.

When she apotheosized motherhood and dwelt on the centrality of sexual expression to feminine fulfillment, Mrs. Sanger seemed merely to dress out in new language nineteenth-century ideas about woman's sacredness and sexual uniqueness. Birth control, as Mrs. Sanger defined it, provided new encouragement—and new technological feasibility—to the Victorian dogmas and pieties that many feminists were striving to escape. In pursuit of sexual and psychological liberation, Margaret Sanger had found in Freud a false liberation and had embraced a confining and deterministic, in some respects reactionary, set of ideas. Hers was eventually to become a characteristic attitude of American women.

CHAPTER 6

The Debate on Morality

In 1922, Katherine Bement Davis published the first statistical study of the use of contraceptives in the United States. Mrs. Davis interviewed 1,000 married women, all either college alumnae or women's club members. Nearly 75 percent, she reported, used contraceptives. Similarly, Robert and Helen Lynd found in Middletown in the mid-1920s that though birth control was "strongly tabooed," the prohibitions against it were losing their effectiveness among the more prosperous classes. "The behavior of the community in this matter of the voluntary limitation of parenthood," said the Lynds, "presents the appearance of a pyramid. At the top, among most of the business group, the use of relatively efficacious contraceptive methods appears practically universal, while sloping down from this peak is a mixed array of knowledge and ignorance, until the base of ignorance is reached." [1]

In spite of the "practically universal" practice of birth control by the middle and upper classes, members of those classes displayed a persistent caution about the subject in public. The editor of *Hearst's Magazine* in 1920 privately acknowledged that "the subject is important and radiant." But, he said, "Mrs. Sanger's specialty is so much like Lydia Pinkham's" that a family magazine could not discuss it.[2] E. A. Ross, ordinarily a courageous man, approved of birth

1. Katherine Bement Davis, "A Study of the Sex Life of the Normal Married Woman," Part I: "The Use of Contraceptives," *Journal of Social Hygiene* 8 (1922): 173–89; Robert S. and Helen Merrell Lynd, *Middletown: A Study in American Culture* (New York: Harcourt, Brace, and World, 1956), p. 125.

2. K. M. Goode to Ada Patterson, October 28, 1920, MSP–LC.

control but hesitated to have his name associated with the American Birth Control League.[3] The National Woman's Party, allegedly an "advanced feminist group," avoided a birth control plank in its 1927 platform for fear of splitting the party and alienating possible supporters.[4] For like reasons, the League of Women Voters three years later declined to consider a resolution that merely called for the study of birth control.[5] In 1929, the National Broadcasting Company refused to carry any speeches on birth control because the subject was "too controversial." [6] Gradually, however, changing attitudes toward the family, women, and sexuality closed the gap between private practice and public repudiation of birth control.

The Lynds associated contraception with "the increasing isolation and mobility of the individual family." Other observers had already noted that among the upper classes the growing sense of the family as a private institution, entitled to self-determination in its innermost affairs, had insulated it from demands to breed more. For all the vigor of Theodore Roosevelt's race suicide pronouncements, said Katherine Anthony, "among the men of his own class he stirred not an echo." The size of the American family continued to shrink, and, as E. A. Ross reported in 1924, of all social groups it was among "the clerical workers, trying to maintain a standard of living beyond their means [that] the effects of birth control show most clearly." A concern for social mobility—for the achievement of a better standard of living and a suitable education for one's children— seemed the principal factor in the decision to limit family size. As parental attention, said the Lynds, "shifted somewhat from child-bearing to child-rearing," there came, inevitably, "increasing regulation of the size of the family." [7]

3. E. A. Ross to Margaret Sanger, October 25, 1921, MSP–LC.

4. *Birth Control Review*, January 1928, p. 6.

5. *New York Times*, May 2, 1930, p. 11.

6. *New Haven Times*, November 20, 1929, clipping, MSP–LC.

7. Katherine Anthony, "The Family," in Harold E. Stearns ed., *Civilization in the United States* (New York: Harcourt, Brace, 1922), p.

Similarly, a changing conception of womanhood influenced attitudes toward birth control. Certainly many elements of the nineteenth-century myth of femininity persisted, often dressed out in the new scientific vocabulary of Freudianism. The Lynds noted that Middletown husbands spoke of women "as creatures purer and morally better than men but as relatively impractical, emotional, unstable, given to prejudice, easily hurt, and largely incapable of facing facts or doing hard thinking." But when the American Academy of Political and Social Science in 1929 discussed "Women in the Modern World," it demonstrated that the old feminine myth was far less compelling than it had once been. The academicians did not debate the merits of the New Woman. No one protested her subversion of the sacred ideals of maternity and wifehood. Rather, the academy treated the woman question as no longer a question at all but as a problem to be solved. The problem was not whether but how women could overcome their victimization by biology and society and become independent.[8]

Again, the academy reflected the sensibilities of an educated class; not every American agreed that women could or should be self-sufficient and free to pursue their own interests. But that conviction was growing. The Federal Council of Churches of Christ in 1929 indicated both the pervasiveness of resentment at women's continuing victimization and the distance of the new feminine ideal from the old. The mother, said the council, "needs to be out of the home as well as in it, and for her children's sake as well as her own." Children, the council implied, should be given "opportunities," not irrelevant parental wisdom. And mothers, in order to provide their offspring with maximum

322; Ray Erwin Farber and Edward Alsworth Ross, *Changes in the Size of American Families in One Generation*, University of Wisconsin Studies in the Social Sciences and History, no. 10 (Madison, 1924), p. 79; Lynd and Lynd, *Middletown*, p. 131.

8. Lynd and Lynd, p. 117; "Women in the Modern World," *Annals of the American Academy of Political and Social Science*, vol. 143 (1929).

opportunities in a fluid society, should have fewer children and should "mother" them less. That suggestion would have appalled the nineteenth-century moralists who insisted on woman's prolific and exclusive maternity; yet it came from a respected, though notoriously "liberal," church body. The proposal measured not the moral bankruptcy of the churches but a new sensitivity to woman's personality and a growing concern for social mobility, especially for the meticulous care one had to exercise in preparing one's children to be socially mobile.[9]

Finally, new ideas about sex affected attitudes toward birth control. Walter Lippmann was only one of many observers who remarked the "immense preoccupation with sex" that characterized the 1920s. Actually, the nineteenth-century preoccupation with sexual gender had begun shifting to the modern concern for sexual instinct at least as early as 1913, when *Current Opinion* announced that it had struck "Sex O'Clock in America." By the 1920s that concern appeared to be an obsession. The generation of the flapper welded nineteenth-century notions of romanticism and scientism into a new outlook on sex. The Victorian cult of love, said Joseph Wood Krutch, the feeling that love was the source "of the most intrinsically valuable of human experiences," reached the 1920s "almost intact." To that romantic notion the twentieth century joined a scientific treatment of sexual matters. Krutch found in Margaret Sanger's principal mentor the perfect embodiment of the new hybrid attitude. Havelock Ellis viewed sex as a "rationalist," said Krutch, but "to Ellis, too, love has its element of transcendental value." [10]

The confluence of romantic optimism and scientific con-

9. Committee on Marriage and the Home, Commission on the Church and Social Services, Federal Council of Churches of Christ in America, *Ideals of Love and Marriage* (New York: Federal Council of Churches, 1929, p. 20).

10. Walter Lippmann, *A Preface to Morals* (New York: Macmillan, 1929), p. 285; Joseph Wood Krutch, *The Modern Temper* (New York: Harcourt, Brace, 1929), pp. 84–95.

fidence was beginning to alter even religious positions on
sex. Nineteenth-century moralists had regarded sexuality as
dangerous and only secondarily, if at all, as a force for good.
The Federal Council of Churches of Christ in 1929 reversed
the emphasis. Though sex could be "destructive," said the
council, "we must start with the assumption that sex is
indeed a creative force." That relatively sanguine approach
helped to remove from sex the cloak of prudery and fear
that had covered it in the nineteenth century. Freud provided the scientific vocabulary that made sex a subject for
respectable conversation and, some said, for experimenta-
tion. Undoubtedly, many committed physical excesses in
the name of science, just as Margaret Sanger committed
sentimental excesses in the name of romanticism. But for a
growing number of people, the union of science and romanticism provided a new context for the discussion of sex
apart from its procreative consequences. As that discussion
progressed, birth control came to be viewed less as a perversion of the natural order and more as the instrumentality
of new, approved possibilities.[11]

By 1931, the President's Committee on Social Trends
reported, 66 percent of the opinions about birth control
expressed in mass periodical publications were favorable.
Fortune magazine reported in 1936 that 63 percent of Americans, including 42 percent of Roman Catholics, believed
"in the teaching and practice of birth control." By 1939,
Henry F. Pringle reported in the *Ladies' Home Journal*,
79 percent of American women favored birth control. Four
years later, according to another poll, that figure had risen
to nearly 85 percent. Margaret Sanger herself was becoming
by the 1930s, a cultural heroine. In 1932, she received the
American Women's Association award for her contributions to womanhood. In 1937, the Town Hall Association
presented her with a medal on the same rostrum from which
she had been forcibly removed sixteen years earlier. Though

11. Committee on Marriage and the Home, *Ideals of Love and
Marriage*, p. 12.

birth control was "still a contentious issue," said Dorothy Dunbar Bromley in 1934, "it has become respectable." [12]

The American churches, the official guardians of respectability, only cautiously and belatedly gave birth control their official attention. The Roman Catholic church, objecting to contraception on strict doctrinal grounds, often carried its dissent into overt action to thwart the birth control movement. But the Protestant churches, too, until well into the 1930s—in at least two cases until the 1950s—refused to sanction contraception and often argued against it with a vigor equal to Rome's. Insofar as American Protestants listened to their churches in such matters, for a long time they could find there no comfort of conscience about contraception.

Well before they ever heard of Margaret Sanger, wrote Walter Lippmann, the churches had decided that "whether or not birth control is eugenic, hygienic or economic, it is the most revolutionary practice in the history of sexual morals." As the custodians of morality, the churches, not surprisingly, resisted the revolution. Mrs. Sanger, who never got over her radical antiecclesiasticism, attributed the churches' defense of traditional moral canons to a self-serving clerical plot. The church tried to keep the sexual instinct in check, she said, because it "has always known and feared the spiritual potentialities of woman's freedom." If that notion seemed a little vague, Mrs. Sanger had more concrete evidence for the church's "moral" objection to birth control. "When the church became a political power rather than a strictly religious institution," she said, "it needed a high birth rate to provide laymen to support its increasingly expensive organization." With such tortured readings of

12. President's Research Committee on Social Trends, *Recent Social Trends in the United States* (New York: McGraw-Hill, 1933), p. 415; *Fortune*, July 1936, p. 158; *Ladies' Home Journal*, March 1938, p. 14; *Fortune*, August 1943, pp. 24, 30; Dorothy Dunbar Bromley, *Birth Control: Its Use and Misuse* (New York: Harper and Brothers, 1934), p. 11.

theology and history, Mrs. Sanger attempted to dismiss the
churches' insistence that birth control was morally problematic.[13]

The issue, however, was not so easily resolved. To answer
the churches' objections, Mrs. Sanger was forced to con-
struct an elaborate defense of the morality of birth control.
There was no moral good, she said, in behavior made
acceptable by the fear of consequences. If only the threat of
pregnancy prevented promiscuous intercourse, birth control
would not make people less moral but simply less hypocrit-
ical. In her view, the defense of any ethical code as divinely
inspired smacked of hypocrisy. Morality was "nothing but
the sum total, the net residuum, of social habits, the codifica-
tion of customs." Since she wished to change social habits,
she said, conservatives naturally regarded her as "immoral."
On other occasions she argued that since morality could be
equated with social mores, and since women had practiced
some sort of birth control in all ages and places, she was in
fact more moral than those who would suppress the spontaneous demand for contraceptive knowledge. Often Mrs.
Sanger confused the moral faculty (the ability to make
choices) with the moral good. Because birth control provided for "individual liberty . . . and personal choice,"
she argued, it was itself morally right. Finally, Mrs. Sanger
frequently admitted that though some individuals might
turn birth control to objectionable ends, the net social good
achieved by reducing prostitution, divorce, and poverty still
made birth control morally acceptable.[14]

That ethical calculus was but an extreme version of the
utilitarian moral theory from which Mrs. Sanger only un-
comfortably strayed. If her pronouncements on the morality
of contraception often appeared confused and contradictory,
it was because they did not easily come to her. For her, the

13. Lippmann, *Preface to Morals,* p. 291; Margaret Sanger, *Woman
and the New Race* (New York; Brentano's, 1920), pp. 179, 173.

14. Margaret Sanger, "The War against Birth Control," *American
Mercury,* June 1924, pp. 231–36.

question was a simple one, really not requiring the elabora-
tions she felt compelled to make. Birth control was obviously morally good, she believed, because it achieved
desirable ends: relief of suffering, prevention of disease,
higher standards of living, sexual liberation. That un-
complicated proposition so illumined Mrs. Sanger's mind
that it blinded her to the objections of other moral schools.
Unable to understand those objections, she never effectively
answered them in debate.

Traditional moralists, trained to believe in a moral order
in which each human act should be judged by catechetical
standards of right and wrong, could not readily agree that
the achievement of commendable results rendered an act
morally correct. In their view, men often had to forego
desirable ends because no licit means were at hand. Where
Margaret Sanger spoke confidently of freedom and capabil-
ity, traditionalists emphasized obligation, restriction, and
sacrifice. They saw moral behavior as controlled behavior,
and, on another level, they regarded moral laws as effective
means of social control. Against that background, traditionalists appraised birth control as a dangerously liberating
device. Contraception freed intercourse from its biological
consequences, and though strict moralists, with Mrs. Sanger,
preferred right conscience to fear as a moral motive, they
nevertheless approved the idea that threatening biological
consequences were a practical moral discipline.

In the Protestant churches, however, traditional moralists
had been on the defensive since the nineteenth century.
Romanticism had encouraged a philosophy that found
moral good in following the intuitions of the individual
conscience, rather than in conforming to reasoned or revealed external standards. The spread of that view coincided with the Darwinian disruption of rationalist religious
thought. The idea of evolution promoted a new theology in
which religious truth was sought less in reason and revela-
tion and more in the history of human experience. The
"empirical reappraisal," writes Stow Persons, "was implicitly

the task of Protestant modernism at the beginning of the twentieth century." [15] By the 1920s, according to another historian of religious thought, "liberalism," or empirical theology, "intellectually dominated" American Protestant thinking. The combined effect of romantic subjectivism and evolutionary empiricism turned the modern moral sense away from the old problem of cultivating general, internalized standards of right and wrong and toward "practical discussion of particular moral issues on which there were serious differences not only of opinions but even of conviction." [16] Liberal clergymen saw their moral function less in terms of education and more in terms of guidance.

In guiding the laity, clerics gave increasing weight both to lay experience and to lay professional opinion as expressions of an empirically revealed divinity. In the liberal view, morality did not inhere in an act itself, but in the state of the individual's conscience measured against the historical experience of his society. The morality of birth control, according to the liberals, was a personal matter, and the church's position should be changed in the light of changing social conditions. When a Roman Catholic cardinal in 1935 condemned birth control as a violation of divine law, thirteen liberal Protestant and Jewish clergymen countered that God "is revealed in the endless sweep of evolution and [His] message is being slowly translated by science into the accents of the human tongue." Since birth control gave "sight and intelligence to what in nature is a blind and groping impulse," it represented, they claimed, an evolutionary advance sanctioned by the Deity. Instead of relying on the Bible and scholastic logic, the liberals urged, the cardinal should reexamine his position on contraception in light of "the evidence, the knowledge, and the experience available in our time." [17]

15. Stow Persons, "Evolution and Theology in America," in Stow Persons, ed., *Evolutionary Thought in America* (New Haven: Yale University Press, 1958), p. 437.

16. Herbert Wallace Schneider, *Religion in Twentieth Century America* (Cambridge: Harvard University Press, 1952), pp. 123, 61.

17. *New York Times,* December 16, 1935, p. 14.

Roman Catholic moralists, however, tended to consider the experience of the church preceptorial—the traditions and teachings of the fathers and theologians—a more authoritative guide to moral judgments than the lay experience from which the liberal Protestants deduced their case for birth control. Catholic teaching stressed the origins of the doctrine on contraception in natural law. God intended marital intercourse primarily for the purpose of procreation, said the church. Certain secondary purposes of intercourse in marriage—such as the relief of concupiscent desires or the expression of connubial affection—were morally licit, but to frustrate unnaturally the primary purpose of intercourse while pursuing its secondary ones perverted the divinely ordained nature of the act. The church thus condemned any device or practice that artificially interfered with the process of insemination, fertilization, and nidation. Though in the practice of the rhythm method insemination occurred when fertilization appeared unlikely, Catholic moralists eventually approved the method because the parties to the act did nothing themselves to interfere with the natural process.

That mechanistic approach precluded any consideration of the motives of a married couple contemplating the use of contraceptives. There were no imaginable extenuating circumstances, the church held, that excused contraceptive practice. The derivation of Catholic doctrine from natural law, said church spokesmen, made compromise on birth control impossible. The church might change ecclesiastical laws, but when natural law was invoked, said Patrick Cardinal Hayes of New York, "for the Catholic the case is closed." Though man had the power to alter the natural procreative process, explained a Jesuit professor in 1931, "he has no moral right to do so." The natural order was more sacred than the order of reason, and man must refrain from employing his rational abilities to pervert nature.[18]

18. *New York Times*, December 9, 1935, p. 5; April 6, 1931, p. 7. See also John T. Noonan, Jr., *Contraception: A History of Its Treat-*

That Appolonian attitude could hardly be expected to win many converts in a nation committed to the control of the environment by the instrumentality of reason. Perhaps sensing that, Catholic spokesmen rarely explained to the American public the church's doctrinal objections to contraception. Catholic statements on birth control usually made passing reference to sinning against nature but most often forsook exegesis for propagandistic bombast. Cardinal Hayes, saying that he felt "embarrassed" to mount the pulpit at St. Patrick's Cathedral to discuss birth control, nevertheless unashamedly branded contraception "diabolical" and "Satanic" and called those who advocated it "prophets of decadence" who were bringing "ruin and disaster to the land and to the civilization that some among us, at least, still cherish." Other Catholic clerics warned that birth control encouraged moral flabbiness. "It leads inevitably to an increase of softness, luxury, and materialism," said John A. Ryan, "and to a decrease of mental and moral discipline, of endurance, and of the power of achievement." In their appeal to the Calvinist moral sense of hard duty and sacrifice, Catholic opponents of birth control resembled no one more than Theodore Roosevelt.[19]

While Catholic propagandists escalated the already apocalyptic rhetoric of Roosevelt and the other moral traditionalists, they often complemented their moral arguments with opposition to birth control on social and economic grounds. There was no danger of overpopulation in the United States, they pointed out, and the greater incidence of contraceptive practice by the socially mobile classes proved that the real motive to utilize birth control was not, as Malthus had said, the downward pressure of population on the means of subsistence, but rather the upward pressure for a

ment by the Catholic Theologians and Canonists (Cambridge: Harvard University Press, Belknap Press, 1965), for a complete discussion of the development of the Catholic position.

19. New York Times, December 9, 1935, p. 1; John A. Ryan, "The Catholic Church and Birth Restriction," in Survey, March 4, 1916, pp. 671–72.

higher standard of living. Moreover, while Catholic spokesmen occasionally admitted the sincerity of the birth control
advocates in trying to alleviate the condition of the poor,
they unanimously insisted that the spread of contraceptive
information was an inappropriate reform measure. Cardinal Hayes called upon reformers to shun birth control and
"so to re-order our economic and social structure as to make
it possible for people to have children and to rear them in
keeping with their needs." [20] Repeatedly citing the social
encyclicals, such as Leo XIII's *Rerum Novarum,* Catholic
foes of contraception indicted maldistribution of wealth
and demanded "less capitalistic control of the labor market,
higher wages, better housing" to relieve the burdens of
large families among the poor.[21]

Catholic leaders did not resort to proposals for economic
reform simply as a last-ditch defense against the birth control movement. From the time of James Cardinal Gibbons
and Archbishop John Ireland the Catholic hierarchy in
America had stood for the same principles of social justice
and welfare that in the Protestant churches had given rise
to the Social Gospel movement. But doctrinal commitment
barred to socially concerned Catholics the pragmatic Protestant reformers' fairly easy acceptance of birth control as
another tool to lift the burdens of poverty. Instead, the
moral orthodoxy of American Catholic reformers led them
to denounce birth control in terms strikingly analagous to
the terms with which orthodox European Marxists had
denounced Malthusianism. As John A. Ryan said:

> To advocate contraception, as a method of bettering
> the condition of the poor and unemployed, is to divert
> the attention of the influential classes from the pursuit
> of social justice and to relieve them of all responsibility
> for our bad distribution and other social maladjust-

20. *New York Times,* December 9, 1935, p. 5.

21. "Report of an Interview with Mr. P. J. Ward of the National
Catholic Welfare Council," March 2, 1926, MSP–SS; see also John
LaFarge, S.J., "Deceit, Fraud and Trickery in Birth Control Propa-
ganda," *America,* April 5, 1941, pp. 708–09.

ments. . . . We simply cannot—those who believe as I do—subscribe to the idea that the poor are to be made responsible for their plight, and instead of getting justice from the Government and more rational social order, they are to be required to reduce their numbers. I repeat that is Toryism.[22]

The sincerity of Ryan's devotion to social justice could not be doubted, but many other Catholics had an unfortunate concept of the just role of the church itself in a pluralistic democracy. In their view, the dictates of the natural law applied equally to all men, whether Catholic or non-Catholic. The church's obligation, ran the argument, was to keep all men, not just Catholics, from the error of contraception.

At times the church confined its opposition to birth control to the exercise of its political right to oppose pro-birth control legislation. When Fr. John J. Burke in the 1920s and Fr. John A. Ryan in the 1930s mobilized the National Catholic Welfare Conference against proposed changes in the federal anticontraception statutes, they only followed their consciences, just as Mrs. Sanger followed hers. And however parochial the belief that what was good for the church was good for the country, the National Catholic Welfare Conference, in advocating its views before Congress, no more surpassed its constitutional prerogatives than did Mrs. Sanger.

On other occasions, however, certain individual clergymen and some Catholic lay groups, in their zeal to thwart the birth control movement, employed less responsible tactics. Some Catholic spokesmen resorted to the same seamy eugenics propaganda that birth control supporters themselves so tirelessly mouthed. One priest warned that, if other religious denominations did not join in opposition to birth

22. U.S., Congress, Senate, Subcommittee of the Committee on the Judiciary, *Birth Control, Hearings on S. 1842*, 73d Cong., 2d sess., 1934, p. 105; U.S., Congress, House, Subcommittee of the Committee on the Judiciary, *Birth Control, Hearings on H.R. 5978*, 73d Cong., 2d sess., 1934, p. 154.

control, their memberships would dwindle while prolific Catholics swelled the ranks of the Roman church. Father Charles E. Coughlin, the notorious "radio priest," said that easily available contraceptive information would decimate the "Anglo-Saxons" while not affecting American Negro and Polish immigrant birthrates. "A hundred years from now," predicted Father Coughlin, "Washington will be Washingtonski" if Congress should legalize contraceptives. Still other Catholic opponents of birth control relied primarily on vilification of Mrs. Sanger and her organizations. They hinted that she perhaps had sinister Bolshevik connections; on one occasion they called her an "enemy and traitor . . . viciously striking at the very roots of preparedness." In 1934, *America*, on most subjects a responsible magazine, called for a congressional investigation of Mrs. Sanger's National Committee for Federal Legislation on Birth Control.[23]

Mrs. Sanger, no novice at name-calling, was thick-skinned enough to withstand such verbal pelting, but she often found her activities physically obstructed by militant Catholic groups. In the 1920s, the Knights of Columbus regularly threatened economic reprisals against hotels and meeting halls that rented their facilities to Mrs. Sanger. At other times, such as the occasion of the first American Birth Control Conference in 1921, some Catholics exploited their political ties to municipal administrations to harass birth control advocates. Under Catholic pressure, the mayor of Boston in 1922, the mayor of Albany, New York, in 1923, and the city council of Syracuse, New York, in 1924 took steps to prevent meetings for the discussion of contraception.[24]

In the 1930s, the Catholic church realized that the attempt to stop discussion of contraception was futile, and aban-

23. *Hearings on H.R. 5978*, p. 129; Guy Emery Shipler, Jr., "Catholics and Birth Control," *Churchman*, April 15, 1941, p. 10; *America*, January 20, 1934, p. 366.

24. *Albany Journal*, January 24, 1923; *Boston Traveler*, April 2, 1922; *Syracuse American*, February 24, 1924, clippings, MSP–LC.

doned that tactic. The church instead concentrated its
energies on mobilizing Catholic leaders and Catholic institutions to block Mrs. Sanger's newest objective: the incorporation of birth control services into community public health
programs. Archbishop John Gregory Murray of Saint Paul,
Minnesota, announced the new tactic in 1935 when he
declared that any Catholic in his archdiocese affiliated with
an association that endorsed, advocated, or facilitated contraception would be denied the sacraments of the church.
Other prelates similarly served notice that no public or
private body with which Catholics were officially associated
could support artificial birth control; if it did, Catholic
members must resign.[25] In the 1940s, private Catholic hospitals attempted to deny their facilities to any doctor who
did not pledge to refuse to give contraceptive advice except
concerning the rhythm method either at the hospitals or in
private practice. Thus the Catholic church, which had already made legislative changes favoring birth control all
but impossible, rendered public and even private administrative action on the subject exceedingly difficult.[26]

The church, however, took one positive step in 1930 when
Pope Pius XI issued his famous encyclical *Casta Conubii
(Of Chaste Marriage)*. The encyclical condemned divorce,
abortion, sterilization, and "the false liberty and unnatural
equality" of the New Woman. It linked the birth control
movement to "a new and utterly perverse morality" which
encouraged "pernicious errors." Those who used artificial
contraceptives, declared the Pope, "sin against nature and
commit a deed which is shameful and intrinsically vicious."
But in spite of the Pope's strong condemnation of "unnatural" birth control, he emphasized that "in matrimony
as well as in the use of the matrimonial rights there are also
secondary ends, such as mutual aid, the cultivating of
mutual love, and the quieting of concupiscence which husband and wife are not forbidden to consider so long as they

25. *New York Times*, August 10, 1935, p. 14.

26. "Memorandum of meeting in Ernst's office," April 14, 1943,
MSP–SS.

are subordinated to the primary end and so long as the intrinsic nature of the act is preserved." Therefore, said the Pope, when "on account of natural reasons, either of time or of certain defects, new life cannot be brought forth," couples could legitimately exercise their marital rights.[27]

The Vatican had given the use of the sterile period qualified approval as early as 1880, but Pius XI's encyclical, along with improved medical information on the nature of the sterile period, did much to soften the church's blanket condemnation of birth control. John A. Ryan, for one, thought that the encyclical should be interpreted liberally to allow the deliberate use of the rhythm method by "any married person with a serious reason for avoiding offspring." [28]

Still, the church continued its opposition to artificial contraceptives and to the ambitious plans of Mrs. Sanger's movement. Ryan and other clerics kept on testifying at congressional hearings against liberalizing birth control laws. But the spread of the rhythm method among Catholics in the early 1930s deprived the church of the argument that wider dissemination of birth control information would corrupt public morals. Catholic spokesmen consequently gave greater emphasis to the demographic and economic dangers of population restriction. Significantly, however, as Ryan's statement showed, many Catholic clergymen now openly recognized individual cases where family limitation might be desirable. As economic theories of underpopulation began to prove false in the late 1930s, and as social

27. *On Christian Marriage* (*Casta Conubii*), encyclical letter of Pius XI, December 31, 1930 (Washington, D.C.: National Catholic Welfare Conference, 1931). In the early days of the church, St. Augustine had been the first theologian to denounce willful sterility. He directed his attack against the Manichees, who practised contraception by confining intercourse to the sterile period as calculated by Greek medicine. Ironically, that first Catholic statement on contraception condemned the very method Pius XI in 1930 endorsed as the one legitimate contraceptive technique for Catholics (Noonan, *Contraception*, pp. 120, 426–27).

28. Noonan, p. 443.

reformers increasingly accepted birth control not as a reprisal against the lower classes, but as a factor in their
rehabilitation, the church had only its orthodox moral doctrine with which to oppose the birth control movement.
And that doctrine, church leaders knew, was of limited
persuasiveness. It made poor propaganda. As a birth control
advocate said in 1934, "It has become increasingly embar-
rassing for Catholics to argue against birth control on any
ground except that of method.[29]

Many people, including many Catholic laymen, came to
feel that when the argument was reduced to a choice between methods it was no argument at all. Some Catholic
clerics reportedly feared that the church's "forbidding,
harshly repressive" position "would drive many from their
religion." Mrs. Sanger claimed that one third of her clinic
patients were Catholics, and while that figure may have
been exaggerated, every parish priest knew of the growing
use of artificial contraceptives among Catholics.[30]

Several of Mrs. Sanger's associates saw in the developing
rift in Catholic opinion about contraception a fruitful
opportunity for the birth control movement. They urged
her to subdue her propaganda so as to emphasize her points
of agreement, rather than conflict, with the Catholic church.
Further, they suggested that she modify her programs in
order to win the good will of liberal elements within the
church. If Mrs. Sanger would stop berating the Catholic
church, they argued, those otherwise loyal Catholics who
disagreed with Rome about contraception might be encouraged to work for a softening of the church's public
opposition to the birth control movement.[31]

29. Guy Irving Burch, "Catholics on Birth Control," *New Republic*,
September 5, 1934, p. 98.

30. *New York Herald-Tribune*, March 9, 1930, clipping, MSP–LC.

31. Florence Rose to Mary Lasker, May 15, 1941, MSP–SS. For a
description of another birth control advocate's approach to conciliating
the Catholic church, see the memo "Population Control" by Edna
Lonigan, dated September 3, 1935, pertaining to the situation in Puerto
Rico (Records of the Office of Territories, National Archives, Washington, D.C.).

But Margaret Sanger could not easily effect even a small reconciliation with the institution she had all her life regarded as the principal agent of evil in the world. She had never been able to understand the church's doctrinal objections to artificial contraception. To the Pope's declaration that birth control frustrated nature, she replied that "the Pope frustrates nature by getting shaved and having his hair cut." [32] Such statements indicated that Mrs. Sanger cared more for polemics and for baiting the church than she did for a strategic compromise or for serious discussion of the moral aspects of birth control. Not surprisingly, therefore, she ignored the urgings of her associates to adopt a conciliatory attitude toward those liberal Catholics who might have been able to help her cause. There could be no truce with the Catholic church while Mrs. Sanger headed the birth control movement.

Toward the Protestant churches Mrs. Sanger always displayed a lesser degree of antagonism, though until about 1930 they offered her little more encouragement than did the Catholic church. Some individual Protestant clerics publicly supported birth control, but for the most part non-Catholic American churchmen either condemned contraception or, more often, officially ignored it. The Federal Council of Churches of Christ in America complained in 1929 that in spite of the increasing knowledge of contraceptives and the need for moral instruction regarding their use, the church had "spent its energies too largely in abstract teaching and institutional activities to the comparative neglect of instruction and pastoral oversight in these practical matters." [33] Protestant silence on contraception resulted largely from the lingering influence of moral traditionalists in church affairs. Though liberal theology "intellectually dominated" American Protestantism by the third decade of the century, many conservatives remained in administrative

32. Margaret Sanger, "My Answer to the Pope on Birth Control," *Nation*, January 27, 1932, pp. 102–04.

33. Committee on Marriage and the Home, *Ideals of Love and Marriage*, p. 5.

control. Especially in the Presbyterian, Methodist Episcopal, and Protestant Episcopal churches, the debate over contraception coincided with struggles for power between liberals and conservatives which made discussion of birth control particularly heated. One of Mrs. Sanger's fieldworkers, for example, after trying unsuccessfully to steer a pro-birth control resolution between warring factions at a Methodist Episcopal convention, observed that "there are more politics in religion, I am inclined to believe, than on the Hill." [34]

In 1931, the Committee on Marriage and the Home of the Federal Council of Churches of Christ in America became the first major American Protestant body to endorse birth control. The lay public, said the committee, had a "right to expect guidance from the church on the moral aspects" of contraception. In the best liberal manner, the committee relied for guidance on medical opinion. "Physicians have long known," the committee reported, that contraceptives were often necessary to preserve maternal health and reduce infant mortality. "Economic considerations" and "the problems of overpopulation," the report continued, provided further grounds for approving birth control. Finally, the committee favored birth control because it facilitated "sex union between husbands and wives as an expression of mutual affection." The committee also added its opinion, obviously aimed at Catholics opposed to changes in anticontraception statutes, "that the church should not seek to impose its point of view as to the use of contraceptives upon the public by legislation or any other form of coercion; and especially should not seek to prohibit physicians from imparting such information to those who in the judgement of the medical profession are entitled to receive it." [35]

The overwhelming majority of the committee endorsed the report, though a minority of three, including the chair-

34. Memo, Helen Countryman to Margaret Sanger, May 16, 1936, MSP–LC.

35. Committee on Marriage and the Home of the Federal Council of the Churches of Christ in America, *Moral Aspects of Birth Control* (New York, 1934).

man, Howard C. Robbins, former dean at Saint John the Divine Cathedral in New York, voted "to uphold the standard of abstinence as the ideal." [36] Outside the committee, the report also evoked a mixed reaction. Catholics, of course, denounced the statement as a pagan document which marked "the liquidation of historic Protestantism by its own trustees." [37] Many Protestant clergymen, on the other hand, "took the position privately that the birth control report was a statement of a situation and of an attitude that was inevitable." Even that unenthusiastic approval was far from unanimous. Within a month of the report's publication, the executive secretary of the Federal Council wrote Margaret Sanger that "the statement on Moral Aspects of Birth Control has aroused more opposition with the Protestant churches than we had expected and has caused some cancellation of subscriptions." The Southern Presbyterian church, he wrote, "may withdraw from the Federal Council on account of this statement." [38] A few months later the Northern Baptist convention announced that the Federal Council "did not speak for the Baptist denomination in endorsing birth control." [39] The Baptists also resolved to reduce their financial support of the council. The opposition proved strong enough to block adoption of the committee's report by the Federal Council as a whole. At the council's meeting in 1932, the delegates referred the matter to the Executive Committee "for study." At the next meeting in 1934, the opposition had so stiffened that the Executive Committee could do no more than issue an innocuous report that took no position on birth control.[40]

36. Committee on Marriage and the Home, *Moral Aspects of Birth Control*, p. 6.

37. *Commonweal*, April 1, 1931, p. 589.

38. Worth M. Tippy to Margaret Sanger, April 14, 1931 and April 22, 1931, MSP–LC.

39. *New York Times*, June 6, 1931, p. 13. The Baptist Convention reiterated its position in 1933; see the *Annual of the Northern Baptist Convention* (St. Louis, 1933), p. 115.

40. Federal Council of Churches of Christ in America, *Quadrennial Report* (New York, 1932), p. 235.

Many Protestant denominations refused to do anything that might appear to approve of contraception. A few weeks after the Committee on Marriage and the Home of the Federal Council issued its report, a Special Commission on Marriage, Divorce and Remarriage of the Presbyterian Church in the United States announced its intention to submit a similar resolution favoring birth control to the Presbyterian General Assembly. The announcement raised a storm of criticism among Presbyterians. One local presbytery drew up a counterresolution stating that "adoption of this declaration would bring deserved criticism and odium upon our beloved church." Soon other presbyteries joined in the protest, and on the eve of the General Assembly the Special Commission, wishing "to avert a deadlock in the General Assembly," withdrew its support. When the assembly convened, however, some delegates who favored birth control prevailed upon the Special Commission to reconsider. They simultaneously made a bid to capture the post of moderator of the General Assembly. The uprising was short-lived. On the fourth day of the assembly the Special Commission changed its mind a third time and deleted from its report any reference to contraception. Conservatives had elected their candidate as moderator. They nearly succeeded in severing all relations with the Federal Council of Churches of Christ, whose liberalism they had always resented, because of its committee's statement on birth control. On the last day of the assembly one delegate protested the absence of any mention of contraception in the Special Commission's final report. He was greeted with "angry murmurs from many parts of the auditorium, and one or two hesitant hisses." The moderator ruled that the subject was "undebatable." The Presbyterian Church in the United States, by the official action of its General Assembly, had nothing to say about contraception.[41]

41. The Presbyterian Church in the United States of America, *General Assembly, 1931, Part I, Journal and Statistics* (Philadelphia, 1931), p. 345; *New York Times*, April 27, 1931, p. 1; May 5, 1931, p. 16; May 20, 1931, p. 21; May 28, 1931, p. 29; May 29, 1931, p. 2; May 31,

In the Methodist Episcopal church, a few local conferences gave their approval to birth control—notably the New York East Conference as early as 1930.[42] But the church as a whole was divided on the issue. While the *Christian Advocate*, a progressive Methodist magazine, welcomed the Federal Council report as "frank and courageous," many Methodist clergymen strongly protested against it.[43] The Bishop of Atlanta announced that the Federal Council's committee, in "sanctioning birth control under certain conditions did not represent the Methodist Episcopal Church South." The committee's report, said the bishop, "I regard as most unfortunate, not to use any stronger words." [44] Another bishop complained that the Federal Council, by suggesting "the practice of unmentionables in human society," had succumbed "to that pagan atmosphere of life which the early church endeavored to cleanse." [45] By 1936, though some local conferences had at least endorsed Mrs. Sanger's proposed changes in the federal anticontraception laws, deep disagreement over birth control still showed plainly at the Methodist Episcopal General Conference in Columbus, Ohio. There, a few liberal delegates presented a memorial endorsing "ethical birth control within the sacred limits of marriage." The committee that considered the memorial, however, recommended nonconcurrence by the conference. "Several delegates," reported the committee, had said that "the church should not touch the subject." The debate on birth control continued for several days, but ended without approval of the memorial. Indeed, the conference closed with the resolution "that it is the major responsibility of Protestant Christianity to urge Christian people to recognize the importance of reproduction rather

---

1931, p. 1; June 2, 1931, p. 21. The United Presbyterian Church in the U.S.A. finally endorsed birth control at its General Assembly in 1959. See Richard N. Fagley, *The Population Explosion and Christian Responsibility* (New York: Oxford University Press, 1960), p. 208.

42. *New York Times*, April 8, 1930, p. 30.

43. *Christian Advocate*, April 2, 1931, p. 421.

44. *New York Times*, April 12, 1931, p. 1.

45. *Christian Advocate*, November 19, 1931, p. 1422.

than on [sic] birth control." [46] One observer noted that the delegates "actually were favoring the principle of birth control but were afraid of the terminology and criticism of members back home." [47] Just as in the Presbyterian church, conservative timidity, in spite of considerable sentiment in favor of birth control, had blocked any meaningful advice to the Methodist Episcopal laity on the morality of contraception.

The Lutheran church proved even more outspokenly opposed to Mrs. Sanger's ideas. Though in 1926 the Convention of the United Lutheran Church in America called for a wider recognition of women's need to express themselves "otherwise than by motherhood," it rebuked contraception. "A chief aim of the married life is the birth of children," said the convention, and in all but exceptional cases "the Church should declare the limitation of birth by artificial means both anti-social and anti-Christian." When the Federal Council statement appeared in 1931, Lutherans almost unanimously condemned it. "It is of prime significance," said Dr. F. H. Knubel, president of the United Lutheran church, "that the present agitation for birth control occurs at a period which is notorious for looseness in sexual morality. This fact creates suspicion as to the motives for the agitation and should warn true-minded men and women against the surrender of themselves as tools for unholy purposes." The United Lutheran Synod of New York resolved that the Federal Council's report on birth control "expressed views distinctly opposed to the moral and spiritual teachings of the Lutheran Church." The same synod also considered withdrawing "all relation with the Federal Council." The relationship of the Lutheran church with the Federal Council, a spokesman said, "was not merely a matter of birth control, although it was birth control that crystallized the issue." Thus among Lutherans, as with

46. *New York Times,* May 7, 1936, p. 1; May 9, 1936, p. 10; May 16, 1936, p. 17; *Churchman,* July 1936, p. 9.

47. Memorandum, Helen Countryman to Margaret Sanger, May 16, 1936, MSP–LC.

Presbyterians and Methodists, birth control became a point of contention between moral optimists, oriented toward the theologically empirical views of the Federal Council, and conservatives, committed to moral traditionalism. And as in the Presbyterian and Methodist churches, Lutheran conservatives retained control. Not until 1956 did Lutheran liberals persuade their church to declare that "by freeing the wife and mother from the fear of too-frequent pregnancy and by limiting the number of children in accordance with the ability of the family to rear and nurture their children properly, conception control may contribute positively to the well-being of the family." [48]

In some churches the clash between liberal theology and traditionalism—so dramatically illustrated in the Scopes trial of 1925—had been resolved by the 1930s in favor of the moral optimists. At the time of the Scopes trial, for example, the National Council of the Congregational Churches of the United States stated its "conviction that there is and can be no conflict between science and religion . . . God makes himself increasingly known through the patient investigations of modern scholars." [49] Liberal theologians, said a Congregationalist writer in 1931, believed that the power of birth control would be used for good, not evil. Religion, he said, would ensure that "progress and knowledge will not outrun the capacity of mankind for self-control." [50]

Religious liberals began generally to accept science just as the Protestant churches were undergoing a great crisis. The laity's growing penchant for divorce forced the

48. United Lutheran Church in America, *Minutes of the 5th Biennial Convention* (Philadelphia, 1926), p. 57; *Lutheran,* April 2, 1931, p. 15; *New York Times,* June 4, 1931, p. 2; United Lutheran Church in America, *Minutes of the 20th Biennial Convention* (Philadelphia, 1956), p. 1138.

49. National Council of the Congregational Churches of the United States, *Minutes of the 21st Regular Meeting* (Boston, 1925), p. 47.

50. Russell J. Clinchy, "Birth Control—An Exposition of the Federal Council Report," *Congregationalist,* May 28, 1931, p. 714.

churches, by the late 1920s, to make some canonical allow-
ances for separation and remarriage or face desertion by
their congregations. Reluctant to accept divorce as anything but the lesser of two evils, ecclesiastical lawmakers
began to consider scientific birth control a positive good if
it lessened connubial tensions and thereby reduced the like-
lihood of separation. Hence the moral optimists, though
they approached contraception with much of the conservatives' fear of spreading immorality, turned the morality
issue on its head. They found a greater good in the conservation of the family than in the containment of sexual
passion. They accepted birth control principally, therefore,
as an instrumentality with which to promote greater marital
stability. That sanction for contraception far outweighed
ancillary considerations such as the utility of birth control
in giving women greater control over their own bodies, or
its effectiveness in alleviating the suffering of the poor. The
liberal churches thus provided further proof, if proof were
needed, of the persistent strength in twentieth-century
America of the commitment to the idea of the family.

When the liberal churches spoke of birth control in relation to the "well-being of the family," they referred only
implicitly to the welfare of offspring. They meant, most
directly, the cultivation of the affective tie between husband
and wife. Thus in yet another way scientific birth control
won approval as it was called upon to foster romantic love.
Liberal clergymen saw romantic love as the last, best hope
for the preservation of the family and hence for the stability
of the social order. The Rabbinical Assembly of America
clearly manifested that attitude when it endorsed contraception as an instrument in the defense of the family
against the centrifugal forces of modernity. "Birth control,"
said the rabbis in 1935, "will not destroy, but rather enhance, the spiritual values inherent in the family." In that
way, they continued, birth control facilitated the overcoming of obstacles "that prevent the proper functioning of
the family under present conditions." In like manner, a
committee of the Philadelphia Yearly Meeting of Friends in

1930 approved birth control because it felt that "the full expression of the sex relation requires a large measure of freedom and spontaneity," which only artificial contraception could provide. Married couples, said the Friends, "vitally need the varied benefits of a rich and harmonious sex experience." Though the Friends also endorsed birth control for eugenic and economic reasons, they concluded that "problems of married life" provided the best case for the moral defense of contraception.[51]

Congregationalists, who had been among the first denominations to embrace liberal theology, extended a similar approval to contraception. Significantly, the Congregational Bureau of Social Service, considering the question of birth control in terms of overpopulation and "race suicide," declared itself "quite unequal for the problem." But the Seminar on the Gospel and the Family and Youth, at the General Council of the Congregational and Christian Churches in 1931, approached birth control in the context of "the moral and spiritual values inherent in and arising from the relation of marriage and the institutions of the home." The ideal of marriage, said the seminar, was "the complete union of one man and one woman." That ideal could not be realized "without mutuality and freedom resulting from physical and spiritual oneness." Therefore, said the seminar's resolution, which the General Council adopted, "we favor the principle of voluntary child bearing, believing that it sacramentalizes physical union and safeguards the well being of the family and society." The integrity and welfare of the family obviously interested liberal Congregational clergymen more than did Mrs. Sanger's pronouncements on eugenics, demography, the high cost of relief, or even the health of the indigent.[52]

In the Protestant Episcopal church, the split between

51. *New York Times*, February 17, 1935, p. 29; Special Committee of the Women's Problems Group of Philadelphia Yearly Meeting of Friends, "A Statement on Birth Control," pamphlet, 1930.

52. General Council of the Congregational and Christian Churches, *Minutes of the First Regular Meeting* (New York, 1931), pp. 164, 205.

liberals and conservatives took shape along the old lines of conflict between the "Protestant" and "Anglo-Catholic" wings of the church. In spite of the historic separation of the English and American churches, in matters of moral philosophy the Protestant Episcopalians often followed the lead of their English brethren, who had long tended toward a Romish position on sexual morals. In 1908, for example, the Lambeth Conference of the Anglican Communion declared that artificial prevention of childbearing "cannot be spoken of without repugnance." The assembled bishops received a report which argued that "the grave immorality of deliberately preventing conception" undermined religious institutions, violated nature, and subverted "high national character." The Anglican theologians in 1908 responded to the growing practice of birth control in England much as the Vatican had responded to the spread of the practice in nineteenth-century France. They appraised contraception not as a humanitarian answer to social ills but as a concomitant of calculating ambition. Rejecting the Malthusian argument that the motive for family restriction was the stress of poverty, the report contended that the real motive "is rather to be found in . . . social ambition; it arises from the wish to escape burdens which might lessen social prestige or limit the opportunities of pleasure; it . . . results in the weakening of character." The committee, borrowing a phrase from Theodore Roosevelt, concluded that "there is the world-danger that the great English-speaking people, diminished in number and weakened in moral force, should commit the crowning infamy of race-suicide, and so fail to fulfill that high destiny to which in the Providence of God they have been manifestly called." The bishops, obviously moved by these arguments, called "upon all Christian people to discountenance the use of all artificial means of restriction as demoralizing to character and hostile to national welfare." [53]

53. Lord Davidson of Lambeth, compiler, *The Six Lambeth Conferences, 1867–1920* (London: Society for Promoting Christian Knowledge, 1929), pp. 310, 327, 399–402.

In 1920, the bishops at Lambeth sounded a less nationalistic note, but remained vigorously opposed to the birth control movement. The conference now acknowledged medical, financial, and social exigencies but said they could not be admitted as sanctions for contraception because "the question cannot be separated from the moral and religious issues involved." The bishops delivered "an emphatic warning against the use of unnatural means for the avoidance of conception." They denounced the idea that sexual union between married couples could be an end in itself. On the contrary, the bishops declared, "we steadfastly uphold what must always be regarded as the governing considerations of Christian marriage. One is the primary purpose for which marriage exists, namely the continuance of the race through the gift and heritage of children; the other is the paramount importance in married life of deliberate and thoughtful self-control." In 1922 and again in 1925 American Episcopalians affirmed their agreement with the 1920 Lambeth statement. Birth control, said the General Convention of the Protestant Episcopal church in 1925, was a "menace to the family." [54]

In spite of the vigor of the Lambeth denunciations of contraception, the bishop's position was susceptible of change. Unlike Roman Catholics, who based their objections to birth control on the doctrine of the immutable nature of the act of intercourse, Anglican theologians couched their arguments against contraception in terms of its dangers to the family and to the nation. That broader context left considerable room for doctrinal adjustment in light of new evaluation of the state of domestic and national affairs.

The Lambeth Conference of 1930 effected such an adjustment. Like so many of the American religious bodies that eventually endorsed birth control, the Lambeth Con-

54. *The Lambeth Conferences, 1867–1930* (London: Society for Promoting Christian Knowledge, 1948), pp. 50–51, 99–105; Protestant Episcopal Church, *Journal of the General Convention, 1925* (N.P., 1926), app. 12, pp. 575–79.

ference liberalized its position on contraception while denouncing the increasing frequency of divorce. "The conditions of modern life," said the conference, demanded a new
recognition of "the biological importance of monogamy."
The conference, calling for "a fresh statement from the
Christian Church on the subject of sex," also adopted the
scientific-romantic appraisal of sex as "essentially noble
and creative," a "holy thing implanted by God in human
nature." Finally, the conference declared that "where there
is a clearly felt moral obligation to limit or avoid parenthood, the method must be decided on Christian principles."

The Lambeth statement was in many ways a watershed.
It manifested many of the ideas that were contributing to
the breakdown of Victorian sexual mores: an increasing
concern for family stability; a respect for the privacy of
family life; a new regard for "the sacredness of personality"; a demand for the "more equal partnership of men
and women"; a recognition of "the need of education,"
according to the best scientific lights, in matters pertaining
to sex; and an acceptance of the optimistic romantic view
of sex as a force for spiritual good. But the Lambeth Conference showed the influence of the past at least as much as
it pointed the way to the future. And not all the bishops
agreed with the path to the future finally chosen by the
conference. The resolution concerning contraception passed
by an unusual divided vote, 193 to 67. Moreover, the resolution itself was a curious mixture of liberal and conservative
views on contraception.

Though the bishops declared that the choice of contraceptive method should be "decided on Christian principles," they pointed out that "the primary and obvious
method is complete abstinence from intercourse (as far as
may be necessary) in a life of discipline and self-control
lived in the power of the Holy Spirit." The bishops reversed their 1920 position on the value of marital intercourse and declared it to have, procreation aside, "a value
of its own"—namely the strengthening of marital love. But

the bishops qualified their approval of such intercourse by linking the morality of willfully preventing propagation to the motives of the couple involved. Explicitly condemning "motives of selfishness, luxury, or mere convenience," they endorsed as a proper motive only "a morally sound reason," without giving any further explanation of moral soundness.[55] And if motive, not method, determined morality, there seemed no reason for the conference to designate abstinence as "the primary and obvious method." One Anglican writer, commenting on the confusing document, noted that "it looks as if Lambeth had not really made up its mind and were attempting to combine with the Christian view, a view of the sexual relation radically distinct." The "radically distinct" view to which he referred, the writer continued, was the "practical Mysticism" in sexual matters preached by Edwardian romantics like Edward Carpenter and popularized by Margaret Sanger.[56]

The bishops at Lambeth did, regrettably, stumble over questions of motive and method. But despite their confusion of traditional and romantic ideas, despite their anomalous prescription of abstinence in the middle of a statement endorsing artificial contraception, the bishops obviously intended to strengthen the family and improve the condition of women by providing new moral sanctions for the practice of birth control.

The *New York Times* called the Lambeth statement "but the slightest concession" to the views of the birth control advocates. American Episcopalians, however, justifiably viewed the bishops' pronouncement as revolutionary. Not all of them welcomed it. The American bishops at Lambeth refrained from condemning the conference's position,

55. *The Lambeth Conferences, 1867–1930,* pp. 164–66, 196–201.
56. J. Conway Davies, "Lambeth, Sex and Romanticism," *Church Quarterly Review* 114 (1932): 60–79; see also Charles Fiske, "The Church and Birth Control," *Atlantic Monthly,* November 1930, pp. 598–605; and W. R. Inge, "Birth Control and the Moral Law," *Atlantic Monthly,* December 1930, pp. 697–703.

but suggested that birth control had no place in "the perfect practice of Christian married life." A year later the
American bishops made their conservative sympathies clear
when they invited Bishop Michael Furse of Saint Alban's,
England, to keynote the Protestant Episcopal Convention
in Denver. Bishop Furse had led the opposition to the birth
control resolution at Lambeth.[57]

The Bishop arrived in America in the midst of a great
debate among Episcopalians about their divorce canons.
Liberals wished to amend the divorce laws in order to stop
the drift of the young from the church. Bishop Furse spoke
for the conservative opposition when he warned that "any
and all changes in the traditional Christian conception of
the sex relationships" would destroy "the whole Christian
ethic" as well as "the whole social order built thereon."
The convention eventually did liberalize the Episcopalian
position on divorce, and in doing so expressed as great a
concern for the stability of the modern family as did any
of the other Protestant bodies. But where other churches
had found in birth control a means of nurturing the marital bond, the Episcopalians declared that "there is no
bond of unity so compelling, so rich and so joy-giving as
that of children." The power of the conservatives proved
too strong to change the 1922 and 1925 decrees on contraception. The convention ended with a call for "an increasing realization of the necessity of children in the
home." The obvious purpose of intercourse, said the convention, "is the procreation of children, and unless children
are born the normal purposes of marriage are not fulfilled.
It is a serious and dangerous thing to thwart them." [58]

Three years later, however, the liberals succeeded in
getting a pro-birth control resolution through the convention, though not without a fight. The resolution scrupu-

57. *New York Times,* August 9, 1930, p. 4; September 17, 1931, p. 11.
58. *New York Times,* September 18, 1931, p. 28; Protestant Episcopal
Church, *Journal of the General Convention, 1931* (N.P., 1932), pp. 480–
81.

lously avoided the words "birth control" and simply endorsed "the efforts now being made to convey such information as is in accord with the highest principles of
eugenics, and a more wholesome family life, wherein
parenthood may be undertaken with due respect for the
health of mothers and the welfare of their children."
Though the statement made no explicit recommendations
about the use or morality of contraceptives, moral traditionalists among the Episcopalian bishops nevertheless objected to it. The Reverend Paul Mathews, bishop of New
Jersey and host to the convention in Atlantic City, led the
protest against the resolution from the floor of the House
of Bishops. "Is it for this house to endorse so dubious a
procedure as this?" he asked. He preferred the church to
remain absolutely silent on the subject. "If this thing is
going on," he said, "let it go on, but why should we endorse
it?"

The bishops engaged in what the *New York Times* called
a "bitter" debate over the resolution. When Mathews and
others began to protest the proposal, Bishop S. Arthur
Huston, its sponsor, snapped: "We have had a lot of
twaddle on this matter from celibate clergy who are about
as far removed from the problems of married life as the
man in the moon." At one point Mathews declared that, if
debate on the subject were limited, "I shall leave this
house forever." He later warned that if the convention
passed the resolution many Episcopalians would be compelled "to decide that their allegiance lies higher." The
friends of the resolution countered that contraception was
already an integral part of the lives of millions of the laity
and therefore deserved more scientific as well as ecclesiastical attention. That argument apparently persuaded the
bishops. By a vote of 44 to 38, they approved the resolution. In the House of Deputies, the resolution passed after
one delegate ironically noted that since the Roman Catholic church had recently approved the rhythm method, the
Episcopalians should at least take some action on birth

control. Thus, reluctantly, haltingly, the Protestant Episcopal church gave its cautious and indirect approval to contraception.[59]

"This puts national convention on record. Hard long battle but worth while," Mrs. Sanger's agents wired from the Protestant Episcopal convention.[60] Even though the Protestant Episcopal resolution only indirectly approved her attempts to change federal anticontraception statutes and made no explicit comment on the morality of birth control, Mrs. Sanger regarded its passage as a great victory. That facile conclusion reflected her continuing conviction that religious objections to contraception simply represented obstacles that her movement must overcome, rather than moral problems that required considered counsel to many conscientious churchgoers. The ease and depth of Mrs. Sanger's own belief in the correctness of birth control disengaged her from the substance of religious discussion of its morality. She well recognized, however, the tactical significance of that discussion, and, at least since 1930, she and her associates had been trying to influence the Protestant debate on contraception. In marked contrast to her relations with Roman Catholics, Mrs. Sanger herself constantly lobbied for birth control with individual Protestant clergymen. She sent her representatives to nearly every church convention in the 1930s. Her book *Motherhood in Bondage*, a collection of the most pathetic and heart-wringing letters she had received over the years from distressed women, she sent to thousands of persons who she felt needed convincing about birth control—including all the bishops attending the 1934 Protestant Episcopal conven-

59. "Birth Control Endorsed," *Churchman*, November 1, 1934, p. 7; *New York Times*, October 16, 1934, p. 28; October 18, 1934, p. 25; October 21, 1934, p. 1; October 23, 1934, p. 12; memo, Hazel Moore to Margaret Sanger, October 20, 1934, MSP–LC.

60. Telegram, "Vandervere Moore" to Margaret Sanger, October 23, 1934, MSP–LC.

tion. She kept up regular communication with Guy Emery Shipler, editor of the Episcopalian magazine *Churchman*, with Dr. Arthur E. Holt and Hubert C. Herring of the Congregational church, with Dr. Ralph W. Sockman of the Methodist Episcopal church, and with Worth M. Tippy of the Federal Council. Through these men she was able to place pro-birth control articles in their respective denominational publications and to encourage the introduction of pro-birth control resolutions at church conventions. In the case of the Federal Council, she personally came to its financial rescue after the flight of regular subscription funds in reaction to the council's birth control report in 1931.[61]

At the church conventions, Mrs. Sanger had her representatives distribute literature, answer questions, and occasionally bolster the courage of an anxious birth control supporter. In at least one instance Mrs. Sanger's efforts had a decisive effect. At the 1934 Protestant Episcopal convention, as the liberal lines began to waver during the floor fight in the House of Bishops, Mrs. Sanger's forces solicited telegrams to the bishops from Robert Latou Dickinson, Adolf Meyer, and other medical authorities, who expressed their support for the resolution under debate. Later, one bishop admitted that "the fact that physicians specializing in obstetrics wanted the legislation" was an important factor in the resolution's passage.[62]

Perhaps predictably, birth control won approval among those churches that boasted the most affluent congregations: Congregationalists, Friends, Reformed Jews, Unitarians, and Episcopalians. Those denominations had also been the most receptive to the doctrines of liberal theology, which proved a middle ground between the highly empirical and utilitarian moral theory of people like Margaret

61. Worth M. Tippy to Margaret Sanger, April 22, 1931; Margaret Sanger to George Blumenthal, July 7, 1933, MSP–LC.
62. Telegram, Hazel Moore to Margaret Sanger, n.d. [probably October 18, 1934], MSP–LC; *New York Times*, October 18, 1934, p. 25.

Sanger and the spiritual formalism of religious traditionalists. Liberal theologians neither simply presumed
that good results rendered the act of contraception good,
nor did they severely insist that it violated immutable
moral precepts. Liberal theology, with its acceptance of
science and its interpretation of lay experience as one
manifestation of the divine plan, joined with a romantic
view of the spiritual fruits of sexuality to provide a framework within which Protestant theologians could find moral
justification for contraception. That justification, however,
was significantly different from the one that Mrs. Sanger
urged.

Significantly, when the Protestant liberals did come to
approve of birth control, the religious sensibilities that
grew out of the Social Gospel movement provided less
sanction for contraception than did a growing concern for
the importance of sexual relations in maintaining marital
stability. Protestant churches, in approving birth control,
spoke not of poverty and health in the slums nor of sexual
liberation as an end in itself. They spoke, rather, about the
cultivation, through sex, of "spiritual values" in the fam-
iles of their faithful. For American Protestants, the conservation of the family carried a greater moral value than
either the social condition of the poor or the traditional
regulation of sexual behavior.

The nineteenth century had regarded sexuality as a
destructive force threatening the social order. Nothing
more dramatically illustrated the obsolescence of that view
by the 1930s than the liberal Protestant's understanding of
sex as an instrumentality for the preservation of marriage.
The sanguine appraisal of sex as the faculty most likely to
stabilize twentieth-century family life testified to the modern
confluence of scientific confidence and romantic optimism.
Liberal Protestants further showed their debt to romantic
ideas when they repeatedly decided to leave the final judgment on the morality of contraception to the individual's
assessment of his own motives. The question of motive
would also finally determine the legality of contraception.

In emphasizing the subjectivity of the morality and the legality of birth control, clergymen and lawmakers alike paid tribute to notions of individualism that were among the chief legacies of the romantics to the modern era.

CHAPTER 7

Birth Control and
American Medicine

At Dr. Johannes Rutgers's clinic in 1915, Margaret Sanger had learned the indispensability of medical support to the success of birth control. Only doctors could ensure a safe and effective contraceptive technique. The New York Court of Appeals' decision in 1918 added, at least for New York State, another imperative: only licensed physicians could prescribe birth control legally. Accordingly, Mrs. Sanger for the next two decades pleaded for medical endorsement of contraception. During that time the tortured relationship between Margaret Sanger and the organized medical profession revealed much about the birth control movement and about the nature of American medicine.

Mrs. Sanger had made scant reference to medical doctors in her pamphlet *"Family Limitation"* and none at all in the *Woman Rebel*.[1] Others, however, had considered contraception an essentially medical question well before Mrs. Sanger learned that lesson in Holland. In the 1830s a Massachusetts physician, Charles Knowlton, had written the most famous of the nineteenth-century "underground" tracts on contraception. In the 1880s and 1890s, medical doctors not infrequently discussed contraceptive techniques in their professional journals. Rarely, however, did they

1. In describing the "French pessary" or cervical cap in "Family Limitation," she said: "Any nurse or doctor will teach one how to adjust it; then women can teach each other." Medical men who saw the pamphlet must have been horrified at the suggestion of an army of New Women practicing lay gynecology. Margaret Sanger, "Family Limitation," 1914, copy in MSP–LC.

mention the subject publicly. Then, in his presidential address to the American Medical Association in 1912, the respected pediatrician Abraham Jacobi cited the high fertility of immigrants, the rising costs of welfare, and the burdens of poverty to substantiate his "indispensable suggestion that only a certain number of babies should be born into the world." [2] Jacobi had been influenced by his friend William J. Robinson, an eccentric physician with his own medical publishing business. Robinson had long believed in contraception, or what he called "prevenception," and had advocated though never actually described it in his various journals and books.[3]

Robinson labored alone for years, with Jacobi his only important convert. But in May 1915, noting the public interest in Margaret Sanger's flight to Europe and William Sanger's arrest, Robinson and the feminist leader Henrietta Rodman arranged an informal discussion of birth control at the New York Academy of Medicine. Though little came of the session, it represented a medical initiative at least indirectly in response to Mrs. Sanger's activities. Most of the discussants came to the meeting already sympathetic toward birth control; four of them—Robinson, Lydia Allen DeVilbiss, Ira S. Wile, and S. Adolphus Knopf —had for some time advocated greater medical participation in the investigation and practice of contraception. Wile and especially Knopf, a tuberculosis specialist, enjoyed substantial prestige among their fellow physicians.[4]

2. *JAMA* 58 (1912): 1735–44.

3. None of Robinson's journals had significant impact on medical thinking or practice. His numerous books, however, enjoyed a substantial popular audience. See, for example, *Fewer and Better Babies, or the Limitation of Offspring by the Prevention of Conception* (New York: Critic and Guide, 1915). Chapter 28, "The Best, Safest, and Most Harmless Means for the Prevention of Conception," consisted of two blank pages, to illustrate Robinson's contention that the law forbade contraceptive information even in scientific journals. Whatever the letter of the law (and the quality of Robinson's journal), many bona fide scientific publications describing contraception had been circulating through the mails, unmolested, for more than 20 years.

4. *New York Sun*, May 20, 1915, clipping, NYAML.

Similarly, a meeting in Chicago in February 1916 presented reputable doctors like Alice Hamilton and Rachelle S. Yarros of Hull House who spoke in favor of birth control. A distinguished guest from New York, Robert Latou Dickinson, one of the country's most eminent gynecologists, urged "that we as a profession should take hold of this matter [of contraception] and not let it go to the radicals, and not let it receive harm by being pushed in any undignified or improper manner." [5]

The rank and file of American medicine did not share that opinion. The associations, academies, and societies which alone could make an innovation such as birth control acceptable to the average doctor refused to endorse it. In late 1916, the New York County Medical Society took the first formal action on birth control of any organized American medical body. A Medical Society committee, studying a proposed amendment to New York's Section 1142, reported its fear that contraceptives, "indiscriminately employed," would undermine personal morality and national strength. The committee suspected that professional abortionists and "sensation-mongers" were behind much of the birth control propaganda. A minority report argued that tuberculosis and epilepsy should be considered legitimate medical indications for contraception and that birth control would end wars, child labor, drunkenness, divorce, poverty, and crime. But the majority countered that Section 1145 already made contraception legitimate for "good and sufficient reasons" (such as serious illness), and renounced any connection between birth control, as a purely medical matter, and social and economic problems. Finally, the committee pointed to medical ignorance of a reliable, harmless contraceptive method. Many "foreign procedures," it insisted, were "absurd, frequently dangerous, filthy, and usually unsatisfactory." It recommended that the Medical Society repudiate "ill-advised legislative enactments and sensational propagandistic movements." [6]

5. See *Surgery, Gynecology and Obstetrics* 23 (1916): 185–90.
6. *Pediatrics* 29 (1917): 17–23.

Medical men generally favored the views of the committee's majority. In an address to the New York Obstetrical Society in January 1917, George Kosmak, a prominent gynecologist, later editor of the American Journal of Gynecology, asked:

> Shall we listen to the unrestrained harangue of the reformer, usually a lay person with little conception of the medical aspects involved, who within the narrow bounds of his or her vision sees the solution of all the faults of our social system eliminated through the dissemination of contraceptive measures? Shall we lend ourselves to the spirit of license which such sentiments naturally must convey?

Kosmak dismissed the birth control advocates as "radical socialists" and "anarchists," whose unscientific literature on contraception contained "arrant nonsense, false reports, and . . . seditious libels on the medical profession." But he did encourage physicians to recommend continence—the only sure method, he said, whatever its liabilities—in cases where pregnancy would endanger a woman's life.[7]

Another writer allowed that birth control was indicated "in all chronic diseases"; beyond that, "economics and medicine are at the parting of the ways." But since there was absolutely no effective contraceptive, and since "the female is harmed by all devices which prevent the entrance of sperma [sic] in the uterine cavity," the only acceptable contraceptive—even in those cases where it was essential to health—was sterilization.[8]

For all their objections to birth control, most doctors clearly did not reject the practice outright. They usually gave guarded approval to contraception in cases with

7. George W. Kosmak, "Birth Control: What Shall Be the Attitude of the Medical Profession toward the Present-Day Propaganda?" *Medical Record* 91 (1917): 268–73; and *Bulletin of the Lying-In Hospital of the City of New York* 11 (1917–18): 181–92.

8. *New York Medical Journal* 105 (1917): 1185–92.

pathologic indications (conditions warranting therapy), but in general they rejected artificial devices in favor of continence or sterilization as the best prophylaxis. That severely qualified approval fell far short of Margaret Sanger's hopes for public support.

At first Mrs. Sanger ascribed medical reticence to moral cowardice and the prejudices of bourgeois doctors insensitive to lower-class suffering and opposed to social justice. To be sure, taking the Hippocratic oath did not automatically liberate a doctor from the values of his place, class, and time. The attitude of most American physicians toward the early birth control movement unmistakably reflected their middle-class upbringing and their commitment to nineteenth-century sexual mores. Yet early medical reaction to birth control derived principally neither from simple cowardice nor from strictly class bias; it owed most, rather, to a relatively new sense of medical professionalism. In commenting on contraception, medical men struck three persistent notes. Doctors had a reflex aversion to anything that smacked of lay medicine, sensationalism, or quackery. They opposed other than pathologic indications for medical treatment. Most forcefully, they rejected any therapeutic technique so untried as artificial contraception. All these themes proceeded from the history of medicine in nineteenth-century America.

The early nineteenth century had witnessed the nadir of public confidence in medicine. American physicians of the age, following the lead of French doctors who had for the first time insisted on scientific method in medical practice, "had so much traditional trash to clear up, and such difficult foundations to lay, that [they were] never able to build a therapeutics that could impress the laity." In other words, a new emphasis on investigation, classification, and accurate diagnosis gave scientific innovators more cause to throw out old cures than to devise new ones. They often retreated to a "therapeutic nihilism" which produced a "cynical distrust of the medical profession . . . during the early Victorian decades." [9]

Americans in the Jacksonian period found reasons besides medical ineffectiveness to mistrust doctors. The democratic and laissez-faire spirit of the age produced a suspicion of all claims to professional privilege. Medical insistence on licensing based on standards of education and orthodoxy smelled of class preference and even of monopoly. Consequently, state legislatures refused to enact—and in some cases repealed—legal controls over the quality of medical education and medical service.[10]

The negative mood of orthodox medicine, the public distaste for professionalism, and the absence of legislative regulation encouraged the widespread popularity of medical faddists such as hydropaths, magnetic and botanical healers, bleeders, and the ubiquitous patent-medicine salesmen. These quacks not only threatened the physician's income and his patient's welfare; they also represented the last-ditch stand of medicine-as-art and therefore blocked public acceptance of the incorporation of the knowledge, techniques and mental habits of science into medical practice. In the battle against quackery, science, more than prestige or pecuniary reward, became the standard for whose honor the orthodox fought. For American medicine in the nineteenth century, quackery became almost as formidable an enemy as disease itself.

The problem of quackery—though most severe west of the Alleghanies, where territorial and population growth had scattered a far-flung rural people willing to accept even the worst medical service—was a national one. To combat it on a national scale, physicians in 1847 organized the American Medical Association, which for the next half-

9. Richard Harrison Shryock, *The Development of Modern Medicine* (Philadelphia: University of Pennsylvania Press, 1936), pp. 241–42.

10. Shryock, pp. 250–55; and Donald E. Konold, *A History of American Medical Ethics, 1847–1912* (Madison: State Historical Society of Wisconsin, 1962), pp. 1–4.

century had as its primary objective the suppression of "irregular" medical practice. The AMA tried to counter the quacks' extravagant claims of therapeutic success by invoking the authority of dispassionate science. Unfortunately, science at first could only condemn irresponsible practices. It offered no alternatives. Indeed, that very negativism had produced the orthodox nihilism responsible for the growth of quackery in the first place.[11]

In the latter half of the century, however, science provided medicine with new knowledge in surgery, endocrinology, hygiene, and chemotherapy. French clinicians successfully demonstrated the necessity of laboratory and clinical tests for accurate diagnosis. The public health movement now gave physicians the techniques of statistical analysis to ascertain the best therapeutic treatment. The scientific attitude, which had heretofore "found its chief service in disclosing the uselessness of traditional remedies," now at last began to provide "positive amelioration and cure." Congress recognized the place of scientific research in medicine when it made a $10,000 grant to the National Board of Health in 1879. And the first meeting of the American Congress of Physicians and Surgeons in 1888 manifested the new strength and confidence of scientific specialists within the profession.[12]

Once scientific knowledge began to produce medical results, orthodox practitioners regularly and persuasively could offer better service than the quacks. Equally important, possession of scientific knowledge became a legally definable standard by which to distinguish legitimate medical doctors from quacks. Science provided both the public confidence and the legal tools that made legislative

11. Konold, pp. 22–28, 71. Quack advertising, especially in newspapers, reached such proportions that one student concluded that by the end of the century "the patent medicine industry had become one of the most corrupting influences on the press." Interestingly, another writer has noted: "One of the most striking and most common forms of quack advertising in the United States was that of abortifacient drugs." (Konold, p. 16; Shryock, p. 243).

12. Shryock, pp. 303, 305, 342; Konold, p. 40.

regulation of medical practice possible. By the early twentieth century, most states had given up their laissez-faire attitude toward medicine and enacted statutory guarantees of scientific medical standards.[13]

The reinstatement of public controls over medical practice represented a victory of regular over irregular medicine but did not signal the end of the war. Organized medicine congratulated itself on public acceptance of scientific medicine but remained constantly vigilant for sniping from outside the perimeter of orthodoxy. It continued to rely on legal controls buttressed by science to repel sorties against the medical establishment.

The long defense of professional integrity, though by the turn of the century largely successful, left a legacy of panicky resistance to any intrusion on orthodox medical practice. Further, the role of science in finally securing that integrity through law, confined medical attention, legally, to those conditions scientifically diagnosable as pathologic, and none others. Finally, the scientizing of therapeutics, accomplished at last, produced a therapeutics balanced precariously between the caution of ignorance and the license of quackery. It was, in short, restricted in scope and extremely sluggish to change.[14]

Robert Latou Dickinson played on the deep-seated fear of quackery among medical men when in 1916 he urged his colleagues who supported birth control to keep it out of the hands of the "radicals." That Margaret Sanger was a radical in the conventional, political sense amplified the predictable medical panic at her paramedical activities. George Kosmak and other doctors heard echoes of the patent-medicine barker when Mrs. Sanger claimed that birth control would end poverty, disease, crime, war, and all manner of social evils. Birth control propaganda

13. Konold, p. 30.
14. For a broader view of the increasing professionalization of medicine, see Robert H. Wiebe, *The Search for Order, 1877–1920* (New York: Hill and Wang, 1967), ch. 5

sounded remarkably like the most extravagant quack advertising against which orthodox medicine had long battled. Most physicians, therefore, opposed Mrs. Sanger as a dangerous, unorthodox interloper. Even those sympathetic to her cause, like Dickinson, sought to reduce or eliminate her personal influence in order to make birth control acceptable to the profession at large.

Doctors who favored contraception also found that they alienated their colleagues when they discussed nonmedical indications. When Abraham Jacobi spoke of immigration, welfare, and poverty in relation to family restriction, he went beyond the dimensions of contraception as a purely medical matter—dimensions within which his fellow physicians would much more willingly have responded. Medical leaders in contraception soon realized the resistance of the profession to "social" indications and confined their discussion to the necessity of birth control in well-defined pathologic circumstances—tuberculosis, heart or kidney disease, and pelvic abnormality.

All advocates of birth control recognized that the major source of medical opposition to the practice lay in ignorance of an acceptable contraceptive technique. Dickinson, in his presidential address to the American Gynecological Society in 1920, noted that ignorance—and ignorance of sex in general—and demanded a systematic effort to overcome it. "What serious study," he asked,

> has ever been made bearing upon the harm or harmlessness of the variety of procedures or concerning the failure or effectiveness of each? Who has or can acquire any considerable body of evidence on these matters but ourselves? What, indeed, is normal sex life? What constitutes excess or what is the penalty for repression in the married? Do we still have to hark back to Luther for an answer? It will take a few professional life-times of accredited histories to gather evidence to submit, but some time a start must be made.[15]

15. *AJOG* 1 (1920): 6.

Mrs. Sanger's move toward respectability during and immediately after World War I helped to allay some medical fears. She stopped carping at bourgeois doctors as she delivered the movement into the arms of middle-class ladies. And she began to acknowledge, reluctantly, her inadequacies as a laywoman and the consequent need for professional involvement. She would retire from the field, she hinted, as soon as doctors stepped in and fulfilled their responsibilities in the matter of contraception.

On the question of indications, however, Mrs. Sanger stood her ground. The unfavorable report of the New York County Medical Society, said the *Birth Control Review*, "furnished the final proof that birth control is not a medical but a social question . . . the economic side is much more important than the purely pathologic." [16] After Judge Crane's 1918 decision, Mrs. Sanger urged New York physicians to give the widest possible construction to Crane's liberal definition of "disease." Medicine, she said, should broaden its conception of its responsibilities to include the amelioration of eugenic, economic, and social problems through the application of medical knowledge.

Mrs. Sanger also squarely faced the doctors' demand for more knowledge of the technical aspects of contraception. At the First American Birth Control Conference in 1921 she announced her intention to open a clinic. The clinic, she said, would of course provide service, as the Brownsville clinic had done. But there the resemblance stopped. Unlike Brownsville, designed primarily as a legal test and publicity stunt, the new clinic would above all be a "first-class" center for medically supervised study of contraceptive techniques. The results of the study, Mrs. Sanger believed, would prove to the world and to the medical profession in particular the desirability and efficacy of birth control. But the doctor who was to be head of the clinic, Lydia Allen DeVilbiss, refused to go ahead until Mrs. Sanger received a proper dispensary license from the State Board of Charities. The board did not grant the license, Dr. De-

16. *Birth Control Review*, March 1917, p. 14.

Vilbiss went off to practice in Florida, and the clinic did not open.[17]

Characteristically, Mrs. Sanger continued her efforts to open a center for contraceptive service and study. By late 1922, she had hired Dr. Dorothy Bocker, a public health officer from Georgia, who "knew practically nothing about birth control technique, but was willing to learn." [18] Dr. Bocker had to operate the "clinic" as her private practice. In compliance with medical ethics, she could not advertise, and in compliance with state law she could prescribe only for a "health reason." Mrs. Sanger leased offices for the clinic across the corridor from the American Birth Control League headquarters at 104 Fifth Avenue. The ABCL, legally able to advocate birth control, but not to prescribe it, could simply refer inquiries to Dr. Bocker's "Clinical Research Bureau" across the hall. It was an arrangement of dubious propriety, conforming to the letter but hardly to the spirit of medical ethics and the New York statutes. Mrs. Sanger warned Dr. Bocker that she might go to jail for her efforts, but offered some consolation: "If this does happen, I believe you will get such a good boost of publicity, that we can put you on the platform lecturing throughout the country for the next two years." [19] Dr. Bocker, hoping to escape harassment long enough to build a body of convincing statistical information on birth control, opened the doors of the Clinical Research Bureau on January 2, 1923.

The bureau, expecting to reach primarily working class women, offered its services free. But because of the lack of advertising and the nature of the ABCL's membership, the "educated classes" were "unduly represented" among the 1,208 patients who came to the clinic in the first twelve months of its operation.[20]

17. *New York Times*, November 13, 1921, p. 18.

18. *Margaret Sanger: An Autobiography* (New York: Norton, 1938), p. 358.

19. Margaret Sanger to Dorothy Bocker, October 17, 1922, MSP–LC.

20. Caroline Hadley Robinson, *Seventy Birth Control Clinics* (Baltimore: Williams and Wilkins, 1930), p. 97; Dorothy Bocker, *Birth*

Dr. Bocker experimented with various contraceptive techniques. The most successful proved to be the combination of a spermacidal jelly with a Mensinga type diaphragm. Mrs. Sanger had procured the basic jelly formula in Germany in 1920, and it was soon being manufactured in the United States.[21] American manufacturers, however, produced only the unsatisfactory "check," or cervical-cap diaphragm, and Federal statutes made it illegal to import contraceptive supplies. Hence the few Mensinga diaphragms the clinic received came from Germany to Mr. Slee's Three-in-One Oil plant in Montreal. From there Slee ran the contraband diaphragms across the Canadian border in oil drums.[22] But even that elaborate operation could not keep the clinic adequately supplied, and Mrs. Sanger therefore encouraged the development of a domestic manufacturing concern to produce a quality Mensinga diaphragm. The Holland-Rantos Company took form in 1925 in response to her request. Mrs. Sanger, to ward off the charge that she was in the birth control movement for profit, scrupulously refrained from any connection with that necessarily commercial enterprise.[23]

The clinic went unmolested and Dr. Bocker continued through 1923 and 1924 to gather information on various contraceptive techniques. She published a report on over a thousand cases in 1924, but since none of her thirteen test series included more than a hundred women, the results were of limited persuasiveness. But the clinic's very existence, and the growing popular response to Mrs. Sanger's propaganda, began to command the interest of doctors.

Control Methods (New York: American Birth Control League, 1924) (report of first year of clinic's operation). The clinic was financed by Mr. Slee and by Clinton Chance, an English friend of Margaret Sanger, who sent her £1000. J. Noah H. Slee to Dorothy Bocker, December 29, 1922; radiogram, Clinton Chance to Margaret Sanger, November 3, 1922, MSP–LC.

21. Bocker, *Birth Control Methods.*

22. Slee, memo, November 25, 1925, MSP–LC.

23. Anne Kennedy, "History of the Development of Contraceptive Materials in the United States," *American Medicine* 41 (1935): 159–61.

One of the most interested physicians in the 1920s was the prominent gynecologist Robert Latou Dickinson. His career as a teacher and lecturer made his triangular face, accentuated by a trim Van Dyke beard, familiar throughout the medical profession. The public knew him as a nature writer and authority on New Jersey's Hudson palisades. His early concern with the pathologic effects of women's dress and traditional avoidance of exercise, and later his sympathetic opinion on birth control, marked him as a progressive ally of the feminist movement. His colleagues honored him in 1920 with the presidency of the American Gynecological Society.

Dickinson knew that the greatest obstacle to medical support for contraception was ignorance of an acceptable technique. The doctors who attended the special medical section of the First American Birth Control Conference in 1921 spent the session warning each other about untested techniques. They doubted the efficacy and especially the safety of nearly every birth control method suggested. Three years later, Dickinson reported: "A guaranteed technique of contraception is not yet worked out." [24] Though the public, in the early 1920s, seemed to be resorting increasingly to *coitus interruptus,* suppositories, intravaginal and intrauterine pessaries, and condoms, medical men generally doubted the propriety of all those devices.[25] Since the meager scientific data on contraception allowed no conclusions as to the effectiveness of any known technique, most doctors, in the nineteenth-century tradition of negative therapeutics, refused to prescribe anything. Abstinence, believed the orthodox, was the only certain contraceptive.[26]

24. R. L. Dickinson, "Contraception, A Medical Review of the Situation—First Report of the Committee on Material Health of New York," *AJOG* 8 (1924): 583–604.

25. Dickinson, "Contraception, A Medical Review"; Katherine Bement Davis, "A Study of the Sex Life of the Normal Married Woman," Part I: "The Use of Contraceptives," *Journal of Social Hygiene* 8 (1922): 173–89.

26. See *Pediatrics* 29 (1917): 17–23; and *Surgery, Gynecology, and Obstetrics* 36 (1923): 435–39.

Some doctors, however, did prescribe birth control; and thousands of women prescribed for themselves without ever consulting a medical authority other than the corner druggist or Margaret Sanger's writings. Against those loose practices the profession waged incessant battle. Medical literature throughout the 1920s abounded in warnings of the harmful effects of contraceptive devices. Often doctors warned of psychological damage, but they chiefly cited hard evidence of physical harm. Writers frequently reported that many commercially advertised douching solutions and suppositories injured the vagina. As for pessaries, Dr. Wilhelm Mensinga had originally advised that his Mensinga diaphragm be left in place between menses, and many doctors and laywomen took Mensinga at his word. The unsanitary conditions that such a practice encouraged led to several reported cases of streptococcus infections and even, some thought, carcinoma of the cervix. Many believed that the damage done by intravaginal devices could lead to permanent sterility.[27]

One device doctors universally rejected: the so-called wishbone, or stem, or gold-pin, cervical cap. Though few if any doctors prescribed it, the high incidence of its condemnation in the medical literature indicated that a great number of women used the "wishbone," with frequently disastrous results. Because this device did not simply cover the cervix, but also extended into the uterine canal, medical authorities hesitated to say exactly how it was supposed to stop conception. If it simply retarded the entry of spermatozoa into the cervix, it was a true contraceptive. If the stem's presence in the uterus prevented nidation of the zygote, then it was in fact an abortifacient, which posed ethical and medical problems of a quite different order. In most cases, however, the "pin" simply failed to work at all. An English doctor who had experimented with it said: "The cervix is kept patent by it, and the way is thus left open for the entry of septic organisms from the exterior

27. *JAMA* 80 (1923): 573; *Surgery, Gynecology, and Obstetrics* 36 (1923): 435–39. One doctor referred to the "so-called occlusion pessary . . . which is left in position weeks at a time."

which may reach the uterus and give rise to pathological conditions. It is not a reliable contraceptive; it often acts as an abortifacient; it has given rise to endo-cervicitis . . . and even death. It is a very dangerous instrument." [28]

No doctor in the 1920s, however sympathetic to birth control, could ignore the medical evidence: there was no reliable contraceptive device; moreover, the increasingly popular "mechanical devices applied to the cervix" seemed "very dangerous" to more than one investigator. Dickinson, reviewing medical knowledge of contraception in 1924, warned: "The largest gap in the clinical reports is on the matter of injury or harm—local, or general, or to the nervous system or morals as the result of the use of any or all of these measures." He especially noted Mensinga's mischievous and unnecessary advice to leave the diaphragm in place for weeks. The medical literature on contraception, concluded Dickinson, was a "library of argument." With regard to efficacy, it was based on hearsay. With regard to safety, the scant evidence seemed to justify medical caution. [29]

Dickinson asked, therefore, for a new program of contraceptive research, designed to find a technique both safe and effective. And to those two requirements he added a third: any effective contraceptive would have to be acceptable to the people intending to use it. To be adopted by the uneducated poor in particular, it must be aesthetically inoffensive, simple, and cheap. "Let us note," he said, "that the sheath and the douche appear to work poorly in the tenement. . . . Indeed, all measures show poorer results in the less intelligent." Even the combined diaphragm and jelly, which the Clinical Research Bureau had tested with some success, chiefly among "educated" women, required the use of a bathroom, and therefore would not work well "in the tenement." Dickinson cautioned researchers that they must

28. Norman Haire, "Contraceptive Technique," *Practitioner* 3 July (1923): 84.

29. *Surgery, Gynecology, and Obstetrics* 36 (1923): 438; Dickinson, "Contraception, A Medical Review."

take into consideration "the inevitable lack of privacy" when they looked for a means "specially adapted . . . to the poor." Doctors repeated that caveat throughout the next two decades, as they increasingly realized that though the diaphragm and jelly technique was tolerably suitable for many women, it was "neither simple nor certain enough to meet the demands of a very large body of women whom it is most desirable to restrain from propagating." In addition to its other drawbacks, it required individual examination and fitting, the kind of medical attention the poor rarely received. When Mrs. Sanger and others tried in the 1930s to bring birth control to rural Southern Negroes and the masses of the Orient, the pressure for a cheap, simple contraceptive increased. Medical technology had to take on a social dimension.[30]

Robert Latou Dickinson realized that only by dissociating birth control from lay propaganda could he secure the kind of scientific investigation that would establish contraceptive techniques acceptable to the medical profession. To Dickinson, Margaret Sanger, though she often proved aggravating to deal with, was a woman of vision and courage, motivated by a high moral purpose. But she was also a professional propagandist; any work associated with her name would risk medical indictment as quackery. The New York Academy of Medicine, in which Dickinson was a prominent member, had already declared, in 1921, that it was "emphatically opposed to the methods, principles, and programs of the Birth Control League." [31] Dickinson noted the warning. To advance the cause of birth control with his colleagues, he would have to avoid Margaret Sanger.

Accordingly, in early 1923 Dickinson drew together a few New York obstetricians and gynecologists to form the Committee on Maternal Health. With the quiet financial backing of Mrs. Gertrude Minturn Pinchot, the committee

30. Dickinson, "Contraception, A Medical Review"; *Medical Journal and Record* 134 (1931): 562–66.
31. *New York Times,* November 22, 1921, p. 16.

intended to carry on "a series of impartial, well-studied clinical tests" of contraception. On March 13, 1923, just a few weeks after Margaret Sanger's opening of the Bocker clinic, Dickinson went before the New York Obstetrical Society to ask for their endorsement of a supervised medical study of birth control. "We all know that contraceptives are generally used," he told the society. "The question is, are they harmful? Are they harmless? Do you know? I don't know. Are they efficacious?" Noting the growth of the birth control movement, he said, "I do not see any other alternative, but for us to guide such a movement to see that it goes slowly, and experimentally, with no publicity, with no general propaganda." He explained his committee's intentions. Would the society back him up? Or, he asked pointedly, "should some Sanger group do it?" [32]

The society polled its members and found that the majority, faced with a choice between studies directed by "some Sanger group" or by Dickinson, greatly preferred the latter. But even in endorsing the study, the society carefully defined its mandate. The society, Dickinson noted, was in "substantial agreement condeming [sic] teaching by specially organized clinics or by nursing organizations as such, or release of information to the general public." [33] The committee therefore gave assurances that it had "no plans at present for alliances or affiliation with any other existing organization. Being a strictly medical and public health project, and its medical policies being outlined and controlled by physicians of recognized standing, it will strictly avoid general publicity." [34] Further, the society's poll indicated that "excessive child-bearing as affecting health, and

32. Dickinson, "Contraception, A Medical Review"; *AJOG* 6 (1923): 351–53.

33. R. L. Dickinson, "Brief Outline of Report of Committee of New York Obstetrical Society," March 1923, records and correspondence of the Committee on Maternal Health in the Office of Dr. Christopher Tietze, Bio-Medical Division, Population Council, in the New York Academy of Medicine, New York, New York. [Hereafter cited as Population Council].

34. *AJOG* 7 (1924): 339–42.

the diseases and conditions wherein pregnancy endangers life are the topics endorsed for study, whereas economic reasons and individual excessive fertility as topics for study are not favored." [35]

The committee, thus pledged to maintain professional integrity and control, and instructed to confine its attention to strictly pathologic indications, began its investigation of contraceptive technique with a poll of the New York Obstetrical Society members. That poll revealed that though many members often prescribed the condom and considered withdrawal and "pessaries and stems" harmful, nearly all complained they had no "actual knowledge or experience of methods that are uniformly successful." [36] Dickinson and an associate next made a thorough "study of the literature . . . from a clinical standpoint, bearing on indications, technique and case histories," and found good reason for the doctors' complaints. "The total clinical material," they reported, "i.e., acceptable reports, covered the histories of 34 patients. This is the sum and substance as far as proving contraceptive measures go. . . . It is the best possible demonstration of the need of our investigation." [37]

To conduct its study of contraceptive techniques, the Obstetrical Society's Committee on Maternal Health set up an office "for reference and record," which was in reality Dr. Dickinson's office in the New York Academy of Medicine Building (although the academy had no official connection with the CMH). The office referred women to any of seven cooperating New York hospitals where they could receive contraceptive information. The CMH purchased the necessary supplies for the hospitals and issued standard-

35. Dickinson, "Brief Outline."

36. *AJOG* 7 (1924): 266–69.

37. "Suggested Communication for the New York Obstetrical Society," October 3, 1923, Population Council. The case histories of which the report spoke should be differentiated from the simple descriptions of contraceptive methods, in which the medical literature abounded. None of those simple descriptions, however, met the standards of scientific medicine held by Dickinson and other leading practitioners.

ized forms on which to record the case histories of the referred patients. The program had little success. The committee was able to supply only condoms and spermacidal jellies. The "cervical cap," the device that attracted the most medical interest, could not be procured in sufficient numbers to conduct adequate tests. Most important, the referral office was "only very moderately patronized. Patients were shy, believing that doctors would not be willing to give advice, judging by their previous experience." The bulk of applicants, concluded Dickinson, "want a special clinic." [38]

A "special clinic" meant just one thing: Margaret Sanger's Clinical Research Bureau. Dickinson had begun his birth control activities precisely because he wished to rescue contraceptive research from the partisanship of "some Sanger group." But the failure of his hospital reference scheme forced him to recognize that the Sanger clinic alone could provide the institutional setting in which to carry on extensive tests.

As the clinic stood, however, neither the CMH nor any other responsible medical organization would go near it. Dickinson noted after a visit to the clinic in early 1924:

> To the medical profession in general and to almost all of the members of the medical group of the C.M.H. the activities of Mrs. Sanger's organization are anathema. Even though such a study as that made by Dr. Dorothy Bocker in the quarters of the American Birth Control League Inc. have [sic] brought out many valuable points and have presented the first open minded clinical study of the subject, nevertheless it would estrange the Obstetrical Society and . . . most of our

38. *AJOG* 7 (1924): 339–42; *AJOG* 8 (1924): 583–604; R. L. Dickinson to Bailey Burritt, November 11, 1925, Population Council; R. L. Dickinson to Charles H. Johnson, November 20, 1926, Population Council. Only Dickinson's prestige had persuaded the hospitals to cooperate in the first place. In 1919, thirty-one New York hospitals had turned down another doctor seeking birth control advice for patients who met the standards set down by Judge Crane in 1918 (*Birth Control Review*, December 1919, p. 5).

own group, were we to cooperate with them or give them advice. The present character of the work is very different from the original Sanger clinic which did not attempt to keep carefully within the law, and which gave out printed slips of instruction. [But] however careful the professional part of the Sanger work may be, many feel that the sale of the *Birth Control Review* on the streets and the agitation for repeal of the law make their movement a dangerous one.[39]

Even the "professional part" of the clinic operation, Dickinson reported to the American Gynecological Society in 1924, fell dismally short of scientific criteria. The information on case history cards was scanty and uneven. Since "the vaginal cap can be obtained with difficulty," test series involving that device were little more extensive than the CMH's own disappointing experiments. The clinic's single attendant physician could not provide "medical inspection or supervision," nor was there any follow-up. In these circumstances, Dickinson concluded, Dr. Bocker's reports were nearly worthless as medical evidence.[40]

When Mrs. Sanger saw Dickinson's report, she immediately sent James F. Cooper, the ABCL's medical director and medical field lecturer, to the CMH "to ask how the criticisms of the league contained in that report could be met." That action enabled Dickinson to convince the New York Academy of Medicine of Mrs. Sanger's good will. The academy therefore authorized Dickinson and his fellow physicians Harold C. Bailey and George Kosmak to undertake an official investigation of the facilities for contraceptive research and service in New York City.[41]

On March 7, 1925, the three doctors visited the Clinical Research Bureau. Kosmak and Bailey strongly objected to the large "propaganda" posters on the clinic walls depicting the horrors of abortion. Dickinson noted evidence of ethical

39. Memorandum, "Relation of Committee on Maternal Health to the Sanger Birth Control Clinic," March 17, 1924, Population Council.

40. *AJOG* 8 (1924): 583–604.

41. *JAMA* 85 (1925): 1153–54.

laxity in the matter of indications: contraceptives were prescribed frequently for women "without evident disqualifi-
cation for child bearing." Further, he complained, sometimes "advice appeared to be given on insufficient evidence
of examination." Kosmak had suspected before he saw the
clinic that "the 'research' idea from all that I can gather is
merely a cover for the otherwise illegal practices of Mrs.
Sanger. The whole thing is in violation of the law and is a
public menace." His visit convinced him that the CMH
should not "develop any relations with the Sanger group."
But he did not confuse his feelings about Mrs. Sanger with
his attitude toward contraception under the proper conditions. "If," he said, "the problem is such that physicians
should participate in its solution, then we ought not to
hesitate about managing such a clinic ourselves, with due
regard to the medical phases alone." [42]

Kosmak's statement was all the encouragement Dickinson
needed. He reported to the New York Academy of Medicine
on March 12, 1925, that few physicians took advantage of
Section 1145, and that the CMH's experiment with hospitals
showed them "reluctant" to carry on clinical tests and in
any case unable to attract a sufficiently large clientele. In
light of those conditions, said Dickinson, "there is for the
time being a need in New York City for a clinic under non-
hospital auspices . . . provided that this special clinic ob-
tains legal sanction from the State Board of Charities and
has an adequate personnel and equipment for diagnosis
and research and an advisory board of gynecologists and
obstetricians of recognized authority to guide its policies
and work, and inspect it regularly." [43]

By the end of November, 1924, Dickinson's report to the
American Gynecological Society had given Mrs. Sanger some
new ideas about her clinic. She now recognized that she

42. "Report of Robert Latou Dickinson to Public Health Committee
on A.B.C.L. Clinic," March 16, 1925; George Kosmak to R. L. Dickinson, February 16, 1925, March 9, 1925, March 26, 1925, Population
Council.

43. Memorandum, R. L. Dickinson to Public Health Committee of
New York Academy of Medicine, March 12, 1925, copy in MSP–LC.

needed more than an attendant physician; she needed top-flight medical support. Dr. Bocker, an unknown, could not attract it, perhaps even impeded it; therefore, despite her loyal service, she must go. Then, when she heard that Dickinson's March report to the academy cited the "need in New York City for a clinic under non-hospital auspices," Mrs. Sanger proposed to Dickinson that the CMH simply take over the Clinical Research Bureau.

Dickinson had contemplated just that; but the actual proposal gave him pause. He knew how doctors felt about Mrs. Sanger and her clinic. On the other hand, his efforts had exhausted all other possibilities for medical testing of contraception. As much as he needed to avoid Margaret Sanger to gain medical approval for birth control, he also needed to be associated with her to secure public support and especially patronage of the clinic. Agonizing over the dilemma, he decided at last to accept Mrs. Sanger's proposal; but he informed her that transfer of the clinic would be possible only if done with due regard for medical ethics and with the full protection of the law. On May 15, 1925, Dickinson called a joint meeting of the CMH and Mrs. Sanger's group from the bureau. Representatives of the two organizations agreed to set up a new body, called the Maternity Research Council, which would undertake

> to provide clinical facilities for such patients as may be entitled to contraceptive advice under the laws of the State of New York and to undertake a scientific investigation of contraceptive methods, under the supervision and inspection of a board of gynecologists and obstetricians and other physicians of recognized authority who shall guide policies and inspect the work; and also to secure from the State Board of Charities a dispensary license for any clinic which may be maintained.[44]

44. "Historical News on Proposed Maternity Research Council," typescript, n.d., MSP–LC.

The last point was critical; if Dickinson was to secure medical backers and ensure the acceptability of the clinic's test results, the operation must be entirely legal. As he told Margaret Sanger, he "felt it essential to the dignity of the undertaking that a license should be obtained so that the clinic would not be supposed to be an underground affair that was merely tolerated." [45] Mrs. Sanger agreed: "I can see the good of the license. I can see the precedent it will establish. I can see the fight practically won by such achievement." [46] Dickinson also knew that he must strip the clinic of every vestige of Mrs. Sanger's propaganda campaign. At a meeting of the MRC incorporators, he recalled her own statement "that research and propaganda did not belong together" and requested her to remove the propagandistic literature and displays which would "raise the strongest objection on the part of the medical men among the incorporators." [47] Assured of Mrs. Sanger's compliance with that request, Dickinson wrote several of his colleagues, asking them to "lend a hand toward removing the Birth Control Clinic from the propaganda influence of the American Birth Control League." Moving with the cautious agility of a nineteenth-century diplomatist, by the end of the year Dickinson had marshaled impressive medical support, including that of William Allen Pusey, former president of the American Medical Association, who had endorsed birth control in his 1924 presidential address. Dickinson and his associates also obtained favorable resolutions on birth control from the New York Obstetrical Society, the Section on Obstetrics, Gynecology, and Abdominal Surgery of the AMA, and the American Gynecological Society. Most importantly, the New York Academy of Medicine, in a signal shift in attitude, incorporated Dickinson's recommendations into its 1925 report. Finally, the Rockefeller-backed Bureau

45. Memorandum, "R.L.D. interview with Margaret Sanger," January 18, 1926, Population Council.

46. Margaret Sanger to R. L. Dickinson, March 29, 1926, MSP–LC.

47. "Minutes of the First Meeting of Incorporators of the M.R.C., November 21, 1925, Population Council.

of Social Hygiene gave the MRC a $10,000 grant to finance its research.[48]

With those impressive credentials, in late 1925 the MRC formally applied to the State Board of Charities for a dispensary license. At their hearing on January 15, 1926, the council's incorporators stressed the necessity for medical control of contraception. On the board's action, said Dickinson, hung the issue of whether the birth control movement would be supervised or unsupervised. "Nothing," he said "can stop it." [49] The council needed a new clinic facility because hospital studies had proved inadequate. As for the existing Clinical Research Bureau,

> it has not been divorced from propaganda nor has it had any medical backing. . . . As it is now, that clinic so-called is under no responsible control. . . . the clinical records of that clinic are not in proper shape for scientific study. A clinic organized under the law and duly licensed under the control of a medical board would not only have better professional supervision but you would have conditions such that you would be getting some experience that would be valuable.[50]

The board asked for a month to sound religious opinion on the matter, and then on February 19 informed Dickinson that it considered a birth control clinic license "inexpedient from the standpoint of public policy." Later, elaborating the board's position, a member explained: "The only excuse for the independent clinic is that the medical profession through its present organization [hospitals and professional associations] is unwilling to foster such clinics

48. R. L. Dickinson to J. Bentley Squire, November 10, 1925, Population Council; R. L. Dickinson to ABCL, October 20, 1925, MSP–LC; "Historical News," MSP–LC; New York Academy of Medicine, Public Health Committee, *Report*, 1925, Archives of the New York Academy of Medicine, New York.

49. "Historical News," MSP–LC.

50. R. L. Dickinson, "Memo for State Board Hearing," January 15, 1926, Population Council.

as the birth control and psychoanalytic movements. As long as the medical profession will not accept these clinics through their organization, it seems to me to be asking a good deal from a lay board such as ours to grant approval." [51] Dickinson was disgusted. He had repeatedly explained the failure of his attempted hospital reference scheme. Likewise, he had often pointed out that professional associations would not accept birth control until a group like the MRC could scientifically demonstrate its desirability. That demonstration required the very clinical tests the board's action rendered impossible. "The real objection," he wrote Margaret Sanger, "was that of certain religious bodies . . . the opposition of the Roman Catholic Church was specifically mentioned and discussed." [52]

The Board of Charities, contradicting its own request of January 15, denied that it had ever "sought or received any communication from the Roman Catholic Church or any Church on this subject." But whatever the board's actual relations with the churches, it was admittedly sensitive to criticism. "The Board," admitted one member, "is too much afraid that a license will be widely exploited as a victory for Mrs. Sanger." [53]

The irony of that comment stung Dr. Dickinson. He saw the license application as a necessary step in taking the medical part of the birth control movement out of Mrs. Sanger's hands. But he seemed unable to escape the liabilities attendant on any association with her name. And even more painful to Dickinson than the board's decision were the slings and arrows of his colleagues. As the clinic continued unlicensed and without adequate medical supervision or inspection, Dickinson came under increasing fire for his unorthodox relation to it. An Illinois medical society in 1925, though not naming Dickinson specifically, noted the increasing involvement of certain prominent

51. "Historical News," MSP–LC.

52. R. L. Dickinson to Margaret Sanger, March 19, 1926, Population Council.

53. "Historical News," MSP–LC

physicians with the birth control movement and resolved that "affiliation in practice with the [ABCL] does constitute an unethical association, and is unprofessional conduct." [54]

All of Dickinson's prestige could not dispel continuing "widespread alarm at the words 'Sanger clinic.' " [55] The ABCL, said the Illinois medical society, failed to distinguish between "sociologic contraception" and "therapeutic contraception." It was a "lay organization essentially sociologic in its aims and programs," and it furnished an extreme example of "the bad social judgement and the bad ethics exhibited by the lay organizations entering or dictating the practice of medicine." [56] As late as 1929, a doctor noted the "persistent rumor" that the clinic did not operate legally. Another doctor claimed to have "evidence" that the clinic "treated patients on other than therapeutic indications." [57]

Indeed, if the clinic stayed within the letter of the law, it did so just barely. Doctors at the clinic searched for "therapeutic" reasons for contraception regardless of the patient's stated reason for wanting it. If the diagnosis could not be stretched far enough, the patient was referred to one of the clinic's physicians in his private practice, where prescription for a nonmedical indication was likely to go unmolested. This procedure was so integral to the clinic's operation that it constituted an important inducement to a doctor to serve on the clinic staff. The "N.H.R." (No Health Reason) referrals—who had to pay the private doctor—could make up a sizable portion of the doctor's clientele. One doctor, in fact, resigned because she was not getting enough N.H.R.s to make her clinic service profitable.[58] In the light of these continuing practices, at best somewhat less than rigorously ethical, many of Dickinson's

54. *American Medicine* n.s. 20 (1925): 655–58; *JAMA* 85 (1925): 908.

55. Louise Stevens Bryant to Samuel W. Lambert, April 7, 1927, Population Council.

56. *American Medicine* n.s. 20 (1925): 655–58.

57. Louise Stevens Bryant to Margaret Sanger, September 21, 1929, and memorandum, Gertrude E. Sturges to R. L. Dickinson and Frederick C. Holden, n.d. [1925], Population Council.

58. Ella M. Hediger to Margaret Sanger, March 22, 1928, MSP–LC.

supporters repeated their old warning against any kind of independent clinic. Dickinson, however, continued to believe that only the Sanger clinic was adaptable to large-scale tests. He persisted through 1926 in seeking some way to bring the clinic under medical control.

Mrs. Sanger in the meantime had made some changes. In anticipation of the MRC take-over, she had moved the clinic to new quarters, detached from the ABCL offices; she had hired a social worker to assist in follow-up studies; and she had appointed a new medical director, Dr. Hannah Stone (who was scarcely better qualified than the unfortunate Dr. Bocker). When the MRC plans had been slow to materialize during the spring and summer of 1925, Mrs. Sanger had recruited on her own a new "advisory board" for the clinic. She tried to enlist physicians, but most doctors preferred to remain aloof until the MRC provided organized professional support. Consequently, a few non-medical scientists dominated the board.[59] Prominent among those scientists were Clarence C. Little, a noted geneticist, eugenicist, and university president; Edward M. East, a biologist and agronomist whose book *Mankind at the Crossroads* had greatly influenced Mrs. Sanger and had established him as a leading prophet of overpopulation; and Leon J. Cole, a zoologist and professor of genetics at the University of Wisconsin. Raymond J. Pearl, a biometrician from Johns Hopkins University, was already a member of the advisory board of the ABCL and had a considerable voice in clinic affairs.

Between these social and biological scientists and Dickinson's medical colleagues there arose considerable bitterness. Each group feared that control of the clinic by the other would constrict or contaminate its own professional interests there. The first hint of trouble came in October 1925, when Little wrote to Dickinson proposing a revision in the original MRC organizational plan. Dickinson, of course, wanted the clinic under exclusive medical management.

59. American Birth Control League, Clinical Research Department, *Report for the Year*, 1925.

Little proposed a tripartite board: medical doctors to oversee service, social workers to supervise the gathering of data, and social and biological scientists to manage the interpretation of the data. "The medical profession," said Little, referring to the CMH's experience with the hospitals, "has already tried to handle the problem alone and has made a mess of it." Medical men had no "right to take over the work in a field which others have tilled for them." The league wanted at least six nonmedical scientists on the clinic's board. "The object of placing these men there," Little concluded, "is quite as much to make sure that advisable and sound methods are employed by the medical men, as it is to place any results of interpretation of data gathered at the clinic before the scientific world." [60]

Dickinson, galled, ignored Little's idea and proposed an "interim working plan" by which the MRC "should take over the control of the new clinic until such time as incorporation was completed and a license from the State Board of Charities procured." The plan was a shrewd ploy on Dickinson's part. By October, when he drew it up, he had come to believe that the State Board would probably refuse the MRC's license application. After that refusal, he knew, the medical incorporators of the MRC would never consent to assume responsibility for the clinic. But if they were already operating the clinic before the refusal became definite, Dickinson gambled that they would remain. True, in that event the clinic would still be unlicensed, which was regrettable, but at least it would be in medical hands. That "very simple beginning," Dickinson thought, could lead to "a very natural growth." But on October 14, Mrs. Sanger took Little's advice and scuttled the plan. The opportunity for Dickinson's *fait accompli* was lost. Moreover, the medical incorporators, seeing the influence of Little and the scientists in Mrs. Sanger's councils, were made even more "wary of beginning until it is understood that medical questions will be fully under medical management." [61]

60. C. C. Little to R. L. Dickinson, October 28, 1925, MSP–LC.
61. Memorandum, R. L. Dickinson to Gertrude E. Sturges, December 30, 1925, Population Council.

Dickinson was so outraged that when Mrs. Sanger approached him in late December with an "interim plan" of her own (one similar to Little's), he simply refused to answer her letter.[62]

The scientists, who should perhaps have been chastised by the experience, continued in their zealous belief that the birth control clinic was more important as a source of sociological information than as a medical service. At the meeting of the MRC incorporators on November 29, 1925, Little, Cole, and East demanded that the clinic provide an "opportunity for scientific investigation from a social and biological point of view." Some years later, East cavalierly dismissed investigation from a medical point of view: "I think there should be no question that the case history report should be available to sociologists, including social workers and biologists. . . . They are the ones that will use the report, not members of the medical profession." Another social scientist, Henry Pratt Fairchild, agreed: "It seems to me that it would be a great mistake if this report were made easily accessible only to the medical profession or even if it were aimed primarily at them." [63]

Margaret Sanger, with her new interests in demography and eugenics, apparently saw greater propaganda utility in social science than in medicine. She revamped the record-keeping procedures of the clinic in 1925, supposedly to correct the medical deficiencies of Bocker's system; but she readily acquiesced in East's demand to include on the case history cards information about the nationality, heredity, religion, occupation, and trade union affiliation of patients at the clinic. Ira S. Wile and other doctors objected to this continued confusion of medical and social matters, but Mrs. Sanger paid no heed.[64]

62. Memorandum, R. L. Dickinson to Gertrude E. Sturges, December 29, 1925, Population Council.

63. "Report of Conference," November 29, 1925, Population Council; E. M. East to Margaret Sanger, June 24, 1931, Henry P. Fairchild to Margaret Sanger, July 13, 1931, MSP–LC.

64. Ira S. Wile to Margaret Sanger, May 14, 1928, Margaret Sanger to John C. Vaughn, May 12, 1928, MSP–LC.

The refusal of the State Board of Charities to grant a license, and continuing suspicion that the clinic breached medical ethics in the matter of indications, had by late 1926 alienated most of the medical men whose support Dickinson had so carefully cultivated. Dickinson himself balked at the influence and obstinacy of the scientists around Margaret Sanger. She dealt him even further discouragement in 1927 when she left for Europe and stayed eighteen months.

When Mrs. Sanger returned to the United States in late 1928, she quit the ABCL and took the clinic with her. The separation of the clinic from the "propaganda" organization that medical men had so often rebuked gave Dickinson new hope. Mrs. Sanger herself approached him with a request for a new medical director and a license from the State Board. He replied that neither was possible until the clinic came "under the direct control of a responsible medical group." [65] A few weeks later, therefore, he went to Mrs. Sanger with a new proposal. Her actions and those of the State Board had killed all chance of support for the clinic from a professional association such as the Maternity Research Council. But after negotiations with the State Board and with the New York Hospital, he now deemed it possible for a new Maternity Research Council (the old group had drifted apart) to operate the Clinical Research Bureau as a legal, fully licensed clinic under the prestigious auspices of New York Hospital. The clinic would be physically separated from the hospital, but "all matters of medical policies including selection of cases, care and follow-up of patients, references, and their affiliations with other medical groups would be in the hands of the Maternity Research Council." [66] All but one of the six medical members of the clinic's advisory board favored Dickinson's plan. The non-

65. "Résumé memo," n.d., Population Council. The exchange between Dickinson and Mrs. Sanger is dated January 3, 1929.

66. Louise Stevens Bryant to Margaret Sanger, February 25, 1929, MSP–LC.

medical scientists, however, still unanimously blocked medical control. Affiliation with the New York Hospital, Leon Cole noted, might "result in tying our hands so that the work of the clinic would be greatly slowed down and might, indeed, suffer a real setback." He referred, of course, to the sociological work the clinic made possible. Similarly, East wrote Mrs. Sanger that "under the present regime there has been a good deal of interest in collecting data of general biological and sociological interest. This is due, of course, to your own interest, and to that of Dr. Cole, Dr. Little, and myself. If the clinic were conducted entirely under medical supervision, would not these activities cease?" [67] Once again, Mrs. Sanger found the warnings of the scientists more persuasive than the need—to which she herself gave such frequent lip service—for medical cooperation. She prepared to tell Dickinson that his latest proposal was unacceptable.

Before Mrs. Sanger formally repudiated Dickinson, however, an event occurred which made his support indispensable. Sometime in late March 1929, a Mrs. McNamara had come to the clinic requesting birth control information. An examination revealed indications for contraception on orthodox medical grounds, and she was duly instructed. Three weeks later she reappeared with a police squad, flashed her badge, arrested two doctors and two nurses, and confiscated the case history records of one hundred fifty patients.

The law clearly protected the physician who prescribed contraception for "health reasons." The police, obviously, expected to find evidence that the clinic's doctors were prescribing in the absence of pathologic indications; but when they confiscated the case histories, they made an egregious blunder. The confiscation violated the confidential relationship between doctor and patient. Mrs. Sanger might find few physicians who would swear to the strict legality of her clinic's operation; but Dickinson could arouse the profession nearly to a man in protest at the seizure of private

67. Leon Cole to Margaret Sanger, March 22, 1929, E. M. East to Margaret Sanger, March 14, 1929, MSP–LC.

records. She asked for his help, which he readily gave. Within the week he persuaded the New York Academy of Medicine to appoint a special investigating committee. The committee lodged a vigorous protest with the commissioner of police, sent representatives to testify in court that Mrs. McNamara's condition warranted contraception to preserve her health, and secured resolutions from various medical groups denouncing the slur on professional good faith and "the attempt to influence the doctors and their freedom of action." In the face of this massive medical support, the judge dismissed the case and the commissioner of police reprimanded the officers responsible for the execution of the raid.[68]

In the wake of the episode, Dickinson made one last attempt to bring the Clinical Research Bureau under medical control. The raid had rekindled the interest of the profession in birth control. Mrs. Sanger herself perceived the opportunity the raid afforded. She told a member of the academy of her renewed desire "to have closer cooperation between the members of the medical profession and the research Bureau." Specifically, she said, she wished to "enlist the supervision of a committee recommended by the Academy." [69] Having seen the vigor and sincerity of the doctors' actions in her behalf, Mrs. Sanger at last seemed willing to loosen her grip on the clinic.

Throughout the summer of 1929, Dickinson labored to put together the new MRC. That fall he persuaded the academy to appoint a committee to investigate the Clinical Research Bureau and stipulate the standards the new MRC would have to meet to secure academy endorsement. The suggestion of endorsement by the academy itself—rather than by an ad hoc professional committee or a hospital— was the boldest proposal yet made. Dickinson now con-

68. Sanger, *Autobiography*, pp. 402–08; R. L. Dickinson, "Control of Conception, Present and Future," pamphlet, 1929, New York Academy of Medicine Library.

69. Margaret Sanger to Dr. J. A. Hartwell, June 3, June 17, 1929, MSP–LC.

sidered it possible because of the sympathetic interest generated by the clinic raid. Stuart Mudd, a doctor close to
Margaret Sanger, tried to show her just how important a
step this could be. Academy approval, he said, would be "of
great value as a precedent in arranging establishment of
clinics elsewhere in the country." With the backing of the
academy, recognized gynecologists would serve on the clinic
board, and they in turn could induce their students, young
interns and residents, to serve on the clinic staff. Financial
support would be more readily forthcoming. The best medical journals would open their pages to clinic reports. (Since
Dr. Stone's reports came from a lay clinic, she had immense
difficulty placing them in a reputable journal.) Endorsement by the academy, he concluded, was an opportunity
not to be missed.[70]

Mrs. Sanger hesitated. "I do not want to release too
quickly," she told Mudd, "the control of a work which it
has taken years to develop." From the beginning, her deal-
ings with Dickinson had been marked by ambivalence. She
needed medical support; she also feared the loss of personal
control. In 1925, she had written James Cooper "Dr. D[ick-
inson] is anxious (wildly anxious) to get in control." She
would have to "go slow in giving too much power." In
early 1929, her reluctance to divest herself of the clinic led
her to say that "contraception . . . is not medicine." In
a bitter note to one of her earliest medical backers, S.
Adolphus Knopf, she pointed out that Dr. Bocker's "theft"
of the clinic records in 1924 had proved "that a paid M.D.
was not the best person to be in control." The best person,
she implied, was herself. When Knopf reminded Mrs.
Sanger of her oft repeated professions that birth control
was primarily a medical matter, she responded tartly: "*You*
are the first person to cast a doubt on my ability or qualifi-
cations as director of the first birth control clinic in the
United States of America." That statement ignored the
nearly universal doubt in the medical world about any

70. Stuart Mudd to Margaret Sanger, June 30, 1929, MSP–LC.

enterprise, especially a clinic, conducted by Margaret Sanger.[71]

By the fall of 1929, Mrs. Sanger had greater reason than ever to keep a tight hold on her clinic. She had quit the American Birth Control League and the *Birth Control Review*; the new federal lobbying organization had not yet taken shape. The clinic, then, was her only institutional connection with the birth control movement. Dickinson sensed her growing reluctance to give it up and asked her in October "to confirm in writing the verbal statement made more than once to Dr. Bryant and myself that you wished to see the clinic turned over completely to the M.R.C." He had little desire to humiliate himself, as he had in 1925, before his committee and before the academy because of Mrs. Sanger's last-minute change of heart. Mrs. Sanger's reply acknowledged that medical supervision "is the main thing our clinic needs now." She would "welcome with open arms," she wrote, "medical supervision and direction." But, she added, she "must consider carefully any proposal to 'turn over completely' a Clinic which has been built up by years of hard sledding and supported by a group of scientists whose opinions must be taken into consideration as well as my own." [72]

Dickinson redoubled his efforts to persuade Mrs. Sanger of the desirability of his plan and to accelerate the investigation of the academy's committee. But Mrs. Sanger's letter warned him that the scientists still had her ear, and the blow he feared fell on November 21, 1929. Deliberately neglecting to inform Dickinson, who was to have presented the MRC plan, Mrs. Sanger called a meeting of her advisory council. Neither did she inform any of the medical men on the council. Acting under C. C. Little's guidance, the council rejected the MRC proposal and adopted a

71. Margaret Sanger to Stuart Mudd, July 17, 1929, Margaret Sanger to James Cooper, November 13, 1925, Margaret Sanger to S. Adolphus Knopf, March 6, 1929, all in MSP–LC.

72. R. L. Dickinson to Margaret Sanger, October 10, 1929, Margaret Sanger to R. L. Dickinson, October 19, 1929, Population Council.

substitute plan to enlist one gynecologist as an inspector and one physician as general manager. Mrs. Sanger sent the president of the academy what was described as a "curt note" informing him of the clinic's decision to reject Dickinson's plan.[73]

By rejecting the MRC plan and the possibility of the academy's support, Margaret Sanger slammed the door on the prospects of any medical endorsement. No specialist, said Dickinson, would serve on the clinic staff alone; and without recognized professional backing, no reputable physician would assume the directorship. The clinic would continue with no supervision of its medical standards. All the professional status that would have come with academy approval was lost. "One of the largest gynecological services in the country," Dickinson wrote regretfully, "a clinic which has never had a gynecologist or obstetrician on its consulting or directing group, nor a director or attending physician with experience above the grade of the lowest dispensary position, elects to continue in this anomalous position." [74] Mrs. Sanger's action, once again promoted by the scientists on the council, and encouraged by her increasing reluctance to lose personal control of the clinic, alienated medical men more than ever. "There is considerable feeling," Dickinson wrote, "that Mrs. Sanger has played fast and loose with the most important committee in the Academy." [75] Another doctor felt that "the careful thought and courtesies extended to the clinic by the Academy and their help in the trial had been such that Mrs. Sanger's recent action should end any aid or counsel." [76]

The effort to bring the Clinical Research Bureau under medical control had persisted for seven years—and accomplished nothing. As Dickinson told the academy, he had been forced to conclude that "it was useless to try to get

73. "Résumé memo," November 21, 1929, Population Council.

74. "Résumé memo."

75. R. L. Dickinson, memorandum, n.d., MSP–LC.

76. R. L. Dickinson, memorandum, December 4, 1929, MSP–LC.

Mrs. Sanger to cooperate with other groups." For her part, Mrs. Sanger, reviewing in 1942 her old correspondence with members of the academy, noted: "These letters indicate . . . our group as *begging* the Medical Profession to come in and supervise. . . . I refused however to hand over a service of humanity to be a football in a political set-up and finally abolished, as the clinic would have been." [77]

The clinic was a political issue for both sides. Moving in the nervous world of medical politics, Dickinson had to pursue his goals with the utmost circumspection, making sure at every step that he had secured the proper form of committee, obtained the requisite organizational backing, and confined his attention to strictly medical matters. Caught between his colleagues' fear of quackery, their aversion to nonmedical indications, and the lack of scientific knowledge of contraception, Dickinson steered a precarious course, only to founder repeatedly. The profession, continuing to avoid official involvement with the birth control clinic, still cited the very impediments that only medical involvement could remove.

Mrs. Sanger, for all her insistence that medical support was indispensable to her clinic, could never quite go far enough to make that support possible. Time after time, just as she approached agreement with Dickinson, she pirouetted away, resolving anew to retain her personal hold on the clinic. Here, as in so many of the skirmishes in Mrs. Sanger's lifelong battle between her head and her heart, emotion prevailed over reason. Though she abandoned her early view that doctors were cowardly bourgeoisie, she never fully understood the historical reasons for the caution with which physicians approached contraception. Failing to understand that, she was often impatient with their demands for exclusive medical control and strict compliance with the letter of the law. Those demands, she thought, were both selfish and subversive. It often seemed to her that doc-

---

77. "Résumé memo," November 21, 1929, Population Council; Mrs. Sanger's notation is dated September 29, 1942, MSP–LC.

tors wanted "to take charge and monopolize the credit" in the movement she had built.[78]

Both she and her scientist-advisers were plagued by the notion that the medical cooperation they so badly needed appeared to be available only at the cost of renouncing their concerns with poverty, eugenics, and demography. Because of these conflicting feelings, all of Margaret Sanger's efforts to respond to Robert Latou Dickinson's offers of help ended only in bitter disagreement.

Dickinson persisted through all the defeats and embarrassments of the clinic episode because he recognized the pressing need for a facility for contraceptive study. Faced with a growing public demand for birth control information, doctors still had no reliable scientific data on contraception. In 1930 the *Journal of the American Medical Association* could only advise an inquiring physician that "we do not know of any method of preventing conception that is absolutely dependable except total abstinence." [79] As late as 1946, Dickinson reviewed the medical literature and concluded: "Neither the clinical work of 23 years of the Sanger Bureau, nor of the clinics of the League or [Planned Parenthood] Federation, nor the 23 years of the National Committee on Maternal Health, with four books and seventy papers related to this subject, had made any striking discoveries." [80]

Researchers in the 1920s and 1930s explored and rejected many contraceptive possibilities. Doctors condemned as potentially dangerous all intrauterine devices, such as the "stem" pessary and the well-known silver "ring" invented by the German Ernst Graefenberg. They doubted the efficacy of such other proposed methods as special vitamin

78. *Birth Control Review*, May 1918, p. 16.

79. *JAMA* 94 (1930): 2806.

80. R. L. Dickinson, "Policy of Future Coordination," notes on meeting of the executive committee of the National Committee on Maternal Health, June 14, 1946, Population Council. The Committee on Maternal Health had added National to its name and concentrated on publishing scientific papers after 1930.

regimens, diathermy to the testicle, and x-ray retardation of ovulation and spermatogenesis.[81] For a time doctors gave great attention to rumors coming out of Russia that researchers there had developed "an almost ideal immunological technique": subcutaneous injections of a spermatic solution which supposedly provided up to a year's sterility. But the rumors about the "spermatoxin" had little substance. Margaret Sanger found nothing when she inquired in person about the Russian experiments in Leningrad in 1933. [82] Mrs. Sanger also personally financed a project in the department of animal genetics at Edinburgh University in Scotland, where biologists, working with mice, were beginning to develop a hormonal anovulant, which years later would make possible the "pill." But in 1930, when the Scottish scientists reported their findings to an international symposium in Zurich, they emphasized the primitive nature of the findings. And they boggled at the social implications of their work. "It is doubtful," they warned, "whether we shall ever wish to obtain a point where these dangerous weapons will be at the disposal of man." [83]

The one contraceptive method the American Medical Association called "free from criticism on religious and social grounds" was restriction of intercourse to the so-called sterile period. Doctors, however, disagreed as to when in the menstrual cycle the sterile period was supposed to

81. Margaret Sanger and Hannah Stone, eds., *The Practice of Contraception* (Baltimore: Williams and Wilkins, 1931), pp. 33–37; résumé of correspondence, Phillip Stoughton to Hannah Stone, July 16, 1936, R. L. Dickinson to Lee K. Frankel, November 2, 1929, MSP–LC.

82. *JAMA* 77 (1921): 42–43; Raymond Squier to D. Kenneth Rose, December 16, 1938, John L. McKelvey to Clair E. Folsome, April 2, 1941, Population Council; *Medical Journal and Record* 125 (1927): 653–57; Sanger, *Autobiography*, p. 442.

83. H. Taylor, "Report on the Hormonic Control of Fertility," in Sanger and Stone, *Practice of Contraception*, pp. 98–104; for Mrs. Sanger's involvement, see the correspondence, B. P. Weisner to Margaret Sanger, July 10, 1928, October 17, 1930, and Margaret Sanger to B. P. Weisner, January 17, 1931, MSP–LC; also, Margaret Sanger, "A Program of Contraceptive Research," typescript, June 5, 1928, MSP–SS.

occur. Dickinson changed his opinion on the matter at least once in the 1920s, and in 1927 confessed that he was still wide of the mark.[84] The following year a leading gynecologist from the Johns Hopkins Medical School said: "The chief benefit which we have derived from the birth control propaganda is the belated recognition . . . that there is no 'safe time' in regard to the menstrual cycle." [85]

By the early 1930s, however, research had produced more definite information on the "safe period." Kyusaku Ogino in Japan and Hermann Knauss in Austria, working independently in the 1920s, had come to identical conclusions: ovulation occurred sixteen to twelve days before the anticipated beginning of the next menses. A couple who avoided intercourse during that period could prevent pregnancy. The work of Knauss and Ogino became known in the United States chiefly through Leo Latz's book, *The Rhythm of Sterility and Fertility in Women*. The book's title was frequently abbreviated to *The Rhythm,* and so the method it described came to be called. Throughout the 1930s the method became increasingly popular. Latz sent thousands of women special calendar-charts by which to calculate their fertile and infertile periods. In marked contrast to its position on most lay medical practices, the medical profession welcomed the rhythm method as "a ray of light" amidst the uncertainties of most contraceptive techniques. The Ogino-Knauss method, the first real advance in contraceptive research in decades, said the American Medical Association, was "more promising than promoting the sale of various mechanical devices, chemical substances and other forms of intricate manipulation." By the end of the decade, however, experience had shown that few women had menstrual cycles regular enough to allow accurate determination of the sterile period. After all the excitement it had

84. First American Birth Control Conference, notes, MSP–SS; R. L. Dickinson, "Contraception, A Medical Review"; R. L. Dickinson, "The Safe Period as a Birth Control Measure," *AJOG* 14 (1927): 718–30.

85. J. Whitridge Williams, "Indications for Therapeutic Sterilization in Obstetrics," *JAMA* 91 (1928): 1237–42.

caused at its introduction, the rhythm method proved an even less adequate contraceptive than the standard diaphragm and jelly.[86]

Clinics and private doctors continued to prescribe the diaphragm and jelly almost exclusively, and the success of that technique depended on individual medical examination and fitting. The extent of that intensive medical attention, in turn, depended on the diffusion of contraceptive knowledge to doctors. Margaret Sanger tried to educate the medical profession when she sent Dr. James F. Cooper to hundreds of county medical societies in the 1920s to speak on birth control and when she sponsored medical symposia, as in Zurich in 1930 and New York in 1934. But the profession continued to scorn any information connected with her or with her clinic as "sensational contributions by fanatical propagandists or hysterical ladies." Dr. Hannah Stone found the leading medical journals closed to all clinic reports. What little information did exist, therefore, was not widely known in the profession. In 1930, only 13 of the 75 American medical schools rated grade-A gave regular courses in contraception. Another 29 gave "incidental instruction," the rest, none. By 1936, nearly half of these schools still gave no instruction.[87] Many doctors came to the Clinical Research Bureau to be taught contraceptive technique, but the bureau could not possibly educate enough doctors to meet the growing public demand. One physician observed in 1932 that the number of doctors "who know little or nothing about contraceptive measures is tragically amazing." [88]

At least part of the responsibility for the tragedy of continuing medical ignorance of contraception had to be laid to Margaret Sanger. Had she relinquished control of the clinic to Dickinson in 1925, she would have facilitated research, opened up the best medical journals for the publication of test results, and made the clinic much more ef-

86. *JAMA* 102 (1934): 452–54; 103 (1934): 756–57.
87. *Medical Times* 58 (1930): 108–18; *AJOG* 31 (1936): 165–68.
88. *Virginia Medical Monthly* 59 (1932): 102.

fective as a training center for physicians interested in contraception. But by frustrating Dickinson's persistent efforts to make birth control acceptable to his colleagues, Mrs. Sanger aggravated a condition similar to that which had plagued all medicine in the nineteenth century. Millions of women, finding no help with regard to contraception from orthodox medicine, turned to the quacks. And as in the nineteenth century, the absence of clear legal regulations exacerbated the situation.

Before 1930, contraceptives could neither be advertised nor sent through the mails legally. A Federal court decision in that year, however, allowed advertisement and shipment of contraceptive devices intended for legal use—in most states, "for the prevention of disease." Under cover of that and similar euphemisms such as "feminine hygiene," a booming business in contraceptives developed rapidly. Scores of unscrupulous profit-seekers swamped the field that Mrs. Sanger had persuaded a single reluctant firm to enter in 1925. One investigator estimated expenditures for contraceptive advertising in 1932 and 1933 at $935,000. Advertisements appeared in newspapers, magazines, and even in the mail-order catalogs of Sears, Roebuck and Montgomery Ward. One unethical manufacturer adopted the name "Marguerite Sanger Company" and moved his headquarters regularly from state to state to avoid prosecution. *Fortune* magazine reported in 1938 that American women spent over $210,000,000 annually for contraceptive materials and that "the medically approved portion of business in female contraceptives is pitifully small . . . as a result . . . millions of women have been duped and thousands of secret tragedies have been enacted." "Contraceptive information today is all under-cover work and devices are being sold at retail in violation of the law so that the entire matter is in about the same position as the Volstead Act," wrote one doctor. The *New Republic* laid the blame for these conditions "on those members of the medical profession who have sidestepped the issue." Although the Federal Trade Commission stopped some of the worst practices, "neither the government, the A.M.A., nor any other organization will give [a woman] any advice as to the relative merits of these products." [89]

George Kosmak and many other doctors had condemned Margaret Sanger in the early days of her activities because they feared that she would bring a flood of quackery in her wake. Mrs. Sanger always had a ready answer: "Just as demand and supply are related to all economic questions, so is propaganda a related part of scientific research in the realms of sex psychology. The medical profession will ultimately meet the issue on the demands of public opinion." [90] In a roundabout way which Mrs. Sanger neither intended nor foresaw, that was what happened in the 1930s. Demand for contraceptives outstripped the supply of medical knowledge and gave rise to a huge birth control industry riddled with quackery and dishonesty. On that sorry product of "public opinion," the organized medical profession did finally, though reluctantly, meet the issue.

As early as 1925, the Section on Obstetrics, Gynecology, and Abdominal Surgery of the American Medical Association, at Dickinson's urging, adopted a resolution requesting amendment of state and federal laws "so that physicians may legally give contraceptive information to their patients." The section referred the resolution to the Board of Trustees in 1927, but they handed it back, noting the "great lack of unanimity of opinion" on the subject. Again, in 1932, the association's executive committee refused a proposal to conduct a study of contraception because birth control was "a controversial subject and the committee be-

89. Randolph Cautley, "Contraceptives in Advertising," article prepared for the Conference on Birth Control and National Recovery, January 15–17, 1934, copy in Population Council; "The Accident of Birth," *Fortune*, February 1938, p. 83; Linsly R. Williams to Mrs. A. Pearson, April 14, 1931, MSP–LC; Elizabeth H. Garrett, "Birth Control's Business Baby," *New Republic*, January 17, 1934, pp. 269–72.

90. Sanger and Stone, *Practice of Contraception*, p. xv.

lieves that it would not be advisable at this time to inject this subject before the profession." [91]

But the growing commercial exploitation of contraception continued forcefully "to inject this subject before the profession." At the 1934 session of the association, a Dr. J. D. Brook pointed to the possible dangers in the "innumerable devices for contraception offered to the public." Backed by several supporting resolutions citing the desperate need for study and regulation, Brook demanded a committee to study the medical aspects of contraception. Still the association refused even to look into the matter.

By 1935, the pressure to take some position on birth control had become overwhelming. Mrs. Sanger had propagandized nearly every member of the AMA's House of Delegates. Doctors sympathetic to birth control pleaded for guidance in the ethics of contraceptive practice and especially in choosing among the hundreds of contraceptive products on the market. All doctors demanded action against the flood of questionably effective and often dangerous devices sold to their patients. Faced with this outcry, the association at last relented and appointed a committee to investigate "contraceptive practices and related problems."

The committee's report in 1936 satisfied no one. While making no judgment on the unethical practices of the contraceptive advertisers, it issued a blast at the relatively respectable birth control organizations. The committee disapproved, it said, "of propaganda directed to the public by lay bodies . . . your committee deplores the support of such agencies by members of the medical profession." With regard to the ethics of indications, the report allowed a long list of medical indications, but dismissed all demographic, eugenic, and especially economic ones. Finally, the report reflected the disappointing state of contraceptive techniques: "Your committee knows of no type of contraception which is reasonably adequate and effective for a large por-

91. R. L. Dickinson to *ABCL*, October 20, 1925, MSP–LC: *JAMA* 88 (1927): 1813; 90 (1928): 1468; 98 (1932): 1897.

tion of the population . . . No contraceptive technic other than actual continence is intrinsically one hundred per cent safe . . . None are dependable for couples who are intoxicated, subnormal, or lacking in self control." Because of the unsatisfactory character of the report, the association instructed the committee to continue its study for another year.

When the committee reported at the 1937 session of the AMA, it manifested an attitude very different from that of 1936. Perhaps because the Second Circuit Court of Appeals had in the meantime clarified the legal status of contraception, perhaps because Margaret Sanger had announced the disbanding of her propaganda organization—the National Committee for Federal Legislation for Birth Control, perhaps because the AMA committee's membership had undergone some changes, the committee submitted a new report which virtually endorsed birth control. It still insisted that clinics be under strict medical supervision, but it refrained from castigating lay organizations in general. Noting the dangers of increasing commercialization of birth control, the committee also asked that the association "undertake the investigation of materials, devices, and methods recommended or employed for the prevention of conception," and report on these investigations to the profession. In order to overcome widespread medical ignorance of contraception the committee asked the association "to promote thorough instruction in our medical schools with respect to the various factors pertaining to fertility and sterility."

Finally, the committee accepted the position Margaret Sanger had been promoting for two decades: that other than pathologic conditions were valid indications for contraception. Medical opinion on permissible indications had been growing more liberal for some time. Doctors at the clinic raid trial in 1929 testified that physicians had come to realize that birth control should be prescribed to ensure the proper spacing of births. Even in normal women, they pointed out, a close succession of pregnancies could destroy good health. In 1935, the *American Journal of Obstetrics and Gynecology* editorially suggested that "sociologists should establish and announce reasons, if such exist, for giving contraceptive advice to individuals." The statement of the AMA committee went far beyond purely medical, and even, in a sense, sociological, indications. Doctors, the committee advised, should no longer insist that contraception be used only in the treatment or prevention of diagnosable disease; they should honor the good faith of their patients who requested birth control. "Voluntary family limitation," the committee said, "is dependent largely on the judgment and wishes of individual parents." [92]

Though Margaret Sanger regarded the indictment of commercial exploitation and the demand for contraceptive education as important victories, she took greatest pleasure in the committee's liberal position on indications. Contrary views on indications had long divided her from otherwise sympathetic physicians. But she had stood her ground and finally won her point. Her old foe, George Kosmak, conceded in 1940 that "the indications, both medical and social, using the latter term in its wider implications, have been established in a more satisfactory manner." [93] Mrs. Sanger, naturally, had not been the only influence in liberalizing medical opinion on the subject. Broadening definitions of health, largely as a result of public health work, and increased legal latitude played important roles. But Mrs. Sanger virtually alone through the years had insisted that birth control was relevant to those expanding conceptions of health; and she had been instrumental in obtaining the legal decisions that made possible wider medical practice of contraception.

Of course, many physicians had backed birth control at considerable risk to their professional reputations. Robert

92. *JAMA* 102 (1934): 2119; 104 (1935): 2336; 106 (1936): 1910–11; 108 (1937): 2217–18. *AJOG* 29 (1935): 460–64. For Mrs. Sanger's attempts to influence the actions of the AMA, see Fred J. Taussig to Margaret Sanger, May 28, 1934, and Prentiss Willson to Margaret Sanger, November 6, 1934, MSP–LC.

93. *AJOG* 40 (1940): 652.

Latou Dickinson put his prestige on the line when he publicly supported Mrs. Sanger, and he and other doctors often thought that if only she would leave them alone they could muster the support of the profession. To be sure, her controversial presence had frightened off many timid physicians, and her stubbornness had often dashed some of Dickinson's most cherished hopes. But for all Dickinson's own courage and dedication, and for all Mrs. Sanger's often unreasoning intransigence, Dickinson could not escape the fact that his profession might have moved even more slowly had it not been for Margaret Sanger.

When the medical profession at last officially endorsed birth control in 1937, many problems remained, especially the continuing lack of an acceptable technique. But the profession had at last taken up its responsibilities as Margaret Sanger had long desired. Undoubtedly many doctors begrudged her her jubilation. But Dickinson, always the gentleman, gave Mrs. Sanger her due. When she received the Town Hall award in 1937, he wired: "Among foremost health measures originating or developing outside medicine like ether under Morton, microbe hunting under Pasteur, nursing under Nightingale, Margaret Sanger's world wide service holds high rank and is destined eventually to fullest medical recognition." [94]

94. Telegram, R. L. Dickinson to Margaret Sanger, January 15, 1937, MSP–LC.

CHAPTER 8

Birth Control and the Law

While Margaret Sanger did battle for birth control with the medical profession, she was also engaged on another front with the law. For more than 20 years after her initial indictment under the Comstock law in 1914, Mrs. Sanger worked to have its statutes nullified either by legislative amendment or judicial interpretation.

The federal Comstock law forbade the mailing, interstate transportation, and importation of contraceptive materials and information.[1] In addition, twenty-two states had "little Comstock laws" which imposed restrictions ranging from New York's confinement of lawful contraception to physicians prescribing "for the cure or prevention of disease," to Massachusetts' prohibition on publishing information and distributing material having to do with contraception, to Connecticut's absolute ban on the "use" of birth control devices. From the beginning of Mrs. Sanger's career until 1930 no court construed the federal statutes with regard to contraception. Nor, with the exception of the New York Court of Appeals' action in Mrs. Sanger's case in 1918, did any state court until 1929 render a decision favorable to the birth control advocates.[2]

1. *United States Code Annotated*, vol. 18, secs. 334, 396 (1927).
2. In Commonwealth v. Allison, 227 Mass. 464 (1917), a Massachusetts court had upheld that state's statutes as a reasonable exercise of the police power. (See ch. 3, n. 17). The Cook County, Illinois, circuit court in 1923 allowed a birth control clinic to open in Chicago in contravention of the strict wording of the *municipal* law. (See *Birth Control and Public Policy*, pamphlet [Chicago: Illinois Birth Control League, 1924]). These apparently were the only other court tests of the state and local laws on contraception.

In the early days of Mrs. Sanger's activity, after the government had dropped its case in the *Woman Rebel* matter, the federal statutes did little to impede her work. She could still legally use the mails to advocate contraception, though not to describe it; and when she actually violated the law by sending plaintive correspondents the addresses of sympathetic doctors, the postal authorities apparently chose to pay no heed.

The state laws were another matter. They directly retarded the establishment of clinics and in some cases thwarted the organization of local leagues to propagandize for birth control. Beginning in 1917, Mrs. Sanger and others repeatedly tried to change those laws, especially in New York. When she had defined birth control as a class issue, Mrs. Sanger had employed the anarchist tactic of direct action, ignoring or deliberately flouting the law. But by 1917, she was moving toward a new definition of her aims in which illegality was inappropriate. Success and support now depended on bringing birth control under the protection of the law. The Brownsville clinic trial confirmed the warnings of her advisers that any attempt to secure a judicial interpretation of the obscenity statutes as unconstitutional was futile. "The law is certainly constitutional," wrote William J. Robinson, "as is any law that is or can be made to appear in the interests of the morals, the welfare and perpetuity of the race. This is not the line on which the law can be fought." [3] She would have to fight in the legislatures, not in the courts. For a season, in 1917, she agreed with Mary Ware Dennett and the National Birth Control League that reform should be sought under the banner of free speech. Accordingly, she supported Mrs. Dennett's amendment, which would have removed the words "for the prevention of conception" from the enumerated list of obscene matters in the New York obscenity statutes.

By 1918, however, Mrs. Sanger had developed a differ-

3. William J. Robinson to "King," April 4, 1917, MSP–LC.

ent idea of the proper form of legislative relief. In January of that year, Judge Crane liberally construed the New York law allowing physicians the right to prescribe contraception "for the cure or prevention of disease." But that opinion still made the legality of contraception dependent on its intended purpose. For other than strictly medical ends, birth control continued to be classified as obscene and unlawful. Judge Crane's decision, said Mrs. Sanger, "does not mean that we are satisfied. We are not." [4] She wanted contraception to be legal for whatever purpose—medical, economic, social, or purely personal. Crane's decision, however, convinced Mrs. Sanger that her best prospect lay in a legislative amendment that would keep control of contraception in medical hands.

Consequently, Mrs. Sanger suggested retaining the enumeration of contraception in the general obscenity statutes. But in Section 1145, which excepted physicians, her amendment struck out the words "for the cure or prevention of disease"; she would retain medical control, while vastly expanding the doctor's discretion. This bill came to be known as the "doctors-only bill," as opposed to Mrs. Dennett's "open bill," which called for simple repeal of the obscenity statutes as they applied to contraception. Mrs. Dennett denounced the doctors-only bill as class legislation which would establish a "medical monopoly" and violate the principles of free speech. In her view, no woman should have to rely on a doctor for contraceptive information nor should any sexual subject continue to be legally designated as obscene. Mrs. Dennett both underestimated the necessity for medical attention to contraception and unrealistically appraised the chances for legislative reform. Mrs. Sanger, by contrast, recognized that contraceptive information "should be given by the kind of persons best suited by training and experience to give it scientifically and accurately. If everyone is permitted to impart information, those who receive it have no guarantee that it is correct or suitable to the individual's phys-

4. Margaret Sanger to Mrs. Wilshire, October 25, 1929, MSP–SS.

ical requirements." [5] She also knew that however laudable the claims of free speech, no legislature was as likely to tamper with its obscenity laws as it was to broaden the scope of medical practice.

Mrs. Sanger succeeded in having the doctors-only bill introduced in the New York legislature in 1921. In 1923, Samuel I. Rosenman—who would in a few years help organize Franklin Roosevelt's first brain trust—sponsored it, and thereafter the bill appeared in every legislative session save one until 1929, always without success. Similar bills met similar fates in sporadic attempts at legislative reform in Connecticut, Pennsylvania, Massachusetts, New Jersey, and California. By the end of the 1920s, no state legislature had altered its statutes on contraception.[6]

Mrs. Dennett persisted with her open bill in New York in 1919, but to no avail. Her failure that year marked the death of the National Birth Control League. No sooner had the NBCL disappeared, however, than Mrs. Dennett formed the Voluntary Parenthood League, with a single, new objective: to remove contraception from the ban of the federal obscenity statutes. Mrs. Dennett later wrote that there had been too much "beating around the bush with State legislation." On the model of the women's suffrage movement, in which Mrs. Dennett had participated, she abandoned the time-consuming, costly, piecemeal effort of state-by-state reform. The federal law, she believed, was the precedent on which state laws were modeled; its eradication would not only allow the free circulation of information and material through the mails; it would also facilitate repeal of the twenty-two remaining restrictive state laws.[7]

5. *Birth Control Review,* April 1918, p. 6; July 1919, p. 8.

6. American Birth Control League, "Laws on Birth Control in the U.S.A.," pamphlet, n.d.; Mary Ware Dennett, *Birth Control Laws: Shall We Keep Them or Abolish Them?* (New York: Frederick H. Hitchcock, 1926), pp. 72–93.

7. See Eleanor Flexner, *Century of Struggle: The Woman's Rights Movement in the United States* (Cambridge: Harvard University Press,

In July 1919, Mrs. Dennett and her co-workers went to Washington to interview potential sponsors for their open bill. After three years of effort, they found a willing legislator at last in Albert B. Cummins, a progressive Republican from Iowa. On January 10, 1923, he placed it in the Senate hopper during the lame-duck session of the Sixty-seventh Congress. Referred to the Judiciary Committee, it died there without a hearing or vote. The following year, Cummins secured a hearing for the bill, but it went unreported. In the Sixty-eighth Congress, the Senate Subcommittee on the Judiciary reported the bill without recommendation, assuring its doom on the Senate floor. Parallel bills sponsored by Congressman William N. Vaile of Colorado fared no better in the House.[8]

By the time of the hearings on the Cummins-Vaile bill in the spring of 1924, Mrs. Dennett had drawn considerable attention to birth control as a political issue on the national level. To her dismay, she had also set the adversary system in operation. Groups opposed to the bill organized nationally to resist its passage. Representatives of various Roman Catholic lay organizations appeared at the hearings and wrote to congressmen to register their opposition. In early 1926, anticipating another attempt to pass the bill, the Catholic, Episcopal, and Lutheran churches were reportedly planning joint action against it. And the doctors, from whom Mrs. Dennett requested "medical endorsement, but not medical monopoly," questioned the wisdom of repealing outright all regulation of contraception.[9]

Robert Latou Dickinson perceived the threat that the open bill posed to his prospects of taking over the Clinical Research Bureau in New York. Religious leaders, aroused to concerted opposition by the bill, would certainly subvert the Maternity Research Council's license application

Belknap Press, 1959), p. 222; Mary Ware Dennett, *Birth Control Laws*, pp. 92–95.

8. Dennett, *Birth Control Laws*, pp. 92–122, 294–98.

9. Dennett, *Birth Control Laws*, pp. 123–65; *Los Angeles Times*, January 22, 1926, *Rochester Herald*, February 7, 1926, clippings, MSP–LC; Annie G. Porritt to Mary Ware Dennett, June 15, 1922, MSP–LC.

before the State Board of Charities. On the other hand, many Protestant clergymen who considered joining the Catholics against the Cummins-Vaile bill looked with some favor on the more responsible doctors-only type of legislation. Therefore Dickinson pointedly informed the churches that neither he nor Mrs. Sanger nor the clinic nor the ABCL had anything to do with the open bill. Similarly, in a letter to the editor of the *Journal of the American Medical Association,* Dickinson reassured his medical colleagues that "the Sanger group seems to have taken no part" in the Cummins-Vaile bill. "In conference with our committee's legal advisors," he wrote, "the ABCL agreed to push such amendments as the one passed in May by the American Gynecological Society"—i.e. a doctors-only bill along the lines of the old New York amendment.[10]

Mrs. Sanger had broken with Mrs. Dennett's legislative program in 1918. In 1925, eager to preserve her fragile links to Dickinson and the medical profession, she dissented from Mrs. Dennett's position more loudly than ever. "To open the U.S. mails for the mothers on the pretext of giving them safe, reliable information is a false assumption," she said. With some prescience she added: "It would only enable them to be exploited through advertisements, quacks, and charlatans." At Dickinson's urging, she sent Anne Kennedy to Washington in early 1926 to explore possible ABCL sponsorship of a federal doctors-only bill. Dickinson hoped to undercut the threatened Protestant-Catholic coalition and hold firm the lines of his medical support by demonstrating clearly the ABCL's opposition to the dangerous open bill, and its espousal of a responsible amendment retaining tight medical control.

But Mrs. Kennedy found the national legislators no more willing to deal with birth control than were those in New York, regardless of the wording of the proposal. And with the breakdown of Mrs. Dennett's Washington operation in

10. R. L. Dickinson to MRC members, February 26, 1926, Population Council; *JAMA* 85 (1925): 1153–54; R. L. Dickinson to Dr. Samuel W. Lambert, February 25, 1926, R. L. Dickinson to John Gardner Murray, January 22, 1926, Population Council.

1926 and the growing improbability of a favorable out-
come to the clinic negotiations in New York, the urgent
need for an alternative federal bill evaporated. Five months
after she had arrived, Mrs. Kennedy closed the Washington
office, thus ending for several years all efforts at legislative
reform on the federal level.[11]

Three years after her unsuccessful expedition, however,
Mrs. Kennedy was back in Washington, looking for new
headquarters for Margaret Sanger, who in early 1929 was
a general without an army. Mrs. Sanger's separation from
the ABCL and the *Birth Control Review* in late 1928 had
left her with no organizational instrument save the Clinical
Research Bureau, which was constrained to operate in
silence, and which Mrs. Sanger at least considered relin-
quishing to Dr. Dickinson. With such limited institutional
connections, she could not hope to hold the position of
preeminence she had so laboriously gained in the birth
control movement. She needed a new organization, with
a new task; and when the uncle of her old friend Juliet
Rublee proposed to give Mrs. Sanger a large sum of money
"to start some big thing—a broadening out of the work,"
she decided upon a big thing indeed: a nationally organized lobbying effort to amend the federal Comstock
law.[12] A national legislative campaign would give Mrs.
Sanger an even larger arena for her energies than had the
ABCL. Characteristically, out of the setbacks and embarrassments of 1928, Mrs. Sanger emerged triumphant in
1929. She never remained long diminished. In the Chicago
home of Mrs. Benjamin Carpenter, the National Committee
on Federal Legislation for Birth Control was established in
April with Mrs. Sanger as chairman.[13]

11. Margaret Sanger to Annie Porritt, December 16, 1925, MSP–LC;
Birth Control Review, March 1924, pp. 68–69; report on 1926 "federal
work," n.d. MSP–LC.

12. Juliet Rublee to Margaret Sanger, August 1, 1928, MSP–SS.

13. *A New Day Dawns for Birth Control*, pamphlet (New York:
National Committee on Federal Legislation for Birth Control, 1937),
p. 16; *Birth Control Review*, October 1929, p. 278.

The National Committee owed its origins both to the imperatives of Mrs. Sanger's personal ambition and to her altered assessment of the most effective type of birth control organization. In Mrs. Sanger's eyes, the situation had changed since Mrs. Kennedy had reported from Washington in 1926 that she should forsake legislative reform for "educational work." It was no longer, she believed, a question of choosing between legislation and education. The ABCL was approaching the limits of its efficacy as an educational tool. Though its program of conferences and lectures had reached and persuaded perhaps millions of middle-class Americans, many millions more remained ignorant or apathetic. Even the convinced kept their opinions, for the most part, private. The National Committee, therefore, by placing the issue of birth control on the forum of congressional politics, could reach a far larger audience than had the ABCL. And the committee could now demand public confirmation of private belief in the form of resolutions supporting the proposed federal amendment. The National Committee would thereby raise and broaden the level of public discussion of birth control. Most importantly, Mrs. Sanger believed that the "Congressional Campaign," as she called it, would greatly increase the involvement of the committed.

Mrs. Sanger also felt by 1929 that the birth control movement had reached the point where it could make no further progress under the pall of potential federal prosecution. Dependence on the good will of federal attorneys no longer sufficed. Despite the infrequency of federal interference, the ever-present threat of possible legal retaliation forestalled many—especially doctors—from taking an active part in the movement. Though doctors probably exaggerated the government's inclination to prosecute, the existence of the federal statutes undoubtedly confused the legal atmosphere, leading many cautious physicians to believe that contraception was illegal even where state laws allowed it. (The federal laws, of course, applied only to use of the mails, to interstate transport, and to importation.) The statutes occasionally hampered the dissemination of contraceptive knowledge throughout the medical profession. Some medical journals refused articles on contraception, because, in the words of one editor, "our journal would be unmailable" with such material included. In December 1929, fourteen Chicago physicians protested the "absurdity" of omitting contraceptive information from medical textbooks in order to keep them mailable. They also blamed the repressive legal atmosphere for the absence of contraceptive instruction in medical schools.[14]

As would become clear in a few years, however, Mrs. Sanger and some of her medical associates in 1929 overestimated the repressive effects of the Comstock law on medical prescription of contraception. So too did Mrs. Sanger misjudge the prospects for judicial, as distinguished from legislative, relief. In a characteristic choice for the dramatic over the deliberate, she resolved to go ahead with a massive congressional lobbying effort.

In a move that quietly marked the distance the birth control movement had come since her frantic protests of 1914, Mrs. Sanger hired a professional consulting firm in 1929 to advise her on the organizational and financial aspects of mounting a federal lobbying campaign. The firm, the John Price Jones Corporation, reported that the anticipated campaign would be handicapped by the continuing dissension in the movement about the proper form of legislative amendment. Although the Voluntary Parenthood League was defunct, Mrs. Dennett still promoted the idea of an open bill. Mrs. Sanger, in spite of her earlier recognition of the superior merits of the doctors-only bill, apparently toyed briefly in 1929 with the idea of an amendment along the lines of the old Cummins-Vaile measure. She did so, perhaps, in an effort to swell the recently reduced ranks of her support; but by 1930 she had finally and firmly committed herself to the same sort of doctors-

14. Gregory Stragnell, editor, *Medical Journal and Record*, to Margaret Sanger, December 1, 1925, MSP–SS; "Statement by fourteen Chicago physicians," December 5, 1929, MSP–LC.

only amendment she had endorsed in New York since 1918. In doing so, she alienated some of her backers—including Mrs. Benjamin Carpenter. But such losses were tolerable. The doctors-only bill would unquestionably protect the national health and welfare better than the open bill. And by adopting the restricted form of amendment Mrs. Sanger shrewdly gathered medical support behind her and appealed also to the cautiously limited liberalism emerging in the Protestant churches.[15]

The consulting firm further warned that the proposed federal campaign would take more money than Mrs. Sanger could command. But the consultants misjudged Mrs. Sanger's phenomenal fund-raising abilities. Her own husband would give tens of thousands of dollars to the work; and her career over the past fifteen years had brought her friendships with some of the nation's wealthiest men and women. When the conversation turned to money, Margaret Sanger could still display the charm and persuasion that had swayed so many audiences on her early lecture tours. From 1932 to 1936, among the worst years of the depression, she and her chief financial assistant, Mrs. Ida Timme, raised more than $150,000 to carry on the federal work. Much of it came from small contributors, but Mrs. Sanger also listed such philanthropists as George Eastman and the Rockefellers among her special benefactors.[16]

Finally, Mrs. Sanger's professional advisers counseled against the federal lobbying effort because it would take too long to "educate" a Congress preoccupied with the depression. Energy could best be spent, they advised, in reuniting the splintered birth control movement, preferably under a leader other than Mrs. Sanger. To that she

15. Report of the John Price Jones Corporation, September 15, 1930; Mrs. Benjamin Carpenter to Margaret Sanger, March 13, 1930, MSP–LC.

16. *A New Day Dawns for Birth Control,* p. 45; John D. Rockefeller, Jr., to National Committee on Federal Legislation for Birth Control, January 2, 1935; Margaret Sanger to George Eastman, November 20, 1929, MSP–LC; Sanger, *Autobiography,* p. 417.

reacted predictably, protesting against the recommendation
that she remove herself from "a position which years of
study, work and consecration has made unique." She had
already consolidated support behind the doctors-only bill;
she would get the necessary money; and she would soon
turn the depression itself into an argument in support of
her cause. She went to Washington in 1930 with a group
of her most devoted personal followers, and in early 1931
opened the National Committee's headquarters at 1343
H Street.[17]

The committee began to build a nationwide organization
with a twofold educational and legislative program. The
committee's strategy was designed to bring the pressure of
public opinion to bear on congressmen both collectively
and individually. The nerve-center of the organization was
the national headquarters in Washington, run by a professional staff which included a salaried minister, a doctor,
and a social worker. That office supervised a tightly inte-
grated operation broken down along regional, state, and
local lines. Each of the four national regions had a director
responsible to Washington headquarters. In every state
a director reported to the regional office. The state directors
oversaw local workers in a system parallel to the organization
of congressional districts. Nearly all the workers at all levels
were women; but in a significant shift from the early days
of the ABCL, many of those women were paid professionals.
In addition to the headquarters staff of trained lobbyists
and organizers, the committee also employed several fieldworkers at salaries up to $300 a month.[18]

The committee utilized many of the same basic propaganda techniques as the ABCL. In 1929, Mrs. Sanger published some of the most heart-rending letters she had re-

17. Margaret Sanger to John Price Jones Corporation, October 8,
1930, MSP–LC; *A New Day Dawns for Birth Control*, p. 16.

18. *A New Day Dawns for Birth Control*, p. 25; National Committee,
Budget, September, 1934 to September, 1935, and "California" folder
in State Files, MSP–LC. In 1934–35, the committee employed ten fieldworkers at $300 a month and thirty-one volunteer fieldworkers.

ceived over the years from desperate mothers, under the title *Motherhood in Bondage*. The committee sent hundreds, perhaps thousands, of copies of the book to civic and political leaders throughout the country and supplemented this appeal to sentiment with a flood of information sheets marshaling facts and statistics to show the relevance of birth control to economic and health problems. The committee also established a lecture bureau, which arranged nearly 2,000 speeches on birth control during the seven years of its existence. And Mrs. Sanger used local, regional, and national conferences on a regular basis to galvanize public interest and maintain the morale of her organization.

The National Committee increased the effectiveness of the old propaganda with vastly superior organization. The centralization of authority that replaced the loose federal structure of the ABCL enabled the committee to mobilize thousands of workers within days for such tasks as fundraising and letter-writing. So tight was the committee's discipline that when its legislative secretary wrote a single unauthorized letter to the Post Office, inquiring about the postal law, she was "rebuked," as Mrs. Sanger wrote her, "for going ahead on your own and not consulting." In the field, the committee's workers were not content merely to arrange a lecture for a local club; they would then cajole the group to pass a resolution endorsing the proposed federal amendment. Often a fieldworker would present the local organization with a form resolution drafted by the National Committee staff in Washington. If a particular body resisted the persuasion of the lecturer and the importuning of the fieldworker, Mrs. Sanger called upon her old radical lessons and counseled discreet "boring from within": the fieldworker should join the organization in question and work quietly but tenaciously to bring it into line. Though local women's clubs were among her primary targets, Mrs. Sanger also sent her agents to nearly every church convention and medical gathering in the country from 1930 to 1936. Wherever they were allowed, committee fieldworkers set up displays, buttonholed delegates, explained, refuted, and begged in the interests of the federal bill. Highly motivated, superbly organized, and soon becoming skilled in the corridor techniques of professional lobbyists, Mrs. Sanger's deputies by 1936 produced nearly a thousand resolutions from organizations large and small favoring the federal amendment.[19]

While the workers in the field were starting their seven-year barrage of resolutions and memorials from all over the country, committee headquarters in Washington concentrated its fire on individual congressmen, senators, and representatives of business, labor, and religious groups. Mrs. Sanger and her assistants, especially Mrs. Hazel Moore and a retired army colonel, J. J. Toy, one of the few men on the committee's payroll, relentlessly went the rounds of Washington offices, explaining their bill, feeling out the depths and edges of the support and the opposition. At the end of 1930, after months of canvassing, they found a sponsor for their bill in Senator Frederick Huntington Gillett, a Massachusetts Republican.

In many ways, Senator Gillett's sponsorship typified the political difficulties the National Committee experienced during its seven years in Washington. Gillett was only a few months away from eighty years of age when he agreed to introduce the bill. Though he had served sixteen terms in the House, in 1930 he was just finishing his first term as a senator. He did not stand for reelection in 1930, and by the time the bill came to a hearing in February 1931, he was an elderly lame-duck senator, without power or influence. In the next three Congresses, Mrs. Sanger's committee had similar misfortune. In the Seventy-second Congress, the bill was sponsored by a second-term Demo-

19. Margaret Sanger to Hazel Moore, October 11, 1935, MSP–SS. See the detailed correspondence between Gladys DeLancey Smith and Margaret Sanger, MSP–LC, for an account of the activities of a fieldworker and her relations with the national office. See especially the memo, Gladys DeLancey Smith to Bernice Wickham, November 14, 1936.

cratic representative from North Carolina, Franklin W. Hancock, and by a politically innocent freshman Republican senator from West Virginia, Henry Drury Hatfield, whom Mrs. Sanger considered a great boon to the cause because he was a surgeon. In the famous New Deal Congresses, the Seventy-third and Seventy-fourth, Mrs. Sanger secured as a sponsor Delaware Senator Daniel Oren Hastings, an outspoken, anti-New Deal freshman Republican whose political influence was measured by his showing in the 1936 election when he ran behind Landon in Delaware. In the House, the bill was sponsored in both Congresses by a seventy-two-year-old Democrat first elected in 1932, Walter M. Pierce, from Oregon. Mrs. Sanger had to settle for such impotent political allies because birth control, in spite of quietly growing public acceptance, was still such an explosive subject that most politicians preferred to avoid it.[20]

Knowing that, Mrs. Sanger was at first led to a curious political strategy: she would try to secure passage of her bill in the lame-duck session of Congress. There, she believed, many congressmen were insulated, by virtue of their recent defeat, from the pressures of electoral politics. Therefore, they were free to vote as their consciences dictated, she reasoned, and no one in good conscience could vote against birth control. In fact, the lame ducks were notoriously powerless to influence any legislation except to block it by filibuster. But Mrs. Sanger's naïve view of American political institutions and simple faith in the self-evident righteousness of the cause dominated the committee's early legislative program. The committee thus de-emphasized political pressure and concentrated on simply enlightening congressmen—especially lame ducks. The preoccupation with lame ducks in the committee's early years retarded a more positive exercise of the old suffragist political tactic of threatened reprisal—a tactic for which the

20. *Biographical Dictionary of the American Congress, 1774–1961* (Washington: Government Printing Office, 1961), pp. 946, 1001, 1023, 1022, 1458; *New York Times*, November 8, 1936, p. 3.

splendid organization of the National Committee left it well equipped.[21]

By 1932, however, the agitation for the Twentieth Amendment abolishing the short congressional session convinced Mrs. Sanger that she should abandon the fatuous lame-duck strategy. The National Committee then began fully to utilize its network of workers and sympathizers to exert maximum political influence on Congress. Having secured only 17 endorsements from various organizations in 1931, the committee obtained 116 in 1932, and hundreds more in the next four years. Mobilizing its representatives in the congressional districts, the committee applied forceful pressure to congressmen on key committees. When Emanuel Celler, for instance, was appointed to the House Judiciary Committee, before which the birth control bill was pending, Washington headquarters instructed the fieldworker in his district to "bring pressure to bear on him immediately. Will you please get signatures from his district. . . . This looks like house to house canvassing." [22] An Illinois representative on the Ways and Means Committee, which considered the bill in 1932, reported receiving "hundreds" of letters from constituents urging approval, and an Indiana senator in the same year had to draft a form reply to his voluminous pro-birth control mail. Dozens of other members of Congress received thousands of similar appeals during the years of the "Congressional Campaign." [23]

Obviously, Mrs. Sanger's committee mounted a far broader, more militant campaign than had Mrs. Dennett's Voluntary Parenthood League. So too did Mrs. Sanger evoke a proportionally larger countervailing movement than had Mrs. Dennett. The National Catholic Welfare Conference

21. Minutes of the Board of Managers, Clinical Research Bureau, October 31, 1932, MSP–LC.

22. Hazel Moore to Martha Vandevere, January 30, 1935, MSP–SS.

23. Margaret Sanger, speech at "Birth Control Comes of Age Dinner," February 12, 1935, copy in MSP–LC.

—composed of all the American bishops, run by a secretariat in Washington, D.C., and designed to oversee the interests of the Catholic church in America—had in Mrs. Dennett's case merely sent a few speakers across town to testify against the Cummins-Vaile bill.[24] But in Mrs. Sanger the NCWC faced a more formidable opponent, and Monsignor John A. Ryan, head of the Social Action Department, had to throw a formidable opposition against her. While the committee mustered almost a thousand endorsements from medical, religious, and social groups, the NCWC produced at least as many petitions from Catholic lay organizations protesting birth control legislation. And at the congressional hearings on the various birth control bills—there were five hearings between 1931 and 1934—the NCWC matched the National Committee witness for witness.

Those hearings provided the forum for a running four-year dialogue between Mrs. Sanger and the chiefly Catholic opposition on the merits of birth control. At the first hearing, before the Senate Judiciary Committee in 1931, Mrs. Sanger spoke of the need for proper medical service to lessen the high rates of maternal and infant mortality. J. Whitridge Williams, obstetrician in chief of Johns Hopkins Hospital, described the difficulty, under the current law, of providing that service when it involved contraception. Mrs. Sanger's other witnesses spoke of eugenics and overpopulation, but the burden of the proponents' testimony emphasized the benefits of birth control to the individual and the family.

The opposition commenced with a canard by a Washington attorney, Ralph H. Burton, who insinuated that the proposed legislation was a subversive plot by the Soviet government "to undermine the moral standards of the coming generation." Representative John W. McCormack of Massachusetts and several other spokesmen, both Catholic and non-Catholic, repeatedly warned of the danger the proposed amendment held for national morals and

24. Dennett, *Birth Control Laws*, pp. 123–65.

family life. Also citing the dangers of immorality, the NCWC and another Massachusetts congressman, John J. Douglas, presented long lists of Catholic organizations opposed to the birth control bill.[25]

At the 1932 hearings in the House, the bill got little help from its sponsor, Franklin Hancock, who said he had "reached no definite and determined view relative to its merits." Mrs. Sanger again claimed that its merits lay in the protection of individual health and the legalization of required medical services. In rebuttal, religious spokesmen, mostly Catholic, repeated their arguments about immorality and the weakening of the family. And again, each side submitted hundreds of petitions in support of its case. Before the hearings had ended, the antagonists had forsaken exposition for invective. Representative McCormack, sitting on the Ways and Means Committee, which took evidence on the bill, accused one witness, Charlotte Perkins Gilman, of making "an attack on the Catholic Church." In the Senate hearings, Canon William Sheafe Chase, an Episcopal clergyman, calling the amendment a "crook's bill," implied that Mrs. Sanger had a pecuniary motive in wanting to open the mails. Mrs. Sanger herself could not resist questioning the credibility of an opposition witness because she was a "childless woman." As had the Senate bill in 1931, both the House and Senate proposals in 1932 died in committee.[26]

In the Senate judiciary subcommittee which sat for hearings on the 1932 bill, Senator Warren R. Austin, a Vermont Republican, cast the deciding vote against a favorable recommendation. His published report repeatedly mentioned the findings of the President's Research Committee on Social Trends in the United States. Those find-

25. U.S., Congress, Senate, Subcommittee of the Committee on the Judiciary, *Birth Control, Hearings on S. 4582*, 71st Cong., 3d sess., 1931.
26. U.S., Congress, House, Committee on Ways and Means, *Birth Control, Extracts from Hearings on H.R. 11082*, 72d Cong., 1st sess., U.S., Congress, Senate, Subcommittee of the Committee on the Judiciary, *Birth Control, Hearings on S. 4436*, 72d Cong., 1st sess., 1932.

ings, he said, had furnished him with "persuasive facts" which had led him to oppose the birth control bill. He cited

> the declining rate of growth of population resulting from the practice of contraception, the economic aspects of agriculture and industry damaged by the decline of the birth rate, the injury to the great group called "labor" [the A.F. of L. had officially protested the birth control bills in 1931 and 1932] and the conflict of the idea of encouraging and facilitating the use of more effective contraceptive practices with the population policy of the United States as influenced by the prevailing depression.[27]

Monsignor Ryan had mentioned the effect of the declining birthrate on the building trades and real estate business in his Senate testimony, but the hearings had generally revolved around the supposedly opposite poles of individual well-being and national morality. Austin's discussion of the relation of birth control to national economic policy sounded a new note.

Margaret Sanger heard that note and was quick to act on it. Nothing she had said so far had swayed "the boneheads, spineless and brainless," as in her exasperation she called the august congressmen. Now she shifted her emphasis. At the next hearing, in January 1934, Monsignor Ryan noted that Mrs. Sanger had moved "from the individual to social grounds. At most hearings previously, the plight of the individual, the individual mother, and the individual family was stressed, and the necessity therefore of bringing contraceptive methods and information to such a person." Now Mrs. Sanger contended that birth control could help relieve the depression.[28] "Population," she said, "is

27. U.S., Congress, Senate, Committee on the Judiciary, *Birth Control, Report to Accompany S-4436*, 72d Cong., 2d sess., Committee Print, copy in MSP–SS.

28. U.S., Congress, House, Committee on the Judiciary, *Birth Control, Hearings on H.R. 5978*, 73d Cong., 2d sess., 1934, p. 150.

pressing upon the relief agencies, upon the dole, upon the other fellow's job. . . . What is to become of the children? of the millions whose parents are today unemployed?" [29] She had evidence submitted before the House Judiciary Committee that families without any employed worker in the household had a birthrate 48 percent higher in 1932 than those with one or more employed workers. Not only did that high birthrate work a hardship on the unemployed; it also swelled the relief rolls, placing the ultimate financial burden on the taxpayers.[30] Making birth control information available to the poor, said Mrs. Sanger, would alleviate misery, ease unemployment, and reduce taxes.

Monsignor Ryan and the NCWC spokesmen made vigorous rebuttal to those arguments. Ryan, an ardent supporter of the New Deal, was just as dedicated a social reformer in his own right as was Mrs. Sanger. To see birth control as a means of reducing the numbers of the unemployed, said Ryan, was a "fantastic" idea. "If we are not well on the way to recovery from this depression by the time any considerable number of children could be born, after the enactment of this bill, then we better get ready for something else in the social order, or a social revolution." [31] And, he added, further reducing the birthrate

29. Speech at "Birth Control Comes of Age Dinner," February 12, 1935, copy in MSP–LC.

30. *Hearings on H.R. 5978*, pp. 76, 11, 69.

31. *Hearings on H.R. 5978*, p. 154. These sentiments were more than mere rhetoric. Although Mrs. Sanger charged later that Ryan was an amateur economist, he had in fact been an influential Catholic voice on political economy for nearly 20 years. In 1919 he authored *Social Reconstruction: A General Review of the Problems and Survey of Remedies,* suggesting such things as minimum-wage legislation, unemployment, health and old-age insurance, public housing, recognition and legal protection of labor's right to organize, and child labor legislation. John T. Noonan says that "he was at his best on social and economic questions." Noonan adds that on birth control, Ryan "did not like to be more rigorous than he felt constrained to be by authority." On April 15, 1932, Father Ryan conferred with Colonel J. J. Toy of the National Committee and spoke favorably about the "doctors' bill." He reportedly viewed strict medical control of contra-

would positively harm, rather than help, economic recovery. In his view, reduced population growth in the United States and Western Europe underlay the agricultural and industrial crises. Smaller populations, or populations growing less rapidly than in the past, spelled decreased consumption, reduced production, and hence greater unemployment.

Ryan quoted at length the noted statistician for the Metropolitan Life Insurance Company Louis I. Dublin, who had long been the nemesis of the pro-birth control population theorists. In numerous books and articles throughout the 1920s Dublin had contended that the American birthrate was dropping toward the point at which the population would fail to maintain, much less raise, its numerical level. In 1930 he concluded that "the effective fertility of our population is separated by a closer margin from the minimum consistent with undiminished numbers than appears on the surface . . . any further

---

ception as a means of stopping drugstore sales of contraceptives. Toy quoted Ryan as saying: "Of course you understand that the Catholic Church can take no conciliatory attitude publicly or officially towards birth control. It would be misunderstood. The press would play havoc with the situation. I think that Mr. Montavon's [of the National Catholic Welfare Conference Legal Department] suggestion that we find a Catholic doctor who might confer with Senator Hatfield [to draft a bill acceptable to Catholics] is a good one." Ryan further suggested that since the church could not make its views known officially, the National Committee could use Edward F. McGrady, lobbyist for the American Federation of Labor and a prominent Catholic, as "a way of getting the right word to the Catholic strength in the House and in the Senate. Now remember that this must be held most confidentially. Any knowledge of my accepting your proposal becoming public would upset everything and create a continuation of controversy and animosity even greater than that which exists now." Despite such conciliatory offers, however, Margaret Sanger continued to regard Fr. Ryan as her arch foe (Report of Col. J. J. Toy, April 15, 1932, MSP–LC). See John Tracy Ellis, *American Catholicism* (Chicago: University of Chicago Press, 1963), pp. 142–43; and John T. Noonan, Jr., *Contraception* (Cambridge: Harvard University Press, Belknap Press, 1965), pp. 422–23. See also Francis Lyons Broderick, *Right Reverend New Dealer, John A. Ryan* (New York: Macmillan, 1963).

decline in fertility would, in the absence of immigration, mean *ultimately* a diminishing population." By 1934, Dublin's influential authority was being incorporated into the "underconsumptionist" theory of the Depression. According to that theory, economic collapse resulted from an insufficiency of purchasing power. Though most of its proponents agreed that the insufficiency stemmed mainly from an uneven distribution of income, many, especially agricultural theorists, laid heavy stress on the slowdown in population growth. The specter of a static or shrinking population haunted economic discussion in the early 1930s. It could be seen in Franklin Roosevelt's Commonwealth Club address in 1932, in Henry Wallace's speeches and writings, and in the questions of the very congressmen taking testimony on Mrs. Sanger's bill. Monsignor Ryan invoked that specter when he told the congressmen that more birth control meant less chance for recovery.[32]

Mrs. Sanger's witnesses, in reply, submitted statements by Wesley C. Mitchell, Robert S. Lynd, and other social scientists, who admitted the decline in the birthrate but minimized its general economic hazards. They warned, however, that "there is danger that legal obstacles to the

32. Louis I. Dublin and Alfred J. Lotka, "The True Rate of Natural Increase of the Population of the United States," in *Metron* 8 (1930): 119. Dublin later realized that he "had approached the population question on the wrong foot." He regretted the fact that he had pointed with alarm to the difference in native and immigrant birthrates: "The implication was certainly there that the newer immigrants and their families were somehow or other of inferior quality when compared with the earlier settlers. . . . But there was no evidence to justify an assumption that the country was being seriously weakened by the recent influx. I realized that I had fallen into the old racial trap and that I had to make amends for the false impression I had given." Dublin also later recognized that his prognosis in 1930 of a declining population was mistaken, and he worked throughout the ensuing decades to call attention to the population explosion. Louis I. Dublin, *After Eighty Years* (Gainesville: University of Florida Press, 1966), p. 140. See also Arthur M. Schlesinger, Jr., *The Crisis of the Old Order, 1919–1933* (Boston: Houghton Mifflin, 1956), pp. 425–26; for Wallace's views, see *Hearings on H.R. 5978*, pp. 151–52, and the questions of Representative Arthur Healey, pp. 40, 58.

democratic spread of birth control information may confine the slower growth in numbers mainly to the relatively
well-to-do classes. Farmers and wage earners surely will
have trouble if they continue to increase at the present rate
while the growth of the total population declines." [33]

The senators, if they heeded at all the arguments before
them, evidently put greater stock in Mrs. Sanger's discussion
of class differences and the high cost of relief than they
did in Ryan's appeal for social reform and greater consuming power. They probably paid even more heed to
Mrs. Sanger's increasingly adroit political maneuvers. She
intensified her pressure on Congress at the outset of the
1934 hearings by scheduling one of her biggest national
conferences, on "Birth Control and National Recovery,"
in Washington at the same time the House hearings began.
The conference generated much favorable publicity and
drew to Washington hundreds of delegates, many of whom
were sent to call on their congressmen. Mrs. Sanger's
lawyers also made a concession to states' rights sentiment
when they amended the birth control bill along the lines
of the Webb-Kenyon act, explicitly rendering the proposed statute inapplicable in those states that already had
anticontraception legislation. Goaded by those moves and
the growing agitation the National Committee was mounting all over the country, the Senate Judiciary Committee,
hoping to get the importuning ladies off its back, reported out the bill and it went on the Senate calendar.[34]

It came up on the last day of the session, June 13, 1934,
and, probably contrary to the Judiciary Committee's expectation, passed in a rush of unanimous votes in the last
hours of the day, just as the Comstock bill which it
amended had passed sixty years earlier. Within minutes,
however, Nevada's Senator Pat McCarran, who had been
off the floor when the bill passed, entered the chamber and
asked for unanimous consent that the vote be reconsidered

33. *Hearings on H.R. 5978*, pp. 61–66.
34. *A New Day Dawns for Birth Control*, p. 23; *Hearings on S. 1842*,
p. 3.

and the bill go over to the next session. Senator Hastings, the bill's sponsor, admitting that the bill would never pass the House in any case, bowed to the traditions of senatorial courtesy and acceded to McCarran's request. The short-lived victory embittered Mrs. Sanger's workers. Hazel Moore, the legislative secretary of the National Committee, had watched the proceedings from the Senate gallery. After McCarran's maneuver she could not contain her ire; as she reported later, she accosted the sergeant at arms of the Senate, and when McCarran passed them she said:

> "Sergeant, arrest this man." "What are the charges?" said the sergeant. "Murder of thousands of women," said I. McCarran laughed and said "I had to object to that bill . . . because I do not believe in murder." To which I answered "Are you accusing us who are backing this bill of being in favor of murder?" "That's what it is," said McCarran. I then said to the Sergeant, "Arrest him for libel," and started on a tirade about an intelligent man making such a statement showing he didn't understand the bill (and probably a lot of other things).[35]

But Mrs. Moore's wrath was only the luminous afterglow of the birth control bill's dying star. After McCarran so abruptly squashed the 1934 legislation, the National Committee never again succeeded in getting a bill even as far as a hearing.

Congressional reluctance to deal further with the birth control bill stemmed in part from a growing feeling that legislation on the subject was needless and redundant. Though Mrs. Sanger had produced many physicians at the hearings who testified that the federal statutes stood in the way of lawful birth control, few could honestly maintain by 1935 that the laws really hampered actual

35. U.S., Congress, Senate, *Congressional Record*, 73d Cong. 2d sess., 1934, 78, pt. 10: 11314; memorandum, "Year of the Devil and Roman Catholics," Hazel Moore, June 13, 1934, MSP–LC.

practice; doctors regularly violated the letter of the anti-contraception statutes with impunity.[36] *American Medicine* said in 1935 that the free flow of contraceptive literature and materials through the mails was "as firmly established as the use of a gummed postage stamp . . . it is highly imaginative to suggest that the postal authorities will enter a court in an attempt to prosecute a physician for receiving or sending contraceptives by mail during the regular procedure of his practice." [37] In early 1936, the American Medical Association's Committee to Study Contraceptive Practices reported that it had been "unable to find evidence that existing laws, federal or state, have interfered with any medical advice which a physician has felt called on to furnish his patients." [38] Similarly, the National Committee on Maternal Health concluded after a 1935 survey that "there was no instance in which medical clinics properly directed or instructing medical students had been interfered with by the Government, nor had texts and material been barred from the mails or common carriers." [39]

The American Birth Control League, existing in the shadow of Mrs. Sanger's notoriety in the early 1930s, had long maintained that the federal laws constituted no real obstacle to birth control work and had gone ahead since 1929 organizing clinics in local communities. In the ABCL's view, Mrs. Sanger's attention to the national Comstock statutes confused the public and actually hindered efforts to establish clinics. Early in 1936, the league issued a pamphlet which stated that "from a survey of federal laws, it is apparent that physicians may proceed in legitimate medical practice to give contraceptive advice and prescribe contraceptive treatment whenever they deem it medically proper." That statement caused an uproar in Mrs. Sanger's National Committee. Guy Irving Burch complained to the ABCL that the pamphlet "suggests that our work is unnecessary."

36. *Hearings on H.R. 5978,* pp. 40, 84.
37. *American Medicine* 41 (1935): 167–70.
38. *JAMA* 106 (1936): 1911.
39. *AJOG* 31 (1936): 166.

Mrs. Sanger set her staff to work digging up evidence of legal interference with birth control. Significantly, of the sixteen cases they reported, all but one were brought under the section dealing with importation. Apparently, the sections pertaining to the mails and interstate transportation were virtually a dead letter.[40]

Mrs. Sanger sent her lawyer, Charles E. Scribner, to confer with the counsel for the ABCL, William J. McWilliams. Morris Ernst, that libertarian battler who had argued numerous birth control cases, also participated in the talks. The lawyers agreed that if the ABCL's statement had not been perfectly correct, it was nearly so. In support of the statement, McWilliams presented a memorandum citing a series of court decisions which Scribner had to admit were "well advanced" toward a construction of the federal laws in line with the amendments Mrs. Sanger was urging. Most significant, in the case of *United States v. One Package of Japanese Pessaries,* Judge Grover Moscowitz of the Federal District Court for the Southern District of New York had just ruled that the troublesome importation section could not be used to stop the import of diaphragms for legitimate medical use. If the government appealed and a higher court upheld that ruling, Scribner wrote, "the law might be established in a much more satisfactory condition than it would be by passing an amendment with limited language . . . it might be broader than any statutory amendment that you could put through Congress now." The only difficulty, Scribner thought, lay in the fact that a decision on the importation law would not directly affect the statutes relating to interstate movement of birth control advice and materials.[41]

McWilliams succeeded in convincing the National Committee representatives that judicial interpretation was a

40. Guy Irving Burch to C. C. Little, March 23, 1936; memorandum, "Summary of Legal References," 1936, MSP–SS.

41. Henry Pratt Fairchild to Marguerite Benson, April 4, 1936, Charles E. Scribner to Margaret Sanger, April 17, 1936, Charles Scribner to Hazel Zborowski, April 24, 1936, MSP–SS.

more profitable avenue of reform than legislative amendment. McWilliams also convinced the ABCL that they should support the attempt to see the *One Package* decision through an appeal. The executive head of the ABCL admitted that "the Federal law must ultimately be changed"; and even the AMA report had conceded that in spite of the absence of interference with legitimate medical practice, "clarification" of the laws was desirable. Thus in the spring of 1936 the attorneys Ernst, Scribner, and especially McWilliams had brought virtually all the factions in the birth control movement together to work for a favorable judicial interpretation of the federal statutes.[42]

The prospects for such an interpretation seemed good. Although the federal Comstock law explicitly banned the mailing, interstate transportation, or importation of "any obscene, lewd, or lascivious or any filthy book, pamphlet, picture, motion-picture film, paper, letter, writing, print, or other matter of indecent character, or any drug, medicine, article, or thing designed, adapted, or intended for preventing conception, or producing abortion, or for any indecent or immoral use," the courts had implied several exceptions to the general prohibitions.[43] With regard to printed matter, in *Swearingen* v. *United States* (1895), the Supreme Court had defined "obscene, lewd, or lascivious" as pertaining to "sexual impurity"; but to fall within the definition, the Court said, the matter in question had to be "calculated to corrupt and debauch the mind and morals of those into whose hands it might fall." [44] In a 1930 case involving Mary Ware Dennett, who had published a pamphlet explaining sexual physiology and functions to children, the Federal Circuit Court of Appeals for the Second Circuit accepted the *Swearingen* definitions, with the important qualification that the "motive" of the defendant in writing and distributing the pamphlet was

42. Marguerite Benson to Charles E. Scribner, March 30, 1936, MSP–SS; *JAMA* 106 (1936): 1911.

43. 18 U.S.C.A. Sec. 334 (1927).

44. Swearingen v. United States, 161 U.S. 446 (1895).

held to be "immaterial." Thus the circuit court dismissed
the relevance of intention which the Supreme Court had
emphasized thirty-five years earlier when it had included
the word "calculated" in its definition of obscenity. The
proof of obscenity, the circuit court now implied, must
inhere in the text itself. That seemed a more rigorous
construction of the law than the Supreme Court had
rendered earlier, but the circuit court went on to say that
"it can hardly be said that, because of the risk of arousing
sex impulses, there should be no instruction of the young
in sex matters." Applying the "rule of reasonable construction," the court declared that the Comstock law "must not
be assumed to have been designed to interfere with serious
instruction regarding sex matters unless the terms in which
the information is conveyed are clearly indecent." [45]

The *Dennett* decision proved a powerful precedent.
Judges repeatedly used its "reasonable" approach in the
following years to clarify further the obscenity laws. In
three notable cases between 1931 and 1934, Judge John
M. Woolsey of the Federal District Court for the Southern
District of New York relied on the *Dennett* decision to
allow the distribution of two books on contraception by
Marie Stopes and *Ulysses* by James Joyce. On August 8,
1934, the second circuit upheld Judge Woolsey's decision
on *Ulysses* and remarked: "It is settled, at least so far as
this court is concerned, that works of physiology, medicine,
science, and sex instruction are not within the statute,
though to some extent and among some persons they may
tend to promote lustful thoughts." [46] Thus McWilliams and
the ABCL appeared to have a solid case when they claimed
that no amendment in the federal laws was necessary to

45. United States v. Dennett, 39 F. 2d 564 (1930). The Swearingen
definitions had also been accepted in Dysart v. United States, 272
U.S. 655 (1926).

46. United States v. One Book Entitled "Ulysses," 72 F. 2d 705 (1934);
see also United States v. One Obscene Book Entitled "Married Love,"
48 F. 2d 821 (1931); and United States v. One Book Entitled "Contra-
ceptions," 51 F. 2d 525 (1931).

open the mails to medical literature on contraception. Such works already moved through the mails without impediment. And the courts since 1930 had consistently protected that movement: bypassing the Supreme Court's earlier test of intention, the judges had returned to the original language of the statutes and held that not intended or putative use, but the nature of the work itself determined the legality of its passage.

With regard to explicit contraceptive advice and contraceptive materials, however, the law took a different turn. The federal statutes left some leeway for the interpretation and reasonable definition of "obscene, lewd, or lascivious," but their prohibition on material pertaining to contraception and abortion was precise and unqualified. Yet in *Bours* v. *United States* (1915), the Court of Appeals for the Seventh Circuit applied the rule of reasonable construction to the Comstock law with regard to abortion. Dr. T. Robinson Bours had appealed his conviction in federal district court for mailing a letter indicating he might perform a therapeutic abortion. The law declared nonmailable any letter giving information "where or by whom any act or operation of any kind, for the procuring or producing of abortion will be done or performed." The court interpreted the word "will" to mean that in order for the accused to be convicted, he would have had to give "indication of a positive intent that the act will be done, not merely that it might perhaps be performed." Dr. Bours had, fortunately, written that he "would have to first see the patient before determining whether I would take the case or not." By invoking that highly technical definition of contingency, the court found Bours not guilty, "irrespective of local statutory definitions" of the legality of abortion. The federal laws, said the court, were not concerned with abortion itself, but only with the use of the mails with regard to abortion. Nevertheless, the court went on to give its views on the scope of the federal abortion statutes. The inclusion of the word "abortion"

in the Comstock law, said the court, indicated "a national
policy of discountenancing abortion as inimical to the
national life." But it was only reasonable, the court continued, to exclude from the ban of the statute "those acts
that are in the interest of national life. Therefore a physician may lawfully use the mails to say that if an examination shows the necessity of an operation to save life he
will operate." Thus, though the wording of the statute
was absolute, the court found an exception for a doctor
exercising responsible medical judgment intended to save
life.[47]

The second circuit, in a curious and at first little-
noticed case in 1930, seemed to extend an analagous exception to doctors prescribing contraception. In *Youngs
Rubber Corporation* v. *C. I. Lee and Co., Inc.*, the plaintiff, a manufacturer of condoms, brought suit against the
defendant for pirating his trademark. The district court
had dismissed the case because the plaintiff's plea failed
to establish that the defendant had misused the trademark
in interstate commerce. On reargument before the circuit
court, new evidence was introduced to show that C. I.
Lee and Company had indeed marketed goods with the
pirated trademark across state lines. That determination
in itself was sufficient cause for the circuit court to re-
mand the case; but Judge Thomas Swan went further. He
anticipated C. I. Lee's next line of defense: that since
both companies were engaged in an illegal enterprise—
interstate transportation of contraceptives—plaintiff could
not bring a suit in equity. The district court would therefore have to determine the merits of the case, and if Judge
Swan did not make clear his view of the merits, he could
expect an appeal on those grounds. Therefore, he said, he
would express his views as to the legality of the interstate
transportation of contraceptives, though such a procedure
was contrary to the court's usual practice of "deciding no
more than is essential to dispose of an appeal."

Swan admitted that, taken literally, the statute seemed

47. Bours v. United States, 229 F. 960 (1915).

to prohibit "the transportation by mail or common carrier of anything 'adapted', in the sense of being suitable or fitted, for preventing conception." But the judge noted that neither the federal statute nor all state statutes forbade the manufacture or sale of contraceptives. Since in New York, at least, birth control devices could be sold at a doctor's order "for the cure or prevention of disease," Swan assumed that "the articles which the plaintiff sells may be used for legal or illegal purposes." With that assumption, Swan seriously qualified the language of the federal statute, which banned the interstate transportation of contraceptives absolutely, without regard to purpose. Swan also departed from the test for obscenity laid down only four months earlier by the same court in the *Dennett* case. The nature of the article mailed or shipped did not determine its legality, said Swan; rather, returning to the rationale of the *Swearingen* and *Bours* decisions, Swan insisted on the paramountcy of the sender's purpose. In effect, Swan read a distinction between legitimate and illegitimate use into the statute. "The intention to prevent a proper medical use of drugs or other articles," he said, "merely because they are capable of illegal uses is not lightly to be ascribed to Congress."

Swan then suggested that intended use "for proper medical purposes" be the determining condition of legality. Going beyond the *Bours* decision, which had made the test of lawful abortion the intention "to save life," Judge Swan indicated that he would grant physicians a good deal of discretion by allowing them to prescribe contraceptives for whatever ends they deemed medically proper. To make his opinion explicit, he said that if the plaintiff's articles were "prescribed by a physician for the prevention of disease, or for the prevention of conception, where that is not forbidden by local law," their use was legitimate. The Federal Circuit Court of Appeals for the Second Circuit thereby outlined a doctrine that, if applied, would virtually nullify the Comstock law with regard to contraceptives: they were capable of a legitimate use, subject only

to the test of intended purpose, and "prevention of conception, where that is not forbidden by local law" was a
"proper medical purpose." Judge Swan's remarks, however,
were in the nature of dicta, since the immediate question
before the circuit court was the establishment of federal
jurisdiction through proof of interstate sales. Swan had
approved the test of intention, but could only suggest its
applicability to contraceptives, since he admitted that "we
do not find it necessary to decide this question in the present case." Nevertheless, Swan had presented the best argument thus far for judicially amending the Comstock
laws.[48]

Three years later, in *Davis* v. *United States* (1933), the
sixth circuit made Judge Swan's remarks the basis for an
important decision. Davis, a wholesale distributor of contraceptives, had been convicted by the federal district court,
which had refused to allow evidence as to Davis's intent
and good faith. The appellate court, however, remanded
the case for a new trial and instructed the lower court
that if testimony showed Davis to have intended his goods
for proper medical use he was not to be judged in violation of the law. The circuit court's decision quoted Swan's
dicta in the *Youngs* case at length, saying: "We cite the
case, not as precedent, but because the soundness of its
reasoning commends itself to us, and because it amplifies
the argument upon which the same court announced
through Judge Augustus N. Hand [in the *Dennett* case]
that the statute must be given a reasonable construction
and relies upon the similar reasoning of Judge Mack [in
the *Bours* decision]." [49]

On the basis of those decisions, McWilliams, Scribner,
and Morris Ernst, who was counsel for the Clinical Research Bureau in the pending Japanese pessaries case, had
every reason early in 1936 to hope that the second circuit
would definitely affirm the position it had suggested six

48. Youngs Rubber Corporation v. C. I. Lee and Co., Inc., 45 F. 2d
103 (1930).

49. Davis et al. v. United States, 62 F. 473 (1933).

years earlier. The Japanese pessaries case involved Section 305 of the Tariff Act of 1930, an outgrowth of the original Comstock law that customs officials had enforced much more rigorously than other government agents had enforced the postal and interstate transportation statutes. A favorable decision on Section 305 would clear away the last effective barrier to the birth control movement in the federal laws. When the government appealed from Judge Moscowitz's decision in the district court, Ernst, in the manner of the "Brandeis Brief," marshaled an impressive amount of medical and sociological evidence. He demonstrated at length the necessity of birth control in the face of several indications, including economic insufficiency. The court did as expected and ordered the release of the confiscated package of pessaries. The logic of Swan's dicta in the *Youngs* case and the sixth circuit's opinion in the *Davis* case culminated in a sweeping decision by Judge Augustus Hand. Though only the importation statute was in question, he said, all three parts of the Comstock law were part of a continuous scheme of legislation and should be construed consistently. The language of that law was clear, said Hand, but it should not be taken literally. Discussing the legislative history of the Comstock bill, Hand noted that in 1873 information on the possible dangers of conception was very meager. The law, he said, should be construed as embracing "only such articles as Congress would have denounced as immoral if it had understood all the conditions under which they were to be used. Its design, in our opinion, was not to prevent the importation, sale, or carriage by mail of things which might intelligently be employed by conscientious and competent physicians for the purpose of saving life or promoting the well-being of their patients."

In obscenity legislation subsequent to the original Comstock Act, Hand pointed out, Congress had qualified its language to stipulate "unlawful" abortion, thus codifying the distinction between licit and illicit abortion which the seventh circuit implied in the *Bours* case. "The same exception," Hand said, "should apply to articles for preventing conception." He noted the illogic of holding that

> abortions, which destroy incipient life, may be allowed
> in proper cases, and yet that no measures may be taken
> to prevent conception even though a likely result
> should be to require the termination of pregnancy by
> means of an operation. It seems unreasonable to suppose that the national scheme of legislation involves
> such inconsistencies and requires the complete suppression of articles, the use of which in many cases is
> advocated by such a weight of authority in the medical
> world.

Judge Hand gave full recognition to the weight of medical authority. "It was significant," Morris Ernst commented later, "that nowhere in its opinion did the court specifically state under what circumstances a doctor was to be free to prescribe a contraceptive. The inference was clear that the medical profession was to be the sole judge of the propriety of prescription in a given case, and that as long as a physician exercised his discretion in good faith the legality of his action was not to be questioned." Thus Hand upheld the distinction between legal and illegal use of contraceptives, the test of intention, and Judge Swan's suggested reliance on medical discretion to determine proper intent.[50]

Mrs. Sanger hailed Hand's decision as "the greatest legal VICTORY in the Birth Control Movement," but those she hoped most to convince—physicians—did not immediately agree with her. The *Journal of the American Medical Association* editorialized that "contraceptive advice, devices, and preparations [are] still contraband." It noted that the National Committee's pamphlet declaring "Now birth control is legal" was "essentially misleading." The

50. United States v. One Package of Japanese Pessaries, 86 F. 2d 737 (1936); Morris Ernst and Alexander Lindey, *The Censor Marches On* (New York: Doubleday, Doran, 1940), p. 165.

One Package decision, said the journal, had nothing to do with "the right of a physician to advise the practice of contraception." It dealt only with importation and applied only in New York, Connecticut, and Vermont, the second circuit's jurisdiction.[51]

Morris Ernst replied that the *One Package* decision did indeed affect the physician's relation to his patient, especially in rural areas, where fear to use the mails to obtain information had been among the principal obstacles to the spread of birth control knowledge. In the months following the decision, the National Committee had circularized every county medical society in the United States, and the responses, requesting technical literature, had come overwhelmingly from rural physicians. The court had also stated explicitly that, though the case before it concerned only importation, the three parts of the Comstock law should be construed consistently. Finally, said Ernst, the weight of the second circuit court's opinion was now added to that of the sixth circuit court in the *Davis* case, and since "conformity of the various circuits is always sedulously strived for," the decision on contraception "thus stands as the last word on the subject." The Solicitor General of the United States had apparently admitted as much when he indicated that he would not seek a Supreme Court review of the circuit court's ruling. State courts, though they were not legally bound to do so, could be expected to "adhere to the normal course of following the lead of the federal government in this regard." Thus, concluded Ernst, the claims of legal victory made by the National Committee "appear to be fully warranted." [52]

In fact, the *One Package* decision had a mixed influence on the legal status of birth control. On the federal level, it effectively removed all obstacles limiting the private doctor's access to contraceptive information and supplies.

51. Margaret Sanger to Mrs. P. B. P. Huse, December 14, 1936, Population Council; *JAMA* 108 (1937): 1179–80.

52. *JAMA* 108 (1937): 1819–20; memorandum, Adelaide Pearson to Mrs. Roseberry, March 28, 1937, MSP–LC.

But debate continued as to the legal—as well as political—propriety of incorporating contraceptive service into federal public health programs. And the courts in some states persistently refused to be persuaded by the federal example. An Illinois judge in 1938 cited the *One Package* decision, but relied more heavily on Learned Hand's concurring opinion than on Augustus Hand's opinion for the majority.[53] Though Learned Hand stated that he was "not prepared to dissent," he admitted that he had "doubts" about the opinion the court was rendering. The law clearly stipulated, he said, "that contraceptives were meant to be forbidden, whether or not prescribed by physicians, and that no lawful use of them was contemplated." If it was true, as he believed, that "many people have changed their minds about such matters in sixty years," nevertheless the statute remained. Proper relief, he implied, might better be sought from the Congress.[54]

In Massachusetts and Connecticut, which had the most stringent anticontraception statutes, the courts seemed more inclined to follow the lead of Learned Hand than that of his cousin. The Massachusetts Supreme Judicial Court, in *Commonwealth* v. *Gardner* (1938), said the federal precedents were not persuasive, especially those that relied, as *One Package* did in part, on Judge Crane's 1918 New York Court of Appeals ruling in *People* v. *Sanger*. That case construed the New York statute which contained a specific exemption for physicians. Judge Swan, in the *Youngs* case, had recognized the importance of such a condition when he noted that articles could be legitimately used for the prevention of conception if "that is not forbidden by local law." But in Massachusetts, said the Supreme Judicial Court, the terms of the law were "plain, unequivocal and peremptory. They contain no exceptions. They are sweeping, absolute and devoid of ambiguity. They are directed with undeviating explicitness against the prevention of conception by any of the means speci-

53. Lanteen Laboratories, Inc., v. Clark, 294 Ill. App. 81 (1938).

54. United States v. One Package, 86 F. 2d 737 (1936).

fied." The situation in Massachusetts, therefore, could be clearly distinguished from that in New York; and relief in Massachusetts, the court insisted, "must be sought from the law-making department and not from the judicial department of the government."

Massachusetts Chief Justice Arthur Prentice Rugg wrote a wretched opinion in the *Gardner* case. He distorted the federal court opinions which he chose to dismiss as unpersuasive. The *Youngs* decision did not, as Rugg said it did, rely on the precedent of *People* v. *Sanger*. Rather, Judge Swan mentioned *People* v. *Sanger* only in his dicta; the actual decision rested on a procedural matter of jurisdiction. And in discussing the *Davis* decision, Rugg asserted: "Again, great reliance was placed upon *People* v. *Sanger*." In fact the *Davis* decision never mentioned *People* v. *Sanger*. Rugg neglected entirely to mention *Bours* v. *United States*, by then a well-established precedent for reading implied exceptions into obscenity statutes. Rugg also, in dismissing the *Youngs* decision, ignored Judge Swan's reasons for going so far in his dicta. Swan was not concerned merely with strict statutory exceptions to the federal laws in local instances. He addressed himself to the broader question of a reasonable interpretation of the federal Comstock law in all circumstances. If Swan could reasonably find exceptions there, so too should Rugg have been able to find them in the Massachusetts anticontraception laws, which were no more sweeping than the federal prohibitions.[55]

In 1940, with Rugg no longer on the bench, the Supreme Judicial Court rejected the trenchant language in which it had described the Massachusetts law only two years earlier and adopted the test of intention to find an implied exception. In *Commonwealth* v. *Corbett*, the defendant, a pharmacist, appealed his conviction for the sale of condoms. Though the law forbade the sale of "any . . . article whatever for the prevention of concep-

55. Commonwealth v. Gardner, 15 N.E. 2d 222 (1938).

tion," the court held that "the words of the statute require proof of an intended use for an illegal purpose, and are not satisfied by mere incidental result." Condoms, said the court, were capable of use for the prevention of disease, which was a legal purpose. Therefore their sale, in the absence of proof of intent to use them for illegal purposes, was legitimate. In effect, following Judge Swan's reasoning in the *Youngs* dicta, though not going as far as he in defining a licit intention, the court had read into the Massachusetts statute a limited form of the exception "for the cure or prevention of disease" which had long existed in New York's Section 1145.[56]

In Connecticut, the courts balked at even that cautious, qualified approval of contraception. In *State* v. *Nelson* in 1940, the Supreme Court of Errors cited *Commonwealth* v. *Gardner* as authority that Connecticut's absolute ban on the "use" of contraceptives was a proper exercise of the police power. The court concluded that "whatever may be our own opinion regarding the general subject . . . if all that can be said is that [the law] is unwise or unreasonably comprehensive, appeal must be made to the Legislature, not to the judiciary." [57] In 1942 birth control advocates argued that the Connecticut statute was unreasonable because it prevented a physician from prescribing contraception to protect his patients from "death, or serious injury to health." But the Supreme Court of Errors, in *Tileston* v. *Ullman,* again refused to exercise that power of interpretation which the federal courts had so consistently employed in liberalizing the Comstock law. The Connecticut statute was clear and unqualified, the court said; the legislature had refused to change it on nine different occasions between 1923 and 1931, when birth control bills had been unsuccessfully promoted at Hartford. As for the medical necessity of avoiding pregnancy, said the court, "the state claims that there is another method, positive and certain in result. It is abstention from inter-

56. Commonwealth v. Corbett, 307 Mass. 7 (1940).
57. State v. Nelson, 126 Conn. 412 (1940).

course in the broadest sense—that is, absolute abstention."
Though it admitted "the frailties of human nature and
the uncertainties of human passions," the court avoided
a judgment on the reasonableness of its suggested alternative. "That," the court said, "is a question for the
legislature. . . . The legislature is the final forum." The
Supreme Court of the United States showed a similar
reluctance to deal with the question. It declined to review
the case, arguing that Dr. Tileston had no standing to
assert a constitutional question since he alleged that not
his but his patient's life was in danger.[58] As late as 1959
the Connecticut courts still resisted a liberal construction
of the law on the grounds that, whatever the medical
necessity, abstention was a viable alternative to contraception.[59]

Though the *One Package* case may have had a somewhat limited legal effect, it had a profound influence on
the course of the organized birth control movement. Mrs.
Sanger had created the National Committee to educate
and to lobby. Its legislative program came to naught, but
Mrs. Sanger regarded its educational effort as ultimately
responsible for the legal breakthrough she considered the
One Package decision to be. Morris Ernst agreed that "the
law process is a simple one—it is a matter of educating
judges to the mores of the day." He added, generously,
that "it is perfectly easy to win a case after Margaret
Sanger has educated the judges, and she has educated any
number of them. I have merely been a mouthpiece." [60]

58. Tileston v. Ullman, 129 Conn. 84 (1942); Tileston v. Ullman,
318 U.S. 44 (1943).

59. Buxton v. Ullman, 147 Conn. 48 (1959). In Poe v. Ullman 367
U.S. 497 (1961), the United States Supreme Court refused to make a
declaratory judgment on the Connecticut statute on the grounds that
no constitutional issue was involved; but in Griswold v. Connecticut,
381 U.S. 479 (1965), the Supreme Court held that the Connecticut law
violated what the Court declared to be a constitutionally guaranteed
right of privacy.

60. Morris Ernst, speech at conference on "Public Health and Birth
Control Laws," December 29, 1936, copy in MSP–LC.

In Mrs. Sanger's view the seven-year encampment in Washington had been a success. After the circuit court's *One Package* decision, the National Committee spent a few months circularizing doctors and public health officers in every state and county, informing them of the new legal status of birth control and urging them to incorporate contraceptive services into local public health programs. Then, in early 1937, Mrs. Sanger decided the National Committee had done its job and she dissolved it.

But though the *One Package* case caused the eventual disappearance of the National Committee, it ultimately brought a new birth control organization into being. When William McWilliams had first presented his memorandum in 1936, Henry Pratt Fairchild, an influential member of the National Committee, saw in the memorandum opportunities beyond the legal. He wrote to the American Birth Control League that "in this position of Mr. McWilliams there may lie the key to a formula that will resolve the difficult situation between the two organizations. . . . It should certainly clear away the great part of the conflicts that confuse the public and impede the work so seriously." [61] That simple beginning led to the formation, in late 1937, of the Birth Control Council of America, which was intended to coordinate the work of the ABCL and Mrs. Sanger's Clinical Research Bureau, and eventually to merge the two groups. [62]

As always, the greatest obstacle to cooperation remained Mrs. Sanger's insistence on paramountcy. She resented every claim the ABCL made to a share in any of the recent successes of the movement. When an impartial consulting firm—the same one Mrs. Sanger had retained seven years earlier—reported in 1937 that "the medical profession today suffers from the notoriety resulting from the work of other [than the ABCL] birth control organizations," Mrs. Sanger called the statement a "knife in the

61. Henry Pratt Fairchild to Mrs. Louise deB. Moore, April 16, 1936, MSP–LC.

62. *JAMA* 109 (1937): 440.

back" by the ABCL. The league, she said, was run by "those whose interest it is to take away credit from others and to snatch it for themselves."

Fortunately for the birth control movement, less self-interested heads than Mrs. Sanger's prevailed. Though Marguerite Benson, the chief executive of the ABCL, took a flexible, conciliatory approach to the merger proposition, most of the cooler heads in the negotiations belonged to men. And when the joint committee of ABCL and Clinical Research Bureau representatives meeting to discuss the merger submitted their recommendations in October 1938, first among them was the suggestion that the president of the new organization be a man. Soon thereafter the two organizations did join, under the presidency of Dr. Richard N. Pierson, a medical doctor, to form the Birth Control Federation of America. A few years later, over Mrs. Sanger's loud protests, the name was changed to Planned Parenthood Federation of America.[63]

The new federation first addressed itself to the task of persuading federal and state governments to include birth control in their public health programs. Mrs. Sanger had believed for years that the assumption of birth control services by public agencies would be a fit and logical culmination of her lifelong campaign. She had urged such action on President Calvin Coolidge in 1925 and President Herbert Hoover in 1930. In that latter year, however, Henry Pratt Fairchild had found Secretary of the Interior Ray Lyman Wilbur less than enthusiastic about Mrs. Sanger's proposals. After an interview, he reported that, "as far as Secretary Wilbur is concerned, any successful approach must entirely exclude any reference to birth control, or contraception or the name of Mrs. Sanger." That same

63. Margaret Sanger to Mrs. P. B. P. Huse, December 20, 1937, "Summary of Recommendations to Joint Committee of A.B.C.L. and Clinical Research Bureau," October 10, 1938; Margaret Sanger to D. Kenneth Rose, August 20, 1956, MSP–SS. Mrs. Sanger protested dropping the phrase she had coined—"birth control"—from the movement's title.

fear of notoriety prevented many public health officers from promoting birth control as vigorously as they would have liked. Though a 1935 survey of local Federal Emergency Relief Administration officials showed that in many states and communities they underwrote the cost of contraception for the indigent, in no case did an administrator care to make his position public. The ABCL sent a field-worker to the South in reponse "to numerous appeals from federal relief administrators" in 1934, and she found them "to a man" in favor of birth control. They were willing to include it in their local programs, however, "on the sole condition that the work be done quietly and without official endorsement from their local committees or from Washington." In Washington, the head of the FERA, Harry Hopkins, expressed personal agreement with the birth control advocates, but had a simple explanation why he would not make birth control an official part of relief work: "because it is illegal." [64]

By 1938, however, the *One Package* decision had finally dissipated the cloud of illegality that had hung over birth control. The new federation had removed Margaret Sanger's controversial name from the singular glare of publicity it had commanded for twenty years. The recent endorsement by the American Medical Association lent birth control a new air of respectability. Moreover, in 1938 nearly four million persons were still on federal relief; and the National Resources Committee reported in May that "recipients of relief are more fertile than the general population." High fertility was an exceptionally acute problem in the blighted South, where the condition of the rural population elicited President Roosevelt's comment that the South was the nation's "number one eco-

---

64. "Report of interview of Henry Pratt Fairchild with Secretary of the Interior Ray Lyman Wilbur," May 5, 1930, MSP–SS; "Survey of Policies of F.E.R.A. administrators," February 25, 1935; report, 1934, ABCL; Hazel Moore, memorandum: "Interview with Harry Hopkins," June 6, 1934, all in MSP–LC.

nomic problem." [65] Mordecai Ezekiel and others in the Department of Agriculture were particularly concerned about the differential urban and rural birthrates. For some, that concern was informed by the same sort of eugenic thinking that had moved birth control theoreticians in the 1920s. Since the problematic Southern rural population was largely Negro, many began to fear the implications of an increasingly prolific indigent black population.[66] When Sam Rayburn, for example, who had never been particularly noted for his support of the movement, heard that birth control was being carried to Southern Negroes, he was reportedly "brought to his feet" with enthusiasm. "Now you're really talking," he said, "when you're getting birth control to them." [67] Finally, a growing number of doctors—especially those in the employ of the United States Public Health Service—were expressing concern for the alarmingly high incidence of maternal mortality in the United States. All these factors seemed to the Birth Control Federation to indicate that the time was ripe for official acceptance of birth control.

Several government agencies had already incorporated some contraceptive services into their programs by 1938, but the reluctance publicly and officially to acknowledge those services persisted. At least one Indian Field Service director reported that she was "doing some work on birth control although we label it under a different name." [68] Officials in the Farm Security Administration, Hazel Moore noted, were providing "all the cooperation we could hope

65. *Historical Statistics of the United States* (Washington: Government Printing Office, 1961), p. 200; *The Problems of a Changing Population*, Report of the Committee on Population Problems to the National Resources Committee (Washington: Government Printing Office, 1938), p. 139.

66. Mordecai Ezekiel to Marguerite Benson, March 10, 1936, records of the Department of Agriculture, National Archives, Washington, D.C.

67. Margaret Sanger to Mary Lasker, January 20, 1942, MSP–SS.

68. Hazel Moore to Florence Rose, February 14, 1938, MSP–SS.

for. . . . we are getting the silent approval of the administrators, Mr. [Will] Alexander and Mr. [Milo] Perkins." [69]
In one state, North Carolina, the State Board of Health
had established birth control in nearly every county. But
even that program had begun with "no publicity" and
with the financial backing not of the state, but of Clarence
J. Gamble, a wealthy physician and generous friend of
the birth control movement. In each of these cases the
secretiveness of the operation hampered its effectiveness.[70]

Mrs. Sanger and federation officials in 1938 formed the
Committee for Public Progress to pressure government
agencies into a full recognition and acceptance of birth
control as an integral part of public health. The committee was composed of several thousand birth control
sympathizers who were periodically instructed to write
letters to various agency officials urging the adoption of
birth control. Mrs. Sanger and some of her medical and
legal advisers—notably Morris Ernst—constituted themselves an informal lobbying group to keep up direct pressure with face-to-face interviews in Washington.

Two pieces of legislation in the late 1930s seemed to
afford Mrs. Sanger and her co-workers the opportunity to
implement their public health program. Title Five of the
Social Security Act of 1938 provided nearly four million
dollars in grants to state maternal and child health services. The Venereal Disease Control Act in 1939 declared
war on venereal disease, the containment of which was
defined, in nearly every state, as a legal purpose for the
employment of contraceptives. The United States Public
Health Service and the Children's Bureau administered
the venereal disease control and social security programs.
The federation pressured these government agencies to
recognize the utility and legality of contraception in stopping venereal disease and improving maternal and child
health.

69. Hazel Moore to Clarence J. Gamble, June 2, 1938, MSP–LC.
70. *North Carolina Medical Journal* 1 (1940): 463–68; *Atlantic Monthly*, October 1939, pp. 463–67.

The Public Health Service had long followed a policy of referring inquiries about contraception to the ABCL and later to the federation.[71] The Children's Bureau, however, under the stern administration of Katherine Lenroot, career bureaucrat, daughter of the controversial Wisconsin Republican Irvine Lenroot, recoiled from even that limited degree of cooperation with the birth control movement. Though the bureau itself had compiled most of the statistical studies demonstrating the shockingly high incidence of maternal deaths due to multiparity, Miss Lenroot refused to acknowledge the relevance of contraception in reducing those deaths. In 1938 she canceled an invitation to Hannah Stone to speak at a conference on baby care, on the grounds that other participants might have been offended by the inclusion of a birth control advocate in the program.[72]

Miss Lenroot's timidity was born of more than a simple reluctance to give offense. Like Monsignor John Ryan and countless others, she feared the prospect of "a civilization with a declining population." [73] But more than that, she feared the prospect of heading a bureau with declining influence. In a classic statement of the defensive caution so common in Franklin Roosevelt's government, one of her subordinates explained Miss Lenroot's position in 1938:

> It seems highly desirable that a newly created organization [the Children's Bureau had begun as a fact-finding agency, interested in labor problems; its health programs were "new" and jealously guarded] does not take on the extra hazards involved in the acceptance of its program by administratively assuming responsibility for an activity which is . . . controversial . . . The first obligation of the welfare department [is] do-

71. Marguerite Benson to Eleanor Dwight-Jones, July 31, 1936, MSP–LC; Marguerite Benson to Dr. Robert Olesen, July 25, 1937, USPHS records, National Archives.

72. Helen Sachs Strauss to Margaret Sanger, May 17, 1938, MSP–LC.

73. Katherine Lenroot to Sidney E. Goldstein, April 26, 1939, MSP–LC.

ing everything possible to build a sound structure which would be so firmly rooted in the governmental pattern of the State and be so well protected against the hazards of political attack that the State, from this time on, would have an effective administrative unit for dealing with the many social problems coming to the attention of a broad public welfare program. [There is] a very real danger which would threaten the entire structure if at this stage of its development, the welfare department became active in the administration of a birth control program.[74]

Miss Lenroot's careful insulation of her agency from "the hazards of political attack" rendered it inaccessible to the influence of Mrs. Sanger, the federation, or even certain government health officials sympathetic to birth control. The Assistant Secretary of the Treasury in charge of public health concluded that "Katherine Lenroot was hopeless." If the birth control advocates were to get anywhere, the Assistant Secretary advised, they "must work through Mrs. Roosevelt." [75]

Eleanor Roosevelt had been among the early financial supporters of the Clinical Research Bureau in New York. In 1940, she lent her immense prestige to the birth control movement when she publicly declared her approval of family planning. But even Eleanor Roosevelt had little sway over Miss Lenroot. She did, however, have some influence with the Surgeon General, Dr. Thomas Parran, and through him, eventually with the USPHS. Morris Ernst—who seemed constantly on the job for the federation in Washington—had tried to persuade Parran in 1938 and 1939 that the Venereal Disease Control Act would allow him to promote birth control, as a preventive hygienic measure, with federal funds. But Parran, somewhat obtusely, said he "did not see the close relationship

74. Mary Irene Atkinson to Mrs. Tom Ragland, July 16, 1938, MSP–LC.

75. Memorandum, Hazel Moore to Florence Rose, December 16, 1938, MSP–LC.

. . . between birth control and venereal diseases." Like Katherine Lenroot, he worried about "a declining total population within the next two decades." Rather than the "purely negative approach of broadcasting contraceptive information," he said, the government should encourage more breeding among the "biologically fit groups." [76]

By 1940, however, while Parran remained cautious, several of his colleagues in the Surgeon General's office had come to agree with the federation about Public Health Service support of birth control. The general counsel of the Treasury, responding to a request by an assistant surgeon general, gave his official opinion in 1939 that the USPHS could legally distribute contraceptive information to physicians and nurses under the terms of the Venereal Disease Control Act. Armed with that legal support, Mark V. Ziegler, R. A. Vonderlehr, and C. V. Aiken, all assistant surgeons general, quietly began to approve state public health programs that included contraceptive services. Mrs. Roosevelt soon lent her active support to Parran's progressive assistants. On March 5, 1941, representatives of the federation, the Public Health Service, the Children's Bureau, and the Department of Agriculture sat down together in the White House at Mrs. Roosevelt's invitation. Though Dr. Parran was unable to attend, he signified his growing sympathy by sending his wife in his stead. [77]

The meeting dealt only with the general outlines of the proper governmental approach to public health and population problems, but it served finally to involve Mrs. Roosevelt directly with the federation's efforts in Washington. Encouraged by her friend and active federation supporter Mrs. Albert Lasker, Mrs. Roosevelt discussed the matter with the President. He was, she reported, entirely in agree-

76. *New York Times,* January 17, 1940, p. 23; "Felton" to Harriet Pilpel, March 18, 1939, Thomas Parran to George B. Lake, June 4, 1938, USPHS records, National Archives.

77. Opinion of the General Counsel, January 23, 1939, USPHS records, National Archives; "Report on Washington D.C. meeting," March 5, 1941, MSP–SS.

ment with the federation's point of view. He felt that Dr. Parran and Miss Lenroot objected to birth control because they feared "certain repercussions from the Catholic Church." Nevertheless, she concluded, "the President is going to speak to both Dr. Parran and Miss Lenroot to see if they can get the whole thing moving." [78] The President himself may not have spoken to the Public Health Service and the Children's Bureau, but Mrs. Roosevelt did. In August she wrote to Parran suggesting that Dr. Mark Ziegler "be placed in charge of any requests from State Health Departments for information on trained doctors for child-spacing program." [79] Two months later, the Surgeon General's office announced that the Public Health Service would review without bias a state health department's request for funds for "a child-spacing program." [80] Early in 1942, Parran stated unequivocally that "planned parenthood programs . . . will receive my approval." [81] He informed Mrs. Roosevelt that he had appointed Dr. Ziegler liaison officer to the Planned Parenthood Federation and to the states on all matters pertaining to contraception. He made it clear, however, that the new policy was only a permissive one. The USPHS would approve state requests, but it would in no case actively propagandize for birth control. [82]

Katherine Lenroot regarded even that moderate policy "a very advanced step." She resented it not only because she feared a declining population, but, again, because she sensed a threat to the existence of her own agency. Already,

78. Eleanor Roosevelt to Mary Lasker, June 17, 1941, copy in MSP–LC.

79. Eleanor Roosevelt to Dr. Parran, August 16, 1941, USPHS records, National Archives.

80. Dr. Warren F. Draper to Mary Lasker, October 17, 1941, USPHS records, National Archives.

81. Dr. C. C. Pierce to D. K. Rose, February 2, 1942, USPHS records, National Archives.

82. Dr. Parran to Eleanor Roosevelt, January 6, 1942, USPHS records, National Archives.

within the bureau itself, some of Miss Lenroot's subordinates had begun to chafe under her negative attitude toward birth control. Sending the standard "no information" form letter to inquiring mothers, said one bureau doctor, "always makes me feel mean." Several doctors in the Children's Bureau wanted at least the authority to refer requests for information to the federation. Public health officers also grumbled about the anomaly of Miss Lenroot's timid administration of public health programs that should logically have been run from the Surgeon General's office. More than one Public Health Service official recommended the absorption of the Children's Bureau into the Public Health Service. Miss Lenroot thus saw herself in beleaguered defense of the Children's Bureau, under attack from within and without. Rather than give ground to appease the assailants, she dug in for a siege.[83]

At a second birth control meeting in the White House, amid the chaos and drama of the day after the Pearl Harbor attack, Miss Lenroot made her position clear. She said that "inclusion of birth control would jeopardize her other programs of maternal and child welfare." She was especially concerned, she said, "about political pressure from Congress." One of the federation representatives responded: "After all, let us remember at whose board we are sitting and under whose roof. I consider this a most historic occasion and the most significant event in the history of the movement since the birth of Margaret Sanger." Miss Lenroot was unimpressed. Under the terms of the statutes, the Public Health Service administered the Venereal Disease Control Act funds, but the Children's Bureau controlled a large part of the Maternal and Child Health funds under Title V of the Social Security Act. Miss Lenroot indicated her intention to tie up those maternal and child health

83. Memorandum, Dr. Katherine Bain to "Eliot," November 17, 1941, Children's Bureau Records, Federal Records Center, Franconia, Virginia; "Interview with Captain Charles Stephenson," October 22, 1941, MSP–SS.

funds rather than allow their use in birth control programs.[84]

In June 1942, Katherine Lenroot asked the solicitor for the Department of Labor two questions: could she "approve a State maternal and child-health plan containing a provision for the furnishing of birth control information and advice," and could she disapprove such a plan. The solicitor noted the weight of medical evidence in support of birth control; he cited the *One Package, Davis, Youngs, Dennett,* and *Bours* cases to substantiate his opinion that "the Chief of the Children's Bureau may lawfully approve a state maternal and child-health service plan containing a provision for the furnishing of birth control information and advice." In answer to the second question, the solicitor concluded that Miss Lenroot could disapprove a state contraceptive program, although, he added, "her right to do so is shrouded with considerable doubt." [85]

Miss Lenroot apparently yielded to the solicitors' argument. She also faced increasing White House pressure and mounting demands for funds from the Public Health Service, which recognized that vital war industries required women workers who would not be disabled by unwanted pregnancies. In May, assured at last of access to Miss Lenroot's Title V funds, the USPHS quietly abandoned its passive policy of approving but not initiating contraceptive programs. The chief of the Division of Industrial Hygiene told the federation that

> there should be a policy of child spacing for women in war industries, under medical supervision. In our future visits to the various States this matter will be brought to the attention of the State Health Officers

84. Memorandum, Edna McKinnon to Florence Rose, December 12, 1941, MSP–LC; "Summary of Conference . . . with Dr. Warren F. Draper," March 12, 1942, MSP–SS.

85. Memorandum, Warner W. Gardner, Solicitor of Labor, to Katherine Lenroot, June 1942, Children's Bureau Records, Central Files, Department of Health, Education, and Welfare, Washington, D.C.

and the industrial hygiene physicians, emphasizing the importance of this phase of conservation of the health of women, and suggesting that for any further information they write you directly.[86]

In that limited, unobtrusive, but significant way, the government had "taken over the job of birth control," as Mrs. Sanger had long desired.

Success came only after Mrs. Sanger had removed herself from the fulcrum of power and publicity in the birth control movement. After the merger of the Clinical Research Bureau and the ABCL, she later reflected, "I spiritually left the front and joined the ranks." [87] Some of her colleagues would have argued that success for the movement had in fact depended on Mrs. Sanger's departure from the front. She had been principally responsible for the eight-year schism that had hobbled the movement through most of the 1930s. And certainly some of her naïve political premises—that conscience could prevail in a lame-duck session of Congress, for example—had hindered the effective operation of the National Committee.

Mrs. Sanger's combative personality had perhaps made more enemies than friends. She was shocked and affronted that religious spokesmen, especially Catholics, had availed themselves of the adversary system and opposed her views before congressional committees. As she grew older, her childhood obsession with supposed Catholic deviousness became more and more exaggerated. One of her associates cautioned her to avoid "emphasis on the religious opposition . . . our victory will never be won that way . . . it is hurting us all the time." Margaret Sanger found it virtually impossible to muster a spirit of conciliation and compromise when she confronted Catholics. Morris Ernst repeatedly urged upon her the desirability of appealing to

86. J. G. Townsend to C. C. Pierce, May 1, 1942, Population Council.

87. Margaret Sanger to Cele Wright, n.d., MSP–SS.

Catholic liberals and of emphasizing the similarities, rather than the differences, between Mrs. Sanger's recommended contraceptive technique and the so-called rhythm method. Roman Catholic opinion on birth control was certainly divided. "Instead of a direct attack on the church," Ernst advised, "your attack should be in widening the division." [88]

Mrs. Sanger paid little heed. She continued and even intensified her attack on the Catholic opposition. The Catholic attack, in turn, often matched Mrs. Sanger in obsessiveness and irresponsibility. The public debate on birth control between Margaret Sanger and Catholic spokesmen consequently produced a strikingly low level of dialogue. Mrs. Sanger often forsook rational explanation of the benefits birth control could effect in order to impugn in acidic terms the eligibility of chaste, infertile clerics to speak on contraception. For their part, Catholic spokesmen made gross charges about the complicity of Russian agents in the birth control movement and about the movement's intention to decimate the Anglo-Saxon and Celtic races. Rarely did they elucidate to the general public the doctrinal grounds on which the church based its view of contraception. Even more rarely did they pause to consider the proprieties of using sectarian morality in a democracy to justify the perpetuation of a legal anachronism that impinged on the freedom of all, not just Catholics. Each side had to share the blame for the degradation of the dialogue on birth control; but to the extent that the church's public behavior was a response to Mrs. Sanger's stimulus, perhaps a less obsessed woman might have initiated a more reasonable discussion.

On the other hand, a less obsessed woman might never have undertaken the propaganda campaign the National Committee mounted—and the committee's seven years of systematic public education did have a profound effect on

88. Ann Wheaton to Margaret Sanger, April 17, 1932, MSP–LC; see also Mary Ware Dennett to Margaret Sanger, February 11, 1931, MSP–LC; Ernst quoted in *New York Times*, January 28, 1942, p. 21.

both Protestant and Catholic attitudes toward birth control. But when the courts, not Congress, ultimately rewrote the birth control laws, they underscored a significant truth: for all her adeptness at propaganda, Mrs. Sanger remained more fascinated by the possibilities of power than by those of persuasion. Though, as Morris Ernst said, Mrs. Sanger had "educated" the judges, which was an exercise in persuasion, the essence of judicial change, she herself could not fully appreciate that exercise. For that reason McWilliams's judicial strategy had initially confused her. She preferred to engage in a yearly numbers game with Catholic representatives before congressional committees, each side annually raising its ante of lists of endorsing or protesting organizations. Margaret Sanger had little sense of law, only of power. And in the arena of American politics, she was no match for Catholic power.

Politicians and bureaucrats feared that their public support of birth control would be profoundly provocative to their Catholic constituents. The threat, whether real or exaggerated, of Catholic political reprisals served as the most effective obstacle to governmental action on birth control.

Because of the threat the Catholic element in political constituencies posed, birth control could make legal progress only through the courts, and administrative progress only quietly. Even the courts at first manifested a certain political sensitivity. In the *Davis* and *Corbett* cases, they allowed the transportation and sale of contraceptives under the fiction that in the absence of positive contrary evidence, devices were intended to be used for noncontraceptive purposes such as the "cure or prevention of disease." The criterion of purpose, which the *Bours* decision applied to abortion, and the *Davis* decision to contraceptives, differed sharply from the doctrine applied to test the obscenity of literature. The *Dennett* decision held that the nature of the object itself, regardless of intended use or audience, determined its legality. By applying the test of intention to abortion and birth control, therefore, the courts avoided meeting those issues foursquare, as they had met the issue of obscene literature. Only after Morris Ernst had introduced evidence of widespread medical practice of contraception in the *One Package* case did the second circuit strip the test of intention of some of its subterfuge. The court no longer insisted on intended use "for the cure or prevention of disease" in order to render contraception legal. Judge Hand now allowed wide discretion to doctors in defining a licit intention for contraception.

In the end, the political and legal aspects of birth control proved inseparable. But in the end, in spite of her political naïveté and legal innocence, Mrs. Sanger won her case. The *One Package* decision made possible precisely what she had demanded for twenty years: medical prescription of contraception for whatever reasons the doctor, in the intimacy of his relationship with the patient, saw fit. And thanks to the timely intervention of Eleanor Roosevelt, Mrs. Sanger at last saw public participation in birth control.

By 1942, her dreams well on the way to full realization, she had "left the front." She went home to Arizona and nursed her failing husband, who died in 1943. She was all alone then, in the big house in Tucson, and she had "lost so much contact," she wrote, "that I would hesitate to go anywhere to speak on Birth Control these days." [89] She must have found it ironic, after all her pushing and pulling to keep the movement going, that the new, businesslike Planned Parenthood Federation often found her and her notoriety detrimental to the cause. It was ironic, too, that the movement she had launched allegedly to free women from the fetters of male tyranny had deliberately called upon a man to lead it. By the end of the war, she was little more than a figurehead in the American birth control movement. Her doggedly militant style now seemed more a liability than an asset.

Despite all her defects of posture and policy, Margaret Sanger, it could be argued, had been indispensable to the

89. Margaret Sanger to Clarence Gamble, February 8, 1943, MSP–SS.

ultimate success of her cause. American society quite possibly needed to go through a phase of rejection and revulsion before it could accept something so new as the widespread practice of artifical contraception. Mrs. Sanger thrived on rejection. She loved combat. She needed enemies. She found joy in evoking revulsion and shock. In temperament and personality, she was the ideal figure to lead and sustain the birth control movement in that early phase. The 1940s brought a new phase, in which birth control began to enjoy substantial social and official acceptance. Not surprisingly, Mrs. Sanger then slipped quietly from the position of leadership she had enjoyed for twenty-five years. So effectively had she educated society that it seemed no longer to need her. That, perhaps, was the final irony.

CHAPTER 9

The Fruits of Rebellion

Birth control has liberated many women—and men—from the burdens of unplanned parenthood. In that sense it can be called a liberal reform. But in many significant ways birth control has served conservative ends. Nothing more pointedly illustrated the potentially conservative implications of her cause than the enthusiastic reception that those eugenicists interested in biological control of allegedly inferior immigrants first gave to Margaret Sanger. The Protestant churches also found conservative utility in birth control when they endorsed it as an instrumentality to aid in the preservation of the family. And the federal government finally gave its quiet support to birth control in the interests of social control in the depression and conservation of human resources in wartime.[1]

Mrs. Sanger herself, after her early immersion in radicalism, spent the rest of her life preaching not to the poor but to the middle class. Though after World War I birth control reformers continued to be concerned with the plight of the prolific poor, in time that concern proceeded less from sympathy with the lower class than from anxiety in the middle class. The poor—especially the Negro and alien poor—became primarily a problem. Birth control, as the means to implement eugenic ideas, seemed the proper solution. But that hope, ultimately, proved chimerical. The Americans who came increasingly to practice birth control

1. Though the government faced a drastic rubber shortage at the beginning of the war, the War Production Board on January 24, 1942 permitted contraceptives, for both men and women, to be manufactured at 100 percent of the 1940–41 production level. Tileston v. Ullman, 26 A.2d 582 at 591 n (1942).

were those most concerned with social mobility—principally the members of the middle class. The very poor have proved either unwilling or unable to practice contraception effectively.

That Margaret Sanger's "shocking" reform, which she announced so defiantly in the *Woman Rebel* in 1914, should eventually have become a middle-class phenomenon was both ironic and appropriate. Mrs. Sanger's radical friends felt the irony keenly when they saw the bourgeoisie become the only self-conscious class in America and saw their comrade turn to serving its purposes and its prejudices. Others must have judged it only appropriate that a woman who had for so long resented her own social station should have led a movement that fitted so well the needs of the mobility-conscious middle class. Her concern for improving standards of living was Mrs. Sanger's most American characteristic.

She was characteristically American, too, in her persistent emotionalism. Hers was a special case of the pervasive anti-rationalism of twentieth-century American thought. With so many of her generation, Mrs. Sanger often allowed her "emotional Me" to triumph over her "head Me." That victory carried certain advantages. It enhanced her extraordinary energy and it contributed to her charismatic leadership of the birth control movement.

But Margaret Sanger's perfervid propagandizing also had its disadvantages. While it no doubt persuaded many of the public, it aggravated her relations with the professionals whose help she so badly needed. Much of Mrs. Sanger's trouble with the medical profession arose on that account. Cautious physicians resisted association with Mrs. Sanger's obstreperousness fully as much as they resisted the simple facts of technological and, some thought, moral innovation.

Similarly, Margaret Sanger, as the leading American spokeswoman for sexual reform, frequently lapsed into romantic extravagances which probably abetted as much as alleviated the frustrations of her feminist followers. Birth control was not, as Mrs. Sanger proclaimed, the simple key to the vexing problem of women's inferior social status.

Moreover, birth control did not miraculously liberate the "feminine spirit" or the "intuitive forward urge within," nor did it automatically produce sexual fulfillment. Yet Mrs. Sanger dwelt on those alluring themes for more than twenty years. Her exaggerated claims may have done more harm than she knew. Kenneth Keniston has recently suggested that the generation of American women who came to maturity in the 1920s and 1930s was singularly disillusioned with the failure of the promises of feminism. Perhaps they were disappointed not only by the sacrifice of their careers to domesticity, as Keniston argues, but also by the failure of connubial sex to provide the pleasures that Margaret Sanger and other romantics had so blithely promised.[2]

Mrs. Sanger's emotionalism was also indictable, as her friends in the eugenics movement would have appreciated, because it was inefficient. Following her "spontaneity theory," Mrs. Sanger long believed that the poor continued to have large families only because the church and the state conspired to withhold contraceptive information. But the very classes that were the most prolific did not demand birth control; the real enemy of her movement was neither the church nor the state but the ignorance and psychology of the masses themselves. Those facts Margaret Sanger never clearly acknowledged. Instead, her peculiar penchant for a dramatic and combative pose led her to an unstrategic deployment of her forces in what she fondly called "my fight for birth control."

Margaret Sanger never fully recovered from the sense of alienation she had felt as a child and a young woman. For all her obvious delight in the social standing leadership in the birth control movement brought her, she never really lost her sense of being an outsider. As a self-conceived combatant and outsider, she preferred to eschew compromise and persuasion and to seek her goals by direct action, defiance, and the attempted exercise of power. And, as with

2. Kenneth Keniston, *The Uncommitted: Alienated Youth in American Society* (New York: Harcourt, Brace, 1965), especially pp. 108–13.

her conduct of the birth control movement, so too with her theory of sexual relations. Woman's sexual goal, said Margaret Sanger, should be not parity but power. Birth control, for her, did not simply liberate; it strengthened women for their combative role in what Mrs. Sanger always regarded as the battle of the sexes.

To many who heard her message, Margaret Sanger was a heroine without equal. Though her personal sacrifices for the movement assuredly never outweighed the satisfactions she derived from her notoriety, the accounts of her self-abnegating crusade grew to legendary proportions. By her sixtieth birthday world opinion had lavishly acclaimed her. H. G. Wells called her "the greatest biological revolutionary the world has ever known." John Dewey spoke of the Sadie Sachs episode as a "Gethsemane" which was "the origin of the devoted, persistent, courageous, unremitting work which has since been done." Helen Keller wrote: "You are among the women I most love because you so labor and suffer that the life of the human race may become sager, finer and more creative. You are a free world-illuminating spirit." John Favill, one of the physicians associated with the birth control movement in the 1930s, told her simply that "your vision, courage and achievement make you the world's greatest woman." [3]

Margaret Sanger merited praise. Though she was often absorbed with self-justification, and though her contrary disposition sometimes hobbled more than it helped her movement, she remained an exceptionally dedicated and dynamic leader in what history must judge as a worthy cause, albeit one whose complexities and potential dangers Mrs. Sanger never fully appreciated.

Yet the praise Margaret Sanger received often seemed out of proportion to her achievement. Part of the hyperbole,

3. Telegram, H. G. Wells to Margaret Sanger, May 20, 1932; John Dewey, speech at presentation of American Women's Association award, to Margaret Sanger, May 20, 1932; Helen Keller to Margaret Sanger, March 13, 1938; telegram, John Favill to Margaret Sanger, May 20, 1932, all in MSP–LC.

undoubtedly, derived from her personal magnetism, which rarely failed to bring those who met her into her orbit. But a larger part reflected Mrs. Sanger's symbolic satisfaction of a pervasive psychological need. American society in this century has not realized its frequently stated ideal of equal status for women. Perhaps, therefore, the apotheosization of a feminist heroine like Margaret Sanger reflects society's recognition of the continuing victimization of women, and the desire, in some way, to find a redemptress. For that role Margaret Sanger, at her best and at her worst, was well suited.

Bibliographical Essay

Chapter 1

The Margaret Sanger Papers in the Library of Congress, Washington, D.C., contain the most complete record of Mrs. Sanger's career and were the principal source of information for this study. The library solicited Mrs. Sanger's papers in the early 1940s. Before she placed them there she had her secretary, Florence Rose, organize the papers and compile a comprehensive, though not too detailed, index. There are now over 250 boxes of material relating to all aspects of Mrs. Sanger's life and career. The Sophia Smith Collection in the Smith College Library, Northampton, Massachusetts, has an unindexed and less valuable assortment of Mrs. Sanger's papers. The Library of Congress collection contains a wealth of material on Mrs. Sanger's activities for birth control between 1914 and 1940. The papers at Smith College refer mainly to Mrs. Sanger's personal life and to her activities in the 1940s and 1950s.

All accounts of Mrs. Sanger's early life must begin, but should not end, with her two autobiographical works, *My Fight for Birth Control* (New York: Farrar and Rinehart, 1931), and *Margaret Sanger: An Autobiography* (New York: Norton, 1938). Both were ghost-written and have the flavor (and reliability) of campaign biographies. Most biographical writing about Mrs. Sanger has suffered from close reliance on these two books. Especially hagiographical and repetitious of Mrs. Sanger's own writings is Lawrence Lader, *The Margaret Sanger Story* (Garden City, N.Y.: Doubleday, 1955). A less comprehensive but more critical account of Mrs. Sanger's life is Chapter 19 in Peter Fryer, *The Birth Controllers* (New York: Stein and Day, 1966).

Henry May, *The End of American Innocence* (Chicago: Quadrangle Books, 1964) provides the best general introduction to the milieu Margaret Sanger found in New York in 1912. Oscar Cargill, *Intellectual America* (New York: Macmillan, 1941) pays special attention to the new ideas about sex that interested the prewar New York radicals and literati. Several of those individuals have left their own accounts of the period. See especially Emma Goldman, *Living My Life* (New York: Alfred A. Knopf, 1931); Floyd Dell, *Homecoming: An Autobiography* (New York: Farrar and Rinehart, 1933); Hutchins Hapgood, *A Victorian in the Modern World* (New York: Harcourt, Brace, 1939); Mabel Dodge Luhan, *Intimate Memories,* vol. 3, *Movers and Shakers* (New York: Harcourt, Brace, 1936); and Will Durant, *Transition* (New York: Simon and Schuster, 1927). Richard Drinnon, *Rebel in Paradise: A Biography of Emma Goldman* (Chicago: University of Chicago Press, 1961) makes special note of Emma Goldman's birth control activity.

Masses and the New York socialist journal *Call* are also indispensable sources of information on literary and political radicalism. The Mabel Dodge Luhan Papers, Beinecke Library, Yale University, New Haven, Connecticut, contain many scrapbooks of clippings and some correspondence about the different personalities who gathered in the Salon Dodge. The Ferrer School, and the group that formed it, have received no detailed study. Leonard D. Abbott, ed., *Francisco Ferrer: His Life, Work and Martyrdom* (New York: Francisco Ferrer Association, 1910), provides an introduction to the man whose memory the New York anarchists honored.

John Spargo, *Socialism and Motherhood* (New York: B. W. Huebsch, 1914) is a good example of so-called radical thinking on women and the family. Most of the ideas that drew Mrs. Sanger's attention, however, came from Europe. See especially Havelock Ellis, *Studies in the Psychology of Sex,* 7 vols. (Philadelphia: F. A. Davis, 1912–29); Edward Carpenter, *Love's Coming-of-Age* (New York: Mitchell Kennerly, 1911); Oliver Schreiner, *Woman and Labor* (New York: Frederick A. Stokes, 1911); and Ellen Key's four volumes, *The Century of the Child* (New York: G. P. Putnam's Sons, 1909). *Love and Marriage* (New York: G. P. Putnam's Sons, 1911), *The Woman Movement* (New York: G. P.

Putnam's Sons, 1912), and *The Renaissance of Motherhood* (New York: G. P. Putnam's Sons, 1914).

Robert Bremner, *From the Depths: The Discovery of Poverty in the United States* (New York: New York University Press, 1964) gives a general account of attitudes toward poverty and how they were changing in the early twentieth century. Roy Lubove, *The Progressives and the Slums* (Pittsburgh: University of Pittsburgh Press, 1962) treats specifically the New York slums which Mrs. Sanger found so appalling. See also Allen F. Davis, *Spearheads for Reform: the Social Settlements and the Progressive Movement* (New York: Oxford University Press, 1967).

Some issues of the *Woman Rebel*, Mrs. Sanger's 1914 newspaper, are preserved in her papers in the Library of Congress. A few other issues are in the New York Public Library.

George Dangerfield, *The Strange Death of Liberal England* (New York: Capricorn Books, 1961) entertainingly describes the English setting into which Mrs. Sanger stepped in 1914. Havelock Ellis's biography, *My Life* (Boston: Houghton Mifflin, 1939), gives Ellis's account of his acquaintance with Mrs. Sanger. For more on their friendship, see Arthur Calder-Marshall, *The Sage of Sex: A Life of Havelock Ellis* (New York: G. P. Putnam's Sons, 1959). Keith Briant, *Marie Stopes: A Biography* (London: Hogarth Press, 1962) is a biography of a leading English personality in the birth control movement and discusses the relationship, not always cordial, between Marie Stopes and Margaret Sanger.

Chapter 2

Still the most rewarding work on the American family is Arthur W. Calhoun, *A Social History of the American Family*, 3 vols. (Cleveland: Arthur H. Clark, 1919). Calhoun should be read in light of the theories brilliantly developed by Phillipe Ariés in *Centuries of Childhood* (New York: Alfred A. Knopf, 1962). Sidney Ditzion, *Marriage, Morals, and Sex in America* (New York: Bookman Associates, 1953) is the standard general work on the subject but is often too

general to be of use to the serious student. On Margaret
Sanger it is, as are most such works, uncritically credulous of
her own writings. John Sirjamaki, *The American Family in
the Twentieth Century* (Cambridge: Harvard University
Press, 1953) gives a general survey of sociological literature
on the subject. Helen I. Clarke, *Social Legislation: American
Laws Dealing With the Family, Child and Dependent* (New
York: D. Appleton-Century, 1940) provides a good introduction to the changing legal view of the family; it should be
supplemented with Fowler V. Harper, *Problems of the Family* (Indianapolis: Bobbs-Merrill, 1952; Rev. ed., 1962).

Michael Ryan, *The Philosophy of Marriage* (Philadelphia: Lindsay and Blakiston, 1870) is a good example of
nineteenth-century concern for the family and for sex ed-
ucation. Frank N. Hagar, *The American Family* (New York:
University Publishing Society, 1905) represents one of the
first twentieth-century criticisms of the state of the family.
Morrison I. Swift, *Marriage and Race Death* (New York:
Morrison I. Swift Press, 1906) is a more alarmist treatment of the same topic. More temperate and valuable are:
Chauncey J. Hawkins, *Will the Home Survive? A Study of
Tendencies in Modern Literature* (New York: Thomas
Whittaker, 1907), which lays responsibility for the disrup-
tion of the American home on the importation of German
and Scandinavian ideas; Lydia Kingsmill Commander, *The
American Idea* (New York: A. S. Barnes, 1907), probably
the best contemporary account of the issues surrounding the
falling birthrate and the emergence of the "new woman";
William E. Carson, *The Marriage Revolt* (London: T. Werner Laurie, 1915), an often cited inquiry into the rising
divorce rates in the early twentieth century. United States
Bureau of the Census, Department of Commerce and Labor,
Special Reports: Marriage and Divorce, 1867–1902, 2 vols.
(Washington: Government Printing Office, 1908), is a broad
statistical survey of divorce and indicates the pervasive concern for the problem in the period. Theodore Roosevelt
offered his views on the condition of the family in *The Foes
of Our Own Household* (New York: George H. Doran,
1917). One should also consult Elting Morison, ed., *The

Letters of Theodore Roosevelt, 8 vols. (Cambridge: Harvard University Press, 1951–54). James Quayle Dealey, *The Family in its Sociological Aspects* (Boston: Houghton Mifflin, 1912) and Edward T. Devine, *The Family and Social Work* (New York: Association Press, 1912) are both scholarly attempts to apply the social sciences to discussion of the family. Bernarr Macfadden, *Manhood and Marriage* (New York: Physical Culture Publishing, 1916) and *Womanhood and Marriage* (New York: Macfadden Publications, 1922) reflect the concern, characteristic of the period, for changing sexual roles in marriage.

J. A. Banks, *Prosperity and Parenthood* (London: Routledge and Kegan Paul, 1954) and J. A. and Olive Banks, *Feminism and Family Planning* (Liverpool: Liverpool University Press, 1964) are illuminating analyses of some of the factors influencing the birthrate in nineteenth-century England. Kenneth Keniston, *The Uncommitted: Alienated Youth in American Society* (New York: Harcourt, Brace and World, 1965), especially Chapter 10, offers some suggestive insights about the nature of American family life in this century.

For the study of modern woman, Simon deBeauvoir, *The Second Sex* (New York: Alfred A. Knopf, 1952) provides an indispensable starting point. A valuable review of other theories of femininity is Viola Klein, *The Feminine Character* (New York: International Universities Press, 1949). See also "The Woman in America," *Daedalus,* Spring, 1964 (Proceedings of the American Academy of Arts and Sciences, Vol. 93, no. 2). Margaret Mead, in *Male and Female* (New York: W. Morrow, 1949), discusses sexual differences from an anthropologist's point of view. Betty Friedan, *The Feminine Mystique* (New York: Dell, 1964) offers a prolix description by a disgruntled feminist partisan of the state of modern American womanhood. Margaret Mead and Frances Bagley Kaplan, eds., *American Women, The Report of the President's Commission on the Status of Women* (New York: Charles Scribner's Sons, 1965), reflects a new official concern for women in American society.

Ernest R. Groves, *The American Woman* (New York:

Greenberg, 1937), now dated, was one of the first attempts at an historical survey of the place of women in American society. Andrew Sinclair, *The Better Half: The Emancipation of the American Woman* (New York: Harper and Row, 1965) is a more recent account of the same subject. Eleanor Flexner, *Century of Struggle: The Woman's Rights Movement in the United States* (Cambridge: Harvard University Press, Belknap Press, 1959) is another general survey, with an especially thorough treatment of the women's suffrage movement. Robert E. Riegel, *American Feminists* (Lawrence: University of Kansas Press, 1963) is good on nineteenth-century feminism. Aileen Kraditor, in *The Ideas of the Woman Suffrage Movement, 1890–1920* (New York: Columbia University Press, 1965), lucidly traces the development of arguments used by the suffragists to promote their cause. Robert W. Smuts, *Women and Work in America* (New York: Columbia University Press, 1959) is a highly informative study of women's work and attitudes toward working women. Christopher Lasch, *The New Radicalism in America, 1889–1963* (New York: Alfred A. Knopf, 1965) contains many perceptive insights on the women's movement around the turn of the century. Alan P. Grimes, *The Puritan Ethic and Woman Suffrage* (New York: Oxford University Press, 1967) emphasizes the essential conservatism of the suffrage movement. William L. O'Neill, "Feminism as a Radical Ideology," in Alfred F. Young, ed., *Dissent: Explorations in the History of American Radicalism* (DeKalb: Northern Illinois University Press, 1968), makes some necessary distinctions between the different kinds of feminists. See also his *Everyone was Brave: the Rise and Fall of Feminism in America* (Chicago: Quadrangle Books, 1969).

Barbara Welter, in "The Cult of True Womanhood," *American Quarterly* 18 (1966): 151–74, discusses the feminine ideal of the early nineteenth century. Egal Feldman, in "Prostitution, the Alien Woman and the Progressive Imagination, 1910–1915," *American Quarterly* 19 (1967): 192–206, makes an interesting comparison for the early twentieth century. See also Robert E. Riegel, "Changing

American Attitudes toward Prostitution, 1800–1920," *Journal of the History of Ideas* 29 (1968): 437–52; and James R. McGovern, "The American Woman's Pre-World War I Freedom in Manners and Morals," *Journal of American History* 55 (1968): 315–33.

Thomas Beer, *The Mauve Decade* (Garden City, N.Y.: Garden City Publishing, 1926) is a good introduction to literary attitudes toward women in the 1890s. Larzer Ziff deals in part with the same subject in *The American 1890s* (New York: Viking Press, 1966). Essential to any study of American attitudes toward women in the period are Henry James's novels *Daisy Miller* (1878), *The Portrait of a Lady* (1881), *The Bostonians* (1886), and *The Wings of the Dove* (1902). William Wasserstrom, *Heiress of All the Ages: Sex and Sentiment in the Genteel Tradition* (Minneapolis: University of Minnesota Press, 1959) discusses the themes of feminine identity and sexuality as treated by James and other authors. Leslie Fiedler, *Love and Death in the American Novel* (New York: Criterion Books, 1960) contains unwieldy, didactic, but invaluable reflections on sexuality (or its absence) in American literature.

Two helpful guides for studying the depiction of women and sexuality in the theatre in this period are T. Allston Brown, *A History of the New York Stage: From the First Performance in 1732 to 1901*, 3 vols. (New York: Dodd, Mead, 1903), and George C. O'Dell, *Annals of the New York Stage*, 15 vols. (New York: Columbia University Press, 1927–49).

Charlotte Perkins Gilman, *Women and Economics* (Boston: Small, Maynard, 1898), *The Home: Its Work and Its Influence* (New York: McClure, Phillips, 1903), and *The Man-Made World, or, Our Androcentric Culture* (New York: Charlton, 1911) are the principal works by the leading feminist theoretician of the period. For a concise review of Mrs. Gilman's ideas, see Carl N. Degler, "Charlotte Perkins Gilman on the Theory and Practice of Feminism," *American Quarterly* 8 (1956): 21–39. Another interesting feminine thinker of the period, who has been long neglected, was

Elsie Clews Parsons. See her *Fear and Conventionality*
(New York: G. P. Putnam's Sons, 1914), *Social Freedom*
(New York: G. P. Putnam's Sons, 1915), and *Social Rule*
(New York: G. P. Putnam's Sons, 1916). Another noteworthy
woman writer was Mary Roberts Coolidge, who wrote,
among other works, *Why Women Are So* (New York: Henry
Holt, 1912). See also: Abba Goold Woolson, *Woman in
American Society* (Boston: Roberts Brothers, 1873); Anna
B. Rogers, *Why American Marriages Fail* (Boston: Hough-
ton Mifflin, 1909); Ida Tarbell, *The Business of Being a
Woman* (New York: Macmillan, 1912); Elizabeth Bisland
Wetmore's anonymously published book *The Secret Life*
(New York: John Lane, 1906); and especially Jessie Taft,
*The Woman Movement from the Point of View of Social
Consciousness* (Chicago: University of Chicago Press, 1916).

For sympathetic male commentary on the "woman question," see: Scott Nearing, *Woman and Social Progress* (New
York: Macmillan, 1912); Walter Lippmann, *Drift and
Mastery* (New York: Mitchell Kennerly, 1914); and Lester
Ward, *Pure Sociology* (New York: Macmillan, 1914), especially chapter 14, where Ward outlined his "gynaecocentric
theory" of human development, an idea that appealed
strongly to Charlotte Perkins Gilman.

One of the first attempts to incorporate new sexual
theories into social science was William I. Thomas, *Sex and
Society* (Chicago: University of Chicago Press, 1907). More
recent and helpful, though overdrawn, are Gordon Rattray
Taylor, *Sex in History* (New York: Vanguard Press, 1954)
and *The Angel-Makers: A Study in Psychological Origins
of Historical Change, 1750–1850* (London: William Heinemann, 1958). For sexual attitudes in the late nineteenth
century, a good starting point is Walter E. Houghton, *The
Victorian Frame of Mind* (New Haven: Yale University
Press, 1957), especially Chapter 13, "Love." Steven Marcus,
*The Other Victorians: A Study of Sexuality and Pornog-
raphy in Mid-Nineteenth Century England* (New York:
Basic Books, 1964) is a brilliant though methodologically

restricted inquiry into Victorian sexual attitudes. Its influence on this study has obviously been great. See also Peter T. Caminos, "Late Victorian Sexual Respectability and the Social System," *International Review of Social History* 8 (1963): 18–48, 216–50.

For a general picture of various aspects of the American mind at the turn of the century, see Henry Steele Commager, *The American Mind* (New Haven: Yale University Press, 1950), and Morton White, *Social Thought in America: The Revolt against Formalism* (Boston: Beacon Press, 1957).

For a partisan account of the impact of new sexual theories, see Floyd Dell, *Love in the Machine Age* (New York: Farrar and Rinehart, 1930). Robert Willson, *The American Boy and the Social Evil* (Philadelphia: John C. Winston, 1905), and Prince A. Morrow, *Social Diseases and Marriage* (New York: Lea Brothers, 1904) illustrate representative attitudes toward masculine and feminine sexuality in the early twentieth century. Freud's influence in America is described best by David Shakow and David Rapaport, in *The Influence of Freud on American Psychology*, Psychological Issues, vol. 4 (New York: International Universities Press, 1964). See also Iago Galdston, ed., *Freud and Contemporary Culture* (New York: International Universities Press, 1957); Benjamin Nelson, ed., *Freud and the Twentieth Century* (New York: Meridian Books, 1957); Hendrik M. Ruitenbeek, *Freud and America* (New York: Macmillan, 1966); and especially Phillip Rieff, *Freud: The Mind of the Moralist* (New York: Viking Press, 1959). R. V. Sampson, in *Equality and Power* (London: Heinemann Educational Books, 1965), argues persuasively that Freud mistakenly insisted on the necessity of inequality and domination in human relationships.

Chapter 3

For a general history of the birth control movement, see Maurice Chachuat, *Le Mouvement du "Birth Control" dans les Pays Anglo-Saxon* (Paris: M. Giard, 1934).

Mrs. Sanger's papers in the Library of Congress and at Smith College are the best sources of information for the organizational history of the movement in the United States. See also *My Fight for Birth Control* and *Margaret Sanger: An Autobiography*. The best study of the early movement is Francis McLennon Vreeland, "The Process of Reform with Especial Reference to Reform Groups in the Field of Population" (Ph.D. diss., University of Michigan, 1929). See also Mary Ware Dennett, *Birth Control Laws: Shall We Keep Them or Abolish Them?* (New York: Grafton Press, 1926). Richard Drinnon, *Rebel in Paradise: A Biography of Emma Goldman* has some material on early propaganda efforts. See also the papers relating to Emma Goldman in the Harry A. Weinberger Memorial Collection, Sterling Library, Yale University, New Haven, Connecticut. The Mable Dodge Luhan Papers in the Beinecke Library, Yale University, contain some material on the early organizational campaign. The *Birth Control Review*, official publication of the New York Birth Control League and later of the American Birth Control League, contains a running chronicle of organizational developments as well as numerous articles on the general subject of birth control.

Chapter 4

The most comprehensive study of American left-wing thought is Donald Drew Egbert and Stow Persons, *Socialism in the United States*, 2 vols. (Princeton: Princeton University Press, 1952). For socialism in the twentieth century, see David Shannon, *The Socialist Party in America: A History* (New York: Macmillan, 1955); and James Weinstein, *The Decline of Socialism in America, 1912–1925* (New York: Monthly Review Press, 1967). See also Eunice Minette Schuster, *Native American Anarchism*, Smith College Studies in History, vol. 18 (Northampton, Mass.: Department of History, Smith College, 1932).

The best introduction to nativist and racist thinking in the United States in this period is John Higham, *Strangers in the Land* (New York: Atheneum, 1963). For a more specific study of a phenomenon that directly affected the birth control movement, see Mark H. Haller, *Eugenics: Hereditarian Attitudes in American Thought* (New Brunswick, N.J.: Rutgers University Press, 1963), which is complemented by Samuel Haber, *Efficiency and Uplift: Scientific Management in the Progressive Era, 1890–1920* (Chicago: University of Chicago Press, 1964), an interesting examination of some of the implications of the idea of "efficiency." Donald K. Pickens, *Eugenics and the Progressives* (Nashville: Vanderbilt University Press, 1968) has a chapter on Margaret Sanger. Mrs. Sanger's own ideas on eugenics can be found in *Woman and the New Race* (New York: Brentano's, 1920), and especially in *The Pivot of Civilization* (New York: Brentano's, 1922). For representative examples of eugenic thinking in the period see: *The Sixth International Neo-Malthusian and Birth Control Conference* (New York: American Birth Control League, 1926); Madison Grant, *The Passing of the Great Race* (New York: Charles Scribner's Sons, 1916); Paul Popenoe, *Applied Eugenics* (New York: Macmillan, 1918); Henry Pratt Fairchild, *The Melting Pot Mistake* (Boston: Little, Brown, 1926); and Ellsworth Huntington, *Tomorrow's Children* (New York: John Wiley and Sons, 1935). G. K. Chesterton, in *Eugenics and Other Evils* (London: Cassell, 1922), points out the dangers inherent in trying to apply eugenic principles in a democratic society. Lee Rainwater, *And the Poor Get Children: Sex, Contraception, and Family Planning in the Working Class* (Chicago: Quadrangle Books, 1960) and the same author's *Family Design: Marital Sexuality, Family Size, and Contraception* (Chicago: Aldine, 1965) demonstrate the proclivity of the prolific to remain prolific, just as Arthur J. Barton and others always feared.

Edward M. East, *Mankind at the Crossroads* (New York: Charles Scribner's Sons, 1928) was one of the first scholarly treatments of the "population explosion." The book, which contradicted the currently voguish "stagnation" theories about population levels and the economy, had a significant influence on Margaret Sanger.

Chapter 5

Denis de Rougemont, *Love in the Western World* (New York: Pantheon, 1956) traces the history of the western tradition of romantic love. For a different view, see Wayland Young, *Eros Denied: Sex in Western Society* (New York: Grove Press, 1964). Probably the most original and perhaps the most influential modern work on romantic love was George R. Drysdale, *The Elements of Social Science* (9th ed. London: E. Truelove, 1871), which was first published in 1855 as *Physical, Sexual and Natural Religion: By a Student of Medicine* (London: E. Truelove, 1855). Mrs. Sanger's views on the subject can be found most easily in *Woman and the New Race* and *The Pivot of Civilization*. See also her *Happiness in Marriage* (New York: Blue Ribbon Books, 1926), which was as close as she ever came to writing a marriage manual. William L. O'Neill, *Divorce in the Progressive Era* (New Haven: Yale University Press, 1967) has some discussion of sexual romanticism as it figured in the divorce controversy.

Chapter 6

The best examinations of social practices and attitudes in the 1920s with regard to family limitation can be found in: Harold E. Stearns, ed., *Civilization in the United States* (New York: Harcourt, Brace, 1922); Robert S. and Helen Merrell Lynd, *Middletown* (New York: Harcourt, Brace, 1929); "The Modern American Family," *Annals of the American Academy of Political and Social Science* 160 (March 1932); and the President's Research Committee on Social Trends, *Recent Social Trends in the United States* (New York: McGraw-Hill, 1933). See also Robert Latou Dickinson and Lura Beam, *A Thousand Marriages: A Medical Study of Sex Adjustment* (Baltimore: Williams and Wilkins, 1931), one of the first surveys of clinical data on sexual behavior.

Both Walter Lippmann, *A Preface to Morals* (New York: Macmillan, 1929) and Bertrand Russell, *Marriage and*

Morals (New York: Horace Liveright, 1929) discuss the morality of the new attitudes. See also Joseph Wood Krutch, *The Modern Temper* (New York: Harcourt, Brace, 1929). Dorothy Dunbar Bromley, *Birth Control: Its Use and Misuse* (New York: Harper and Brothers, 1934) gives a good review of the debate on birth control in the early 1930s, and has a helpful bibliography. Edwin M. Schur, ed., *The Family and the Sexual Revolution* (Bloomington: Indiana University Press, 1964), is an anthology that brings the debate up to the 1960s.

A good survey of the institutional and intellectual developments within American Protestantism in this century is Herbert Wallace Schneider, *Religion in 20th-Century America* (Cambridge: Harvard University Press, 1952). On liberalism, see Lloyd J. Averill, *American Theology in the Liberal Tradition* (Philadelphia: Westminster Press, 1967); and Kenneth Cauthen, *The Impact of American Religious Liberalism* (New York: Harper and Row, 1962). See also chapters 10 and 11 in Stow Persons, ed., *Evolutionary Thought in America* (New Haven: Yale University Press, 1950), for the impact of Darwin on moral theory and theology. Richard M. Fagley, *The Population Explosion and Christian Responsibility* (New York: Oxford University Press, 1960) discusses at length Protestant attitudes toward contraception.

The best sources for religious opinion on birth control are the periodical publications of the various denominations. Occasionally rewarding, but extremely difficult to use because they are not usually indexed, are the official records and journals of church conventions.

A few Protestant clergymen spoke out publicly, though often anonymously, for birth control. See, for example, A Priest of the Church of England, *The Morality of Birth Control* (London: John Bale, Sons and Danielsson, 1924). For one notable layman's comment on the Lambeth Conference of 1930, see T. S. Eliot, *Thoughts after Lambeth* (London: Faber and Faber, 1931).

For Roman Catholic attitudes toward birth control, **see**

especially John T. Noonan, Jr., *Contraception: A History of its Treatment by the Catholic Theologians and Canonists* (Cambridge: Harvard University Press, Belknap Press, 1965), a monumental work of scholarship which traces the development of Catholic doctrine on contraception from the first century to the twentieth. While Noonan is critical of the present Catholic position, Alvah W. Sulloway, in *Birth Control and Catholic Doctrine* (Boston: Beacon Press, 1959), is still more critical. John Rock, *The Time Has Come: A Catholic Doctor's Proposal to End the Battle over Birth Control* (New York: Alfred A. Knopf, 1963) is a statement of faith by a liberal Catholic physician who played an important role in developing the hormonal anovulant pill. Dorothy Dunbar Bromley, *Catholics and Birth Control: Contemporary Views on Doctrine* (New York: Devin-Adair, 1965) reflects the growing dissatisfaction of many Catholic laymen and some clergymen with Rome's immobility on the issue of contraception.

Chapter 7

Richard Shryock, *The Development of Modern Medicine* (Philadelphia: University of Pennsylvania Press, 1936) is the standard history of modern medicine and is especially good on public attitudes toward the medical profession in the nineteenth century and on the controversy over quackery. A more detailed study of that controversy is Donald E. Konold, *A History of Medical Ethics, 1847–1912* (Madison: State Historical Society of Wisconsin, 1962). A general work with some material relevant to the birth control movement is George Rosen, *A History of Public Health* (New York: M.D. Publications, 1958). James G. Burrow, *AMA: Voice of American Medicine* (Baltimore: Johns Hopkins Press, 1963), though otherwise a thorough study of that organization, does not discuss its reaction to the birth control movement. Norman E. Himes, *Medical History of Contraception* (Baltimore: Williams and Wilkins, 1936) is the standard work on the subject. Himes, though not a medical doctor, treated the technical as well as the sociological aspects of medical involvement with birth control. He considered Margaret Sanger important for having promoted the "democratization" of contraceptive practices.

Margaret Sanger and Hannah Stone, eds., *The Practice of Contraception* (Baltimore: Williams and Wilkins, 1931), the proceedings of the Seventh International Birth Control Conference in Zurich, Switzerland in 1930, summarizes the state of medical knowledge of contraception in the 1920s. See also Robert Latou Dickinson, *Control of Conception* (Baltimore: Williams and Wilkins, 1931) and *Techniques of Conception Control* (Baltimore: Williams and Wilkins, 1931). Dickinson's National Committee on Maternal Health published many works on fertility and contraception in the Medical Aspects of Human Fertility series. Caroline Hadley Robinson, in *Seventy Birth Control Clinics* (Baltimore: Williams and Wilkins, 1930), describes in detail the clientele and the operating procedures in a sample of clinics.

The archives of the New York Academy of Medicine in New York provided some information on the activities of Robert Latou Dickinson and the Committee on Maternal Health. Unfortunately, most of the material in the archives is not available to scholars, but two large boxes of Dickinson's papers are in the office of Dr. Christopher Tietze, Bio-Medical Division, Population Council, in the New York Academy of Medicine. Those papers were indispensable to understanding the complexities of the relationship between Mrs. Sanger and the medical profession. Lura Beam, *Bequest from a Life: A Biography of Louise Stevens Bryant* (Privately published, 1963), a copy of which is in the superb library of the New York Academy of Medicine, shed some light on the role Dickinson's secretary played in the long negotiations with Mrs. Sanger.

Morris Fishbein, *The Medical Follies* (New York: Boni and Liveright, 1925) and *Fads and Quackery in Healing* (New York: Covici, Friede, 1932), and Rachel Lynn Palmer and Sarah K. Greenberg, *Facts and Frauds in Woman's Hygiene: A Medical Guide Against Misleading Claims and Dangerous Products* (New York: Vanguard Press, 1936) all emphasize the limits of medical knowledge of contraception and condemn the proliferation of contraceptive devices sold without prescription.

Professional medical journals proved the most valuable source of information for this part of the study. The many journals published over the past hundred years contain a rich untapped vein of raw material for social history. The *Index Medicus* and the *Index Catalogue of the Library of the Surgeon-General's Office, United States Army* provide valuable guides to that material.

Chapter 8

Mrs. Sanger's several attempts to persuade Congress to change the Comstock law are recorded in: United States, Congress, Senate, Subcommittee of the Committee on the Judiciary, *Birth Control, Hearings on S. 4582*, 71st Cong., 3d sess., 1931; United States, Congress, Senate, Subcommittee of the Committee on the Judiciary, *Birth Control, Hearings on S. 4436*, 72d Cong., 1st sess., 1932; United States, Congress, House, Subcommittee of the Committee on Ways and Means, *Birth Control, Extracts from Hearings on H.R. 11082*, 72d Cong., 1st sess., 1932; United States, Congress, House, Subcommittee of the Committee on the Judiciary, *Birth Control, Hearings on H.R. 5978*, 73d Cong., 2d sess., 1934; United States, Congress, Senate, Subcommittee of the Committee on the Judiciary, *Birth Control, Hearings on S. 1842*, 73d Cong., 2d sess., 1934. For a sympathetic view of Mrs. Sanger's principal adversary before Congress, see Francis Lyons Broderick, *Right Reverend New Dealer: John A. Ryan* (New York: Macmillan, 1963). For a less sympathetic view, see Paul Blanchard, *American Freedom and Catholic Power* (Boston: Beacon Press, 1949). For a comparison with England, see Robert E. Dowse and John Peel, "The Politics of Birth Control," *Political Studies* 13 (1965): 181–97.

A good general account of the legal atmosphere Mrs. Sanger found so oppressive is Robert W. Haney, *Comstockery in America* (Boston: Beacon Press, 1960). Heywood Broun and Margaret Leech, *Anthony Comstock: Roundsman of the Lord* (New York: Albert and Charles Boni, 1927) is the standard biography of that vigorous defender of the public morals. See also Morris L. Ernst and Alexander Lindey, *The Censor Marches On* (New York: Doubleday, Doran, 1940), especially chapters 9 and 10.

Carol Flora Books, "The Early History of the Anti-Contraceptive Laws in Massachusetts and Connecticut," *American Quarterly* 18 (1966): 3–23, gives the nineteenth-century background to the protracted legal fight over birth control in two states.

Alvah W. Sulloway, in *Birth Control and Catholic Doctrine*, Chapter 5, describes the general development of case-law history with regard to contraception. See also Peter Smith, "The History and Future of the Legal Battle over Birth Control," *Cornell Law Quarterly* 49 (1964): 275. Other legal aspects of birth control are discussed in Jack Hudson, "Birth Control Legislation," *Cleveland-Marshall Law Review* 9 (1960): 245; and Joseph L. Dorsey, "Changing Attitudes toward the Massachusetts Birth Control Law," *New England Journal of Medicine* 271: (1964): 823.

Some material on the involvement of the federal government with birth control can be found in the records of the Department of Agriculture, the Works Progress Administration, and especially the United States Public Health Service, all in the National Archives, Washington, D.C. The records of the Children's Bureau are in the Central Files, Department of Health, Education and Welfare, Washington, D.C., and in the Federal Records Center, Franconia, Virginia. There is also some material relating to the development of birth control programs in Puerto Rico in the records of the Office of Territories in the National Archives.

Selected Bibliography

Manuscript Collections

Franconia, Virginia. Federal Records Center. Children's Bureau Records.

New Haven, Connecticut. Yale University. Beinecke Library. Mabel Dodge Luhan Papers.

New Haven, Connecticut. Yale University. Sterling Library. Harry A. Weinberger Memorial Collection.

New York, N.Y. New York Academy of Medicine. Archives.

New York, N.Y. Population Council. Bio-Medical Division. Office of Dr. Christopher Tietze. Robert Latou Dickinson Papers.

Northampton, Massachusetts. Smith College. Sophia Smith Collection. Margaret Sanger Papers.

Washington, D.C. Library of Congress. Margaret Sanger Papers.

Washington, D.C. National Archives. United States Department of Agriculture Records.

Washington, D.C. National Archives. United States Public Health Service Records.

Washington, D.C. National Archives. Works Progress Administration Records.

Washington, D.C. United States Department of Health, Education, and Welfare. Children's Bureau Records.

Periodicals

Birth Control Review, 1917–38.
Call (New York), 1910–16.
Masses, 1912–16.
Woman Rebel, 1914.

Articles

Brooks, Carol Flora. "The Early History of the Anti-Contraceptive Laws in Massachusetts and Connecticut." *American Quarterly* 18 (1966): 3–23.

Cominos, Peter T. "Late Victorian Sexual Respectability

and the Social System." *International Review of Social History* 8 (1963): 18–48, 216–50.

Degler, Carl N. "Charlotte Perkins Gilman on the Theory and Practice of Feminism." *American Quarterly* 7 (1956): 21–39.

Dorsey, Joseph L. "Changing Attitudes toward the Massachusetts Birth Control Law." *New England Journal of Medicine* 271 (1964): 823.

Dowse, Robert E., and John Peel. "The Politics of Birth Control." *Political Studies* 13 (1965): 181–97.

Feldman, Egal. "Prostitution, the Alien Woman and the Progressive Imagination, 1910–1915." *American Quarterly* 19 (1967): 192–206.

Hudson, Jack. "Birth Control Legislation." *Cleveland-Marshall Law Review* 9 (1960): 245.

Lader, Lawrence. "Three Men Who Made a Revolution." *New York Times Magazine*, April 10, 1966, p. 8.

Lasch, Christopher. "Divorce and the Family in America." *Atlantic*, November, 1966, pp. 57–61.

McGovern, James R. "The American Woman's Pre-World War I Freedom in Manners and Morals." *Journal of American History* 55 (1968): 315–33.

Obituary of Margaret Sanger. *New York Times*, September 7, 1966, p. 1.

O'Neill, William L. "Feminism as a Radical Ideology." In *Dissent: Explorations in the History of American Radicalism*, ed. Alfred F. Young. DeKalb: Northern Illinois University Press, 1968.

Potter, David M. "American Women and the American Character." *Stetson University Bulletin* 62 (1962).

Riegel, Robert E. "Changing American Attitudes toward Prostitution 1800–1920." *Journal of the History of Ideas* 29 (1968): 437–52.

Smith, Peter. "The History and Future of the Legal Battle over Birth Control." *Cornell Law Quarterly* 49 (1964): 275.

Welter, Barbara. "The Cult of True Womanhood." *American Quarterly* 18 (1960): 151–74.

Books

Abbott, Leonard. *Francisco Ferrer: His Life, Work and Martyrdom*. New York: Francisco Ferrer Association, 1910.

Ariés, Phillipe. *Centuries of Childhood*. New York: Alfred A. Knopf, 1962.

Averill, Lloyd J. *American Theology in the Liberal Tradition*. Philadelphia: Westminster Press, 1967.

Banks, J. A. *Prosperity and Parenthood*. London: Routledge and Kegan Paul, 1954.

Banks, J. A., and Olive Banks. *Feminism and Family Planning*. Liverpool: Liverpool University Press, 1964.

Beam, Lura. *Bequest from a Life: A Biography of Louise Stevens Bryant*. Privately published, 1963.

Beauvoir, Simone de. *The Second Sex*. New York: Alfred A. Knopf, 1952.

Beer, Thomas. *The Mauve Decade*. Garden City, N.Y.: Garden City Publishing, 1926.

Blanshard, Paul. *American Freedom and Catholic Power*. Boston: Beacon Press, 1949.

Bremner, Robert. *From the Depths: The Discovery of Poverty in the United States*. New York: New York University Press, 1964.

Briant, Keith. *Marie Stopes: A Biography*. London: Hogarth Press, 1962.

Broderick, Francis Lyons. *Right Reverend New Dealer: John A. Ryan*. New York: Macmillan, 1963.

Bromley, Dorothy Dunbar. *Birth Control: Its Use and Misuse*. New York: Harper and Brothers, 1934.

———. *Catholics and Birth Control: Contemporary Views on Doctrine*. New York: Devin-Adair, 1965.

Broun, Heywood, and Margaret Leech. *Anthony Comstock: Roundsman of the Lord*. New York: Albert and Charles Boni, 1927.

Burrow, James G. *AMA: Voice of American Medicine*. Baltimore: Johns Hopkins Press, 1963.

Calder-Marshall, Arthur. *The Sage of Sex: A Life of Havelock Ellis*. New York: G. P. Putnam's Sons, 1959.

Calhoun, Arthur W. *A Social History of the American Family*. 3 vols. Cleveland: Arthur H. Clark, 1919.

Cargill, Oscar. *Intellectual America*. New York: Macmillan, 1941.

Carpenter, Edward. *Love's Coming-of-Age*. New York: Mitchell Kennerly, 1911.

Carson, William E. *The Marriage Revolt*. London: T. Werner Laurie, 1915.

Cauthen, Kenneth. *The Impact of American Religious Liberalism*. New York: Harper and Row, 1962.

Chachuat, Maurice. *Le Mouvement du "Birth Control" dans les Pays Anglo-Saxon*. Paris: M. Giard, 1934.

Chesterton, G. K. *Eugenics and Other Evils*. London: Cassell, 1922.

Clarke, Helen I. *Social Legislation: American Laws Dealing with the Family, Child, and Dependent*. New York: D. Appleton-Century, 1940.

Commager, Henry Steele. *The American Mind*. New Haven: Yale University Press, 1950.

Commander, Lydia K. *The American Idea*. New York: A. S. Barnes, 1907.

Coolidge, Mary Roberts. *Why Women Are So*. New York: Henry Holt, 1912.

Dangerfield, George. *The Strange Death of Liberal England*. New York: Capricorn Books, 1961.

Davis, Allen F. *Spearheads for Reform: the Social Settlements and the Progressive Movement*. New York: Oxford University Press, 1967.

Dealey, James Quayle. *The Family in its Sociological Aspects*. Boston: Houghton Mifflin, 1912.

Dell, Floyd. *Homecoming: An Autobiography*. New York: Farrar and Rinehart, 1933.

————. *Love in the Machine Age*. New York: Farrar and Rinehart, 1930.

Dennett, Mary Ware. *Birth Control Laws: Shall We Keep Them or Abolish Them?* New York: Frederick H. Hitchcock, 1926.

Devine, Edward T. *The Family and Social Work*. New York: Association Press, 1912.

Dickinson, Robert Latou. *Control of Conception*. Baltimore: Williams and Wilkins, 1931.

———. *Techniques of Conception Control*. Baltimore: Williams and Wilkins, 1931.

———, and Lura Beam. *A Thousand Marriages: A Medical Study of Sex Adjustment*. Baltimore: Williams and Wilkins, 1931.

Ditzion, Sidney. *Marriage, Morals, and Sex in America*. New York: Bookman Associates, 1953.

Drinnon, Richard. *Rebel in Paradise: A Biography of Emma Goldman*. Chicago: University of Chicago Press, 1961.

Drysdale, George R. *The Elements of Social Science*. 9th ed. London: E. Truelove, 1871.

Durant, Will. *Transition*. New York: Simon and Schuster, 1927.

East, E. M. *Mankind at the Crossroads*. New York: Charles Scribner's Sons, 1928.

Egbert, Donald Drew, and Stow, Persons. *Socialism in the United States*. 2 vols. Princeton: Princeton University Press, 1952.

Eliot, T. S. *Thoughts after Lambeth*. London: Faber and Faber, 1931.

Ellis, Havelock. *My Life*. Boston: Houghton Mifflin, 1939.

———. *Studies in the Psychology of Sex*. 7 vols. Philadelphia: F. A. Davis, 1912–29.

Ernst, Morris, and Alexander Lindey. *The Censor Marches On*. New York: Doubleday, Doran, 1940.

Fagley, Richard M. *The Population Explosion and Christian Responsibility*. New York: Oxford University Press, 1960.

Fairchild, Henry Pratt. *The Melting Pot Mistake*. Boston: Little, Brown, 1926.

Fiedler, Leslie. *Love and Death in the American Novel*. New York: Criterion Books, 1960.

Fishbein, Morris. *Fads and Quackery in Healing*. New York: Covici, Friede, 1932.

———. *The Medical Follies*. New York: Boni and Liveright, 1925.

Flexner, Eleanor. *Century of Struggle: The Woman's Rights Movement in the United States.* Cambridge: Harvard University Press, Belknap Press, 1959.

Friedan, Betty. *The Feminine Mystique.* New York: Dell, 1964.

Fryer, Peter. *The Birth Controllers.* New York: Stalin and Day, 1966.

Galdston, Iago, ed. *Freud and Contemporary Culture.* New York: International Universities Press, 1957.

Gilman, Charlotte Perkins. *The Home: Its Works and Its Influence.* New York: McClure, Phillips, 1903.

———. *The Man-Made World, or, Our Androcentric Culture.* New York: Charlton, 1911.

———. *Women and Economics.* Boston: Small, Maynard, 1898.

Goldman, Emma. *Living My Life.* New York, Alfred A. Knopf, 1931.

Grant, Madison. *The Passing of the Great Race.* New York: Charles Scribner's Sons, 1916.

Grimes, Alan P. *The Puritan Ethic and Woman Suffrage.* New York: Oxford University Press, 1967.

Groves, Ernest R. *The American Woman.* New York: Greenberg, 1937.

Haber, Samuel. *Efficiency and Uplift: Scientific Management in the Progressive Era, 1890–1920.* Chicago: University of Chicago Press, 1964.

Hager, Frank H. *The American Family.* New York: University Publishing Society, 1905.

Haller, Mark H. *Eugenics: Hereditarian Attitudes in American Thought.* New Brunswick, N.J.: Rutgers University Press, 1963.

Haney, Robert W. *Comstockery in America.* Boston: Beacon Press, 1960.

Hapgood, Hutchins. *A Victorian in the Modern World.* New York: Harcourt, Brace, 1939.

Harper, Fowler V. *Problems of the Family.* Indianapolis: Bobbs-Merrill, 1952; rev. ed. 1962.

Hawkins, Chauncey J. *Will the Home Survive? A Study of*

Tendencies in Modern Literature. New York: Thomas Whittaker, 1907.

Higham, John. *Strangers in the Land*. New York: Atheneum, 1963.

Himes, Norman E. *Medical History of Contraception*. Baltimore: Williams and Wilkins, 1936.

Houghton, Walter E. *The Victorian Frame of Mind*. New Haven: Yale University Press, 1957.

Huntington, Ellsworth. *Tomorrow's Children*. New York: John Wiley and Sons, 1935.

James, Henry. *The Bostonians*. New York: Random House, Modern Library, 1956.

———. *Daisy Miller*. New York: Dell, 1963.

———. *The Portrait of a Lady*. Boston: Houghton Mifflin, 1963.

———. *The Wings of the Dove*. New York: Dell, 1963.

Keniston, Kenneth. *The Uncommitted: Alienated Youth in American Society*. New York: Harcourt, Brace and World, 1965.

Key, Ellen. *The Century of the Child*. New York: G. P. Putnam's Sons, 1909.

———. *Love and Marriage*. New York: G. P. Putnam's Sons, 1911.

———. *The Renaissance of Motherhood*. New York: G. P. Putnam's Sons, 1914.

———. *The Woman Movement*. New York: G. P. Putnam's Sons, 1912.

Klein, Viola. *The Feminine Character*. New York: International Universities Press, 1949.

Konold, Donald E. *A History of Medical Ethics, 1847–1912*. Madison: State Historical Society of Wisconsin, 1962.

Kraditor, Aileen. *The Ideas of the Woman Suffrage Movement, 1890–1920*. New York: Columbia University Press, 1965.

Krutch, Joseph Wood. *The Modern Temper*. New York: Harcourt, Brace, 1929.

Lader, Lawrence. *The Margaret Sanger Story*. Garden City, N.Y.: Doubleday, 1955.

Lasch, Christopher. *The New Radicalism in America, 1889–1963.* New York: Alfred A. Knopf, 1965.

Lippmann, Walter. *Drift and Mastery.* New York: Mitchell Kennerly, 1914.

———. *A Preface to Morals.* New York: Macmillan, 1929.

Lubove, Roy. *The Progressives and the Slums: Tenement House Reform in New York City, 1890–1917.* Pittsburgh: University of Pittsburgh Press, 1962.

Luhan, Mabel Dodge. *Intimate Memories.* Vol. 3, *Movers and Shakers.* New York: Harcourt, Brace, 1936.

Lynd, Robert S., and Helen Merrell Lynd. *Middletown.* New York: Harcourt, Brace, 1929.

Macfadden, Bernarr. *Manhood and Marriage.* New York: Physical Culture Publishing, 1916.

———. *Womanhood and Marriage.* New York: Macfadden Publications, 1922.

Marcus, Steven. *The Other Victorians: A Study of Sexuality and Pornography in Mid-Nineteenth Century England.* New York: Basic Books, 1964.

May, Henry. *The End of American Innocence.* Chicago: Quadrangle Books, 1964.

Mead, Margaret. *Male and Female.* New York: W. Morrow, 1949.

———, and Frances Bagley Kaplan, eds. *American Women: The Report of the President's Commission on the Status of Women.* New York: Charles Scribner's Sons, 1965.

Morison, Elting E., ed. *The Letters of Theodore Roosevelt.* 8 vols. Cambridge: Harvard University Press, 1951–54.

Morrow, Prince A. *Social Diseases and Marriage.* New York: Lea Brothers, 1904.

Nearing, Scott. *Woman and Social Progress.* New York: Macmillan, 1912.

Nelson, Benjamin, ed. *Freud and the Twentieth Century.* New York: Meridian Books, 1957.

Noonan, John T., Jr. *Contraception: A History of its Treatment by the Catholic Theologians and Canonists.* Cambridge: Harvard University Press, Belknap Press, 1965.

O'Neill, William L. *Divorce in the Progressive Era*. New Haven: Yale University Press, 1967.

———. *Everyone was Brave: the Rise and Fall of Feminism in America*. Chicago: Quadrangle Books, 1969.

Palmer, Lynn, and Sarah K. Greenberg. *Facts and Frauds in Woman's Hygiene: A Medical Guide Against Misleading Claims and Dangerous Products*. New York: Vanguard Press, 1936.

Parsons, Elsie Clews. *Fear and Conventionality*. New York: G. P. Putnam's Sons, 1914.

———. *Social Freedom*. New York: G. P. Putnam's Sons, 1915.

———. *Social Rule*. New York: G. P. Putnam's Sons, 1916.

Persons, Stow, ed. *Evolutionary Thought in America*. New Haven: Yale University Press, 1950.

Pickens, Donald K. *Eugenics and the Progressives*. Nashville: Vanderbilt University Press, 1968.

Popenoe, Paul. *Applied Eugenics*. New York: Macmillan, 1918.

President's Research Committee on Social Trends. *Recent Social Trends in the United States*. New York: McGraw-Hill, 1933.

Priest of the Church of England, A. *The Morality of Birth Control*. London: John Bale, Sons and Danielsson, 1924.

Rainwater, Lee. *And the Poor Get Children: Sex, Contraception, and Family Planning in the Working Class*. Chicago: Quadrangle Books, 1960.

———. *Family Design: Marital Sexuality, Family Size, and Contraception*. Chicago: Aldine, 1965.

Rieff, Phillip. *Freud: The Mind of the Moralist*. New York: Viking Press, 1959.

Riegel, Robert E. *American Feminists*. Lawrence: University of Kansas Press, 1963.

Robinson, Caroline Hadley. *Seventy Birth Control Clinics*. Baltimore: Williams and Wilkins, 1930.

Rock, John. *The Time Has Come: A Catholic Doctor's Proposal to End the Battle over Birth Control*. New York: Alfred A. Knopf, 1963.

Rogers, Anna B. *Why American Marriages Fail.* Boston: Houghton Mifflin, 1909.

Roosevelt, Theodore. *The Foes of Our Own Household.* New York: George H. Doran, 1917.

Rosen, George. *A History of Public Health.* New York: M.D. Publications, 1958.

Rougemont, Denis de. *Love in the Western World.* New York: Pantheon, 1956.

Ruitenbeek, Hendrik M. *Freud and America.* New York: Macmillan, 1966.

Russell, Bertrand. *Marriage and Morals.* New York: Horace Liveright, 1929.

Ryan, Michael. *The Philosophy of Marriage.* Philadelphia: Lindsay and Blakiston, 1870.

Sampson, R. V. *Equality and Power.* London: Heinemann Educational Books, 1965.

Sanger, Margaret. *Happiness in Marriage.* New York: Blue Ribbon Books, 1926.

―――. *Margaret Sanger: An Autobiography.* New York: Norton, 1938.

―――. *My Fight for Birth Control.* New York: Farrar and Rinehart, 1931.

―――. *The Pivot of Civilization.* New York: Brentano's, 1922.

―――, ed. *The Sixth International Neo-Malthusian and Birth Control Conference.* 4 vols. New York: American Birth Control League, 1926.

―――. *Woman and the New Race.* New York: Brentano's, 1920.

―――, and Hannah Stone, eds. *The Practice of Contraception.* Baltimore: Williams and Wilkins, 1931.

Schneider, Herbert Wallace. *Religion in 20th-Century America.* Cambridge: Harvard University Press, 1952.

Schreiner, Olive. *Woman and Labor.* New York: Frederick A. Stokes, 1911.

Schur, Edwin M., ed. *The Family and the Sexual Revolution.* Bloomington: Indiana University Press, 1964.

Schuster, Eunice Minette. *Native American Anarchism.*

Smith College Studies in History, vol. 18. Northampton, Mass.: Department of History, Smith College, 1932.

Shakow, David, and David Rapaport. *The Influence of Freud on American Psychology*. Psychological Issues, vol. 4. New York: International Universities Press, 1964.

Shannon, David. *The Socialist Party of America: A History*. New York: Macmillan, 1955.

Sinclair, Andrew. *The Better Half: The Emancipation of the American Woman*. New York: Harper and Row, 1965.

Sirjamaki, John. *The American Family in the Twentieth Century*. Cambridge: Harvard University Press, 1953.

Smuts, Robert W. *Women and Work in America*. New York: Columbia University Press, 1959.

Spargo, John. *Socialism and Motherhood*. New York: B. W. Huebsch, 1914.

Stearns, Harold E., ed. *Civilization in the United States*. New York: Harcourt, Brace, 1922.

Sulloway, Alvah W. *Birth Control and Catholic Doctrine*. Boston: Beacon Press, 1959.

Swift, Morrison I. *Marriage and Race Death*. New York: Morrison I. Swift Press, 1906.

Taft, Jesse. *The Woman Movement from the Point of View of Social Consciousness*. Chicago: University of Chicago Press, 1916.

Tarbell, Ida M. *The Business of Being a Woman*. New York: Macmillan, 1912.

Taylor, Gordon Rattray. *The Angel-Makers: A Study in Psychological Origins of Historical Change, 1750–1850*. London: William Heinemann, 1958.

————. *Sex in History*. New York: Vanguard Press, 1954.

Thomas, William I. *Sex and Society*. Chicago: University of Chicago Press, 1907.

United States, Congress. House. Subcommittee of the Committee on Ways and Means. *Birth Control, Extracts from Hearings on H.R. 11082*, 72d Cong., 1st sess., 1932.

United States, Congress. House. Subcommittee of the Committee on the Judiciary. *Birth Control, Hearings on H.R. 5978*, 73d Cong., 2d sess., 1934.

United States, Congress. Senate. Subcommittee of the Committee on the Judiciary. *Birth Control, Hearings on S. 4582*, 71st Cong., 3d sess., 1931.

United States, Congress. Senate. Subcommittee of the Committee on the Judiciary. *Birth Control, Hearings on S. 4436*, 72d Cong., 1st sess., 1932.

United States, Congress. Senate. Subcommittee of the Committee on the Judiciary. *Birth Control, Hearings on S. 1842*, 73d Cong., 2d sess., 1934.

United States, Department of Commerce and Labor. Bureau of the Census. *Special Reports, Marriage and Divorce, 1867–1906.* 2 vols. Washington: Government Printing Office, 1908.

Vreeland, Francis McLennon. "The Process of Reform with Especial Reference to Reform Groups in the Field of Population." Unpublished Ph.D. Dissertation, University of Michigan, 1929.

Ward, Lester. *Pure Sociology.* New York: Macmillan, 1914.

Wasserstrom, William. *Heiress of All the Ages: Sex and Sentiment in the Genteel Tradition.* Minneapolis: University of Minnesota Press, 1959.

Weinstein, James. *The Decline of Socialism in America, 1912–1925.* New York: Monthly Review Press, 1967.

[Wetmore, Elizabeth Bisland]. *The Secret Life.* New York: John Lane, 1906.

White, Morton G. *Social Thought in America: The Revolt Against Formalism.* Boston: Beacon Press, 1957.

Willson, Robert. *The American Boy and the Social Evil.* Philadelphia: John C. Winston, 1905.

Woolson, Abba Goold. *Woman in American Society.* Boston: Roberts Brothers, 1873.

Young, Wayland. *Eros Denied: Sex in Western Society.* New York: Grove Press, 1964.

Ziff, Larzer. *The American 1890s.* New York: Viking Press, 1966.

Index